FROM GEORGE WASHINGTON TO COL. ELIAS DAYTON, 26.7.1777

"The necessity of procuring good Intelligence is apparent & need not be further urged—All that remains for me to add is, that you keep the whole matter as Secret as possible. For upon Secrecy, Success depends in Most Enterprizes of the Kind, and for want of it, they are generally defeated, however well planned and promising a favorable issue.

> I am Sir
> Yr. Most Obed. Sev."

THE BALLANTINE ESPIONAGE/INTELLIGENCE LIBRARY

is the first cohesive collection of true chronicles of the greatest, most important, and most intriguing events in the history of international espionage and intelligence gathering. The series offers astonishing new information for the professional and an exciting introduction for the uninitiated. The books delve deeply into the people, events, and techniques of modern espionage—the puzzles, wiles, ruthlessness, romance, and secrets of this endlessly fascinating world.

Written by eyewitnesses or experts, they read "like fiction." But they are undeniably more powerful, because they are *true* . . .

ⓑⓑ ESPIONAGE/INTELLIGENCE LIBRARY ⓑⓑ

ABEL

LOUISE BERNIKOW

WITH A NEW PERSPECTIVE
BY THE AUTHOR

BALLANTINE BOOKS • NEW YORK

For Burt, who got it together.
And Peter, who kept it alive.

ISBN 0-345-30212-5

Printed in Canada

Originally published in hardcover by Trident Press, a division
of Simon & Schuster, Inc.

First Ballantine Books Edition: March 1982

AUTHOR'S NOTE

THIS book is about the front of the store and the back of the store—Rudolph Abel as he appears in public records, and as he comes through in the talk of people who knew him somewhere along the way. Had several people not shared with me their experience of the man called Abel, I would have had little to add to what already exists on the subject. I am, in this respect, especially grateful to Mr. William F. Tompkins, Mr. and Mrs. Harvey Dinnerstein, Mr. and Mrs. David Levine, and Mr. and Mrs. Daniel Schwartz.

I have the usual debts to friends and colleagues, those who arranged access to material I would not otherwise have encountered, those who read and talked the manuscript through with me. I particularly want to acknowledge the help of Peter Maas, the best investigative reporter around; of Paul Lazarus, my editor, whose perception and judgment are so extraordinary that he ought to be writing his own books; of Gil Eisner, the truest friend; and of Burt Silverman, my silent partner, who conceived and researched the book with me, whose spirit shaped every page of it, and without whom it would never have come to be written.

INTRODUCTION

IN Brooklyn Heights, a man in a painting studio struggles with oil on canvas most of the day, plays Segovia skillfully on his guitar, and reads Henry Miller's novels. He has several close friends in the building—painters, younger men, "Bohemian" as they would have been called in the early 50s, when this story takes place. The friends enjoy the wit, intellect, and warmth of this man, who calls himself Emil Goldfus, retired photofinisher. Some make paintings or drawings of him. One, Burt Silverman, has Goldfus to his wedding.

At the same time, Goldfus is a Soviet agent with the code name "Mark." He has a cipher, the apparatus for reducing messages to microdots, a radio transmitter. Moscow sends an assistant named Reino Hayhanen, whose code name is "Vic." These two are an interesting pair. "Mark" is fastidious, intellectual, a perfectionist. "Vic" is sloppy, inept, a drunkard. They appear to be Don Quixote and Sancho Panza, except the feeling between the two spies is not rollicking camaraderie, but increasing sullenness on Sancho Panza's part, mistrust and disapproval on Don Quixote's. "Mark" orders his assistant back to Moscow (for reprimand? for further training?) and, instead, "Vic" walks into the American Embassy in Paris, defects, and leads the authorities to "Mark."

It is June, 1957. The man is arrested, and another name emerges: Colonel Rudolph Ivanovich Abel. Under this name, he stands trial in September of that year, goes to prison, and is exchanged five years later for the American U-2 pilot Francis Gary Powers.

Abel's story is a fiction writer's dream. The central character, Abel, is complex. Everyone who knew him used words like "dignity" and "integrity" to describe him. The plot moves along at a natural clip, suspense at every turn, the themes of discovery and betrayal on all sides.

Atmospherically, the story is worthy of Le Carré; thematically, it echoes Conrad, for it is a story of intersecting secret lives. But the story is factual, not invented, and some of the facts grow more elusive and mysterious.

Abel confessed to being a Soviet citizen. The paraphernalia of spying was littered about the hotel room in which he was arrested and the artist's studio in which he worked. Hayhanen testified at Abel's trial that the two had met, that they were conducting espionage. But there was no indication of the substance of the espionage. The talk at the time was that Abel must have been involved in stealing atomic secrets. There were feeble attempts to link him with the Rosenbergs, but no real evidence emerged. And no further clues to what he was after have come to light in the quarter of a century since his trial or in the years since this book was first published. No forlorn American citizens have confessed to having been recruited by Abel. No national secrets have, to the best of anyone's knowledge, turned up in the possession of the Kremlin with Abel as their only likely courier. No triumphant announcements have come from our intelligence agencies about the peril to our lives averted by Abel's capture. The case is still open.

In spy novels, the agent always has a specific assignment. He moves in, steals a secret, recruits his agent, makes his kill, and moves on. In life, things go more slowly and less coherently. In those aspects of life ruled by bureaucracies, this is even more true. Intelligence work is dull, deadening, often ineffectual, often random. There may have been no specific goal in mind for Rudolph Abel beyond accomplishing his placement, adding a second agent, constructing an apparatus for future use.

Hayhanen's defection is another puzzle. Abel made a mistake. Against all rules of procedure and common sense, he allowed Hayhanen to visit the Brooklyn Heights studio once, allowed his two worlds to cross. It is difficult to understand how Abel tolerated Hayhanen's ineptitude from the beginning and why he did not disappear when Hayhanen, en route to Moscow, failed to turn up. The speculation that Hayhanen had been "reached" by American intelligence agents before his departure for Moscow is persistent. These questions arise in the course of the story as I told it in 1970. They are not dismissible, and the years have not laid them to rest.

There is no official record of Hayhanen's life after the trial. Shrouded in a new identity, he was moved to parts unknown. The government said he died soon afterward of natural causes. Unofficially, Hayhanen left some tracks in Keene, New Hampshire. He spent his days watching television and drinking. Then rumor takes over. The story begins to resemble a B-movie. Some say he died in a car accident. (Unsavory fellows whose profiles could not be made out—and which side were they on?—knocked him off the road.) The accident is not traceable. The General Counsel of the CIA said, when this book was published, that he believed the natural death version but that the accident made a better story. A newsman in York, Pennsylvania, uncovered evidence that a man he believed to be Hayhanen had lived there. Loose ends. The story is full of them.

Some things, however, become clearer. One of these is the place of Abel's story in our history. It is very much a Cold War story. The trial, in 1957, took place at the end of a period that had seen the American government violent (some would have said "vigilant") in its search for subversives and Soviet agents in the civilian population. It was a small step, in official eyes, from dissent to treason. Citizens were asked to "name names." The climate of suspicion was intense. There was a "Communist" under every bed. Abel's capture seemed to vindicate these policies and this period. The case was used to fan anti-Soviet feeling, to rouse fear in the citizenry ("Anyone you know could be a KGB agent"), and to justify greater and greater defense spending. The attitude of the government and the press can be described only as righteous indignation and outraged innocence.

In 1960, Francis Gary Powers was shot down as he piloted a U-2 plane over the Soviet Union. He had been, he claimed, just pushing buttons, but the button-pushing resulted in photographs of military installations below. At first, President Eisenhower denied that the United States was engaged in espionage; but Powers and his equipment were paraded for the world by Soviet authorities, and the denial was rescinded. The U-2 "incident" marked the end of a faltering innocence and naiveté on the part of the American public. We were not so clearly the "Good Guys" in white hats in a world of black-hatted "Bad Guys" who did disgusting things like spying.

Abel was exchanged for Powers in 1962. It was called "the trade of the century." Powers died a few years ago, in the crash of the helicopter from which he reported traffic conditions in southern California. Although Powers had nothing to do, personally, with Abel, his story illuminates Abel's. The U-2 flights established the primacy of technology in intelligence work. Dame Rebecca West wrote to me, on the publication of this book: "I agree that now almost all espionage is useless—the machine is the best reliable spy nowadays." Abel's story stands out more starkly, then, because there is a great deal of what is human in it, because there is a man of many dimensions at the heart of it, and because the juggling of identities that his life as a spy required is, unlike button-pushing, familiar to all of us.

Abel died of lung cancer in Moscow in 1971. His death put an end to any expectations that he would, like Gordon Lonsdale or Kim Philby, provide further revelations. It stilled my fantasies and hopes of meeting the man whose life I had recreated. This book did reach him, and he had lent it to a friend before he died. I still wonder, from time to time, whether the character who parades through these pages was recognizable to him.

After Abel's death, Western newsmen "stumbled" on his grave in a Moscow cemetery and reported that what had been suspected all along was true: Abel was not Abel. His real name was William Fischer, or William Gerryko-vich Fischer, as the gravestone read. There was an etched portrait of Abel/Fischer on the stone. Eventually, pieces of his life story began to emerge. Henry Fischer, his father, had left Russia for England in 1900. The family was originally German. William was born in Newcastle upon Tyne in 1903, and he grew up in a household where political activity was daily life. His father was deeply involved in the British labor movement, an early member of the Communist Party, and a man devoted to the overthrow of the Tsar. His mother was a midwife; that is the only available information about her. As a boy, then, "Willie" went to meetings, helped his father carry propaganda among factory workers, and listened to talk of the Party. After the October Revolution, the family returned to Russia. Henry Fischer's memoirs, published in Moscow in the 1920s, recount several conversations with his spiritual and political mentor, Lenin. He does not mention his son, who apparently did not remain long in Russia. William received training as an intelligence agent (what other options were available to a young, bright, ambitious, political young man at the time?) and returned to England before the decade was over. Thus began the career that ended in Brooklyn Heights.

These facts are consistent with Abel's character. They fit. The English background is borne out in what his Brooklyn friends called "a slight Scottish burr" in his voice, the involvement in the workers' movement makes legitimate his easy conversations about labor history, the facility with which certain songs came to him as he strummed his guitar. It is an interesting background. In contrast, Hayhanen's life before he came to this country reflected laborious progress through the labyrinth of an intelligence bureaucracy; Abel's, on the other hand, speaks not only of adventure and cataclysmic world events, but of commitment to an idea. It is hard not to think of Abel as a "type" and perhaps one of the last of that "type" we might call "Old World." And it is hard not to notice that what the spy manuals suggest does, in fact, apply in practice, for Abel's "cover" in Brooklyn Heights was close to what he actually was.

Journalists operate under difficult conditions in Moscow. "Accidental discoveries" are rare. Abel's grave, and the revelation of his identity, were obviously meant to catch the eye of Western newsmen and the information was meant to be transmitted. What prompted the Soviet government to reveal the truth? The same thing, apparently, that prompted the American government to produce the sensational trial it did in 1957. The case lends itself to propaganda on both sides. In Moscow, in the years after Abel's exchange, he appeared in print and on television claiming to have destroyed crucial evidence before the eyes of the FBI agents who arrested him. The tombstone is, perhaps, the last of these boasts and the last attempt to belittle American intelligence agencies. Its public function is one last, rueful piece of propaganda: the Americans never knew who he was, after all.

But the propaganda is, in the end, far less interesting than the man was. Burt Silverman was his friend, although he knew Abel as Goldfus, and the only clandestine aspect to their association was late-night conversations in the Brooklyn studio on the subject of art history. Silverman painted his friend sitting in his crowded studio, an up-ended shortwave radio at the end of the table. He called the portrait "The Amateur." The friend in the painting is as real as the spy on the front page of the world's newspapers less than a year later. The radio is real and became the subject of testimony at Abel's trial. The sense of betrayal and a shock that can only be called metaphysical on the part of Abel's painter friends was genuine and irreparable.

Colonel Abel was a cog in a machine, but Goldfus was an extraordinary individual. Abel's world was grounded in duplicity and deception, but Goldfus had an actual talent for friendship. His intellect was not only immensely developed, but protean and flexible. He was caught in a web larger than himself, yet his own activities helped spin that web. As Silverman said, he was both agent and victim of the Cold War. These ironies of character and situation remain and, as time passes, grow deeper and more resonant.

ONE

It was chilly on the Quebec pier, November 14, 1948. At five minutes past one, friends and relations were waiting for the incoming ship with their collars turned against the wind. The S.S. *Scythia* trundled in and settled along the dock. The *Scythia* had carried her 1,587 passengers from Cuxhaven, Germany, without incident. As the passengers disembarked, foreign accents called out. The wind was sharp. Andrew Kayotis came down the gangplank.

No one met him. Kayotis, according to his papers, was fifty-three years old, single, destined for Detroit. He was nearly six feet tall, he sloped a little when he walked, and he looked lanky. His face was narrow—hawklike—his most prominent features a set of bushy eyebrows and a long, aquiline nose. He had a weak jaw line. As always, he wore gray: slacks, a tweed jacket, shirt without tie. Nothing fit quite right. The outfit came off as shabby or, as he would like it nondescript.

Customs and immigration officials worked quickly. Kayotis produced his papers, had his American passport stamped—and was gone.

Andrew Kayotis was a dead man. He had been a naturalized American citizen, living in Detroit, who took a trip to his native Lithuania in July 1947. There he died. Friends in Detroit had known him to be in bad health. It was no surprise, then, when they began to receive letters from a Lithuanian hospital and, after a while, no letters at all. The timely end for Mr. Kayotis. For the KGB, the Soviet State Security Service, the beginning. Someone got hold of Kayotis's papers and eventually a man known as Colonel Rudolph Ivanovich Abel became Andrew Kayotis.

The new Kayotis had no trouble booking passage from Cuxhaven, disembarking at Quebec, and crossing the border into the United States. His usefulness done with, Kayotis was buried. He never turned up again. Colonel Rudolph Ivanovich Abel, stripped of the Kayotis identity, became nobody. And quickly disappeared.

Wherever he wandered, he left no trace until early in 1950, when Rudolph Abel rented a furnished apartment in New York City. He signed the lease for the premises at 216 West 99th Street, New York. The name he wrote was Emil R. Goldfus. Like Andrew Kayotis, the real Goldfus was dead. Abel, using his name, carried a birth certificate, issued in New York County, borough of Manhattan, certifying that Emil Robert Goldfus had been born in that city on August 2, 1902, that he was a white male, and that his parents had originally been citizens of Germany. The certificate is genuine. How Abel got it no one knows. There was, however, another document about Goldfus that Colonel Abel did not carry: a certificate of death. Young Emil Goldfuss [sic], white male, born of German parents, says the document on file in New York City, died there on October 9, 1903. He was a little over a year old.

The new Goldfus was longer lived. First, he moved into a four-story red brick building on the West Side. He lived quietly. As he walked the streets of the Upper West Side—brownstones and looming apartment houses, Broadway full of shops, none elegant, all catering to family needs: bakeries, supermarkets, candy stores, dry cleaners —as he walked among the population of that community: immigrants, their sons and daughters, professional people, teachers, shopkeepers, and old folks—he melted into the crowd.

The colonel fit well. His manner was "old world." Something out-of-date about him, charming, sad. He looked like a displaced professor, a disinherited European intellectual. And thus he might have presented himself to his neighbors.

Abel played Goldfus well. It was his first role in this country; the first mask he took on. Goldfus was, as Abel acted him, a quiet, well-educated, semiretired photographer. Later, Abel would make his character more expansive; he would take up drawing, painting, and woodworking. He would take in some friends. He would take on a past. For the moment, in 1950, Goldfus spent his time getting on record. He turned up as a depositor at the 96th

Street branch of the East River Savings Bank. E. R. Gold-fus, photographer, began, on June 12, 1950, to be a reg-ular customer. Small deposits every few months—between one and three hundred dollars each time. An occasional withdrawal. Just what one expects from a forty-eight-year-old photographer who does not look to be doing well. The only odd thing about Goldfus at the bank was that he was carrying on the same small-scale banking all over the city. Odd, but not sinister.

"The Russians have placed any number of bets," Dean Acheson is reported to have said in 1947. "If they win any one of them, they win them all."

Abel masked as Goldfus was one of those bets, es-tablishing his cover. Setting up shop. A simple operation. It meant having documents in which he was called Gold-fus and getting himself known around the neighborhood by that name. The best people for that role are shopkeep-ers; they press your suits and sell you cigarettes and say, "Good morning"; eventually, "Good morning, Mr. Gold-fus." And nothing more. And you are ready.

While Goldfus was banking and eating modest meals in neighborhood cafeterias and buying his pipe tobacco in the candy store, Rudolph Abel was keeping an eye out. He was making sure that the cover was going over well, that he was not being watched, that he had made it. As he wandered around the neighborhood, Goldfus was just taking a walk and Rudolph Abel was looking for things that would be useful.

All kinds of things; all kinds of uses. Transportation sys-tems, for one. Abel was well prepared, for public trans-portation in assigned cities is drummed into KGB agents before they leave Moscow. So Emil Goldfus, unobtrusive, rode the buses and subways all over New York, and Ru-dolph Abel, methodical, kept track. He had a high old time disentangling the IRT lines that stopped near his 99th Street apartment. His job was to know everything: how long the express train took to travel from 96th and Broadway to Times Square, where to change for the Bronx lines, how to connect with Lexington Avenue. There was an entire city to master, so Goldfus rode and rode. He never owned a car and rarely took taxis.

Sometimes, Emil Goldfus took himself to the movies. He had no penchant for "arty" films, and given his choice, he preferred to immerse himself in a good adventure story. But he did not always have that choice, for Rudolph Abel was after something else. So he went often to the Symphony Theatre at 96th Street and Broadway, examined the place carefully and found it more suitable than the four other movie houses in the neighbhood. The Symphony had a front entrance and a large side door—suitable, then, for meetings. One man could leave by the front door, one by the side. And there was Riverside Park, slope of green along the Hudson River. There Emil Goldfus sat on benches, strolled the paths over the West Side Highway, read his newspapers. But Rudolph Abel was not out for the air; he was there, too, working. In the park he searched for likely "drop" sites—places where he could leave microfilmed messages in hollowed-out containers.

If Emil Goldfus made any friends, they have kept quiet. No one has appeared who knew him at 99th Street. In 1951 he moved to Riverside Drive and 74th Street, a more pleasant apartment with a view of the Hudson River. He signed the lease as Goldfus and paid his rent on time. No one knew him there, either. No friends. Out of the question. Abel's mission was clearly, the first years he lived in New York, to become anonymous, to make the mask of Emil Goldfus, photographer, his own. Lonely, tedious, absolutely necessary task.

On the side, he took on another personality. This one was Milton, an Englishman. Unlike the other roles he played, Abel did not provide Milton with supporting documents. No certificates of birth or death. But there was a personality. And three acquaintances.

A lady called Lona Teresa Petka, a Polish girl, had worked as a governess in Manhattan and then married Morris Cohen from the Bronx. Morris played at the American dream for a while, won a football scholarship after high school, did well at college, and went to graduate school. But there had grown in him all that time another dream. In 1937 he joined the Abraham Lincoln Brigade.

When Abel-as-Milton knew Cohen and his wife, the couple were in their mid-thirties. Morris had served in the Quartermaster Corps during the Second World War, taken a course at Columbia University's Teachers College, begun to teach elementary grades in the New York City public schools. Lona worked from time to time in a li-

brary. They were living on East 71st Street and they had
been dedicated Communists for many years.

The third acquaintance was a friend of the Cohens, a
much younger man. Milton's relationship with him was
mysterious. It was or was not professional; Milton was or
was not trying to recruit the younger man as part of his
job. Paul Owen,* the young man, says that they were
introduced in Central Park one day. They talked. At first,
Milton was very interested in Owen's political outlook. He
encouraged Owen to air his anti-Establishment bias, his
gadfly reaction to the positions the American government
was taking toward communism in the country and around
the world. Milton listened, interested:

Harry S Truman, President, piano player, man from
Missouri. Postwar prosperity for the country; recession
and recovery. No catastrophes on an international scale
for a while. Shivers, sometimes. For instance, the State
Department announces it has abandoned hope of saving
China from the Communists. No further aid to Chiang
Kai-shek. By December 1949 Chiang set up on the island
of Formosa. At home, there were murmurs that our China
policy had failed because of Communist influence inside
the government. Small talk at the end of 1949, bigger the
next year. It began with the dropouts, those loyal Communists who had suddenly seen the light. Elizabeth Bent-
ley. Whittaker Chambers. They, and more, told all about
the "Communist Conspiracy" in our midst and they
named names. Alger Hiss. William Remington. The Russians exploded an atomic bomb in 1949; people worried.
Communists and traitors—who could tell the difference?
The models of respectability were not what they seemed
—Hiss; Judy Coplon. Welcome the age of anxiety.

On Lincoln's birthday, 1950, the junior senator from
Wisconsin spoke to a ladies' club in Wheeling, West Virginia. He had a small national reputation and big ideas;
in his pocket, he said, there was a list of known Communists in the State Department. It had begun.

By late spring and early summer of 1950, the newspapers were laden with talk of disaster. Nothing was getting any better; everything was worse. The bomb, the

* Pseudonym.

bomb; its shadow over everyone, ominous. The threat of
nuclear war no longer the preoccupation of a few odd
fanatics. In great earnest, with life itself at stake, the
conspirators who had helped Klaus Fuchs betray the "secret" of the atomic bomb were sought. Daily, the number
of names on Senator Joseph McCarthy's list changed:
there were more, there were fewer "known" Communists
in government. A barometer of the growing, diminishing,
growing hysteria. Suddenly, the American "accomplice"
of Klaus Fuchs was found in Philadelphia. Harry Gold,
the little chemist, talked and talked and talked. The papers promised more arrests. On June 16, David Green-
glass was arrested as part of the "A-Bomb Conspiracy,"
Julius Rosenberg at his Lower East Side home the next
day. On June 25 the North Koreans crossed the Thirty-
Eighth Parallel.

All of which disturbed Paul Owen. He talked to Milton about it as it was happening throughout 1950. Then,
just before the arrest of Julius Rosenberg, Owen's friends,
Lona and Morris Cohen, disappeared. Milton and Owen
continued to see one another. Paul thought his older
friend a likable fellow, sophisticated, sensitive, genuinely
interested in photography and painting. He had a pleasant, wry humor. Owen did some painting and some sculp-
ture; gradually the political aspect of their association
wore away and Milton became just a man. Someone Owen
went to the movies with, cooked dinner with, had picnics
with. Talked about his work with. Talked about women
with.

Milton was prudish. He disapproved of the way Paul
lived: Paul, young, attractive, was living a good life in
his own apartment; he had several girl friends. Milton
was shocked. But then Milton would turn around and be
shocking. They would be sitting in a restaurant; an attractive woman would go by, Milton would ogle her, his
eyes twinkling, grinning. He would say to his friend, ap-
preciatively, *"Fantastiche!"*

Late in 1953, Abel left the Upper West Side and
moved to Brooklyn. He had been in the United States for
five years. Whatever contacts he had made during those
years were never discovered, except for the Cohens and
Owen. Whatever he was doing as *rezident,* he kept it well
hidden. If he was doing anything. Aside from combing

the Upper West Side for likely drop sites, he does not seem to have done much. Just, as was required, set himself up. Get things running. Plant himself. Establish cover, then emerge.

The mask this time was Emil Goldfus, again. As Goldfus-photographer, he rented studio space in a cavernous seven-story ogre of a building, the Ovington Studios, on the wasteland edge of Brooklyn Heights. The building was full of artists and writers who paid from thirty-five to seventy dollars a month for mostly clean, spacious, skylighted work spaces. Most had their homes elsewhere. Goldfus signed his lease for a fifth-floor studio space and took a room in a boarding house on Hicks Street, nearby. He set up shop. He moved some things into his studio in December and came and went for several weeks unnoticed.

One wintry morning, 1954, Goldfus waited on the street floor for the building's only elevator. By the time it arrived, a second, younger man was waiting, too. They got in. The elevator began a weary ascent; its operator, who was also superintendent of the building, stared straight ahead at the inner gate, the outer set of glass doors. No one spoke. The walls were green, a yellow light bulb dangled. The elevator ascended, very slowly, creaking loudly.

The other passenger was Burt Silverman, a painter in his mid-twenties, who rented a studio on the fifth floor. Silverman had taken the place in February 1953 when he was fresh from an army life of murals and posters and signs in Camp Atterbury. He needed and found the time and place to paint seriously, without interruption. He came early and worked late and had no friends in the building. That morning, he was reading his mail and paying little attention to the other man.

As the elevator neared the fifth floor, Silverman looked at Emil Goldfus. He saw a man nearly thirty years older than himself, dressed in an obviously old but clean tan raincoat, holding a hat in his hand. Goldfus nodded. Silverman nodded. They left the elevator at the fifth floor without a word.

Like thousands of elevator encounters. Only something stuck in Silverman's mind. Perhaps a painterly thing: Goldfus had a striking look, provocative sharp features, open gaze, dignity, composure. Something about his manner. Something interesting. Weeks later, Silverman was in his studio. He had been sweeping the floor, and the door to the hallway was half open.

"Excuse me," there was a soft knock. Goldfus stood there. "I saw your door open and I thought it was a good time to say hello."

"Sure. Come in."

A little stiff, a little awkward, he came in.

"Hello. I'm Emil Goldfus."

"Burt Silverman."

He stood in the middle of the room and looked around. Silverman had been doing single-figure portraits, a large painting of construction workers, and a bizarre picture showing four army men on K.P. pouring blood out of a milk pitcher.

He turned to face Burt. "I have a studio just down the hall." He was dressed in baggy gray slacks, nearly shapeless tweed jacket—also gray—shirt and tie. "Have you been here long?"

"Few months. Just got out of the army."

Burt looked at his own painting. Goldfus looked, too. He began to pace the studio as he talked, peering at one or another of the canvases, while Burt watched him.

A lean frame, topped by a squarish head, bald. As Goldfus leaned closer to look at a canvas and nodded his head, the window light caught his baldness. He looked like a bird. A tall man, but not quite, maybe six feet, you could not tell, really, for he stooped.

Goldfus was talking as he looked around.

"I am retired. I worked as a photofinisher for years and saved enough to retire to paint."

He seemed to like Burt's painting.

Small talk. Burt told Goldfus that he painted most of the day, collected unemployment insurance, was not married. On his side, Goldfus told little. Burt liked him—liked his eyes, especially: cold, piercing as he concentrated on one of the paintings, then warm, witty when he turned to talk.

Burt slumped in the chair.

Goldfus threw his jacket on the daybed and took a pack of Winston cigarettes from his shirt pocket. He had a faint accent, but Burt could not place it. He said "Burt" with a soft, rolling "r," nearly Scottish. His speech was paced slow, reserved, holding back, as though he thought the sentences in his head before he spoke them. Vaguely British, too.

Eager to talk about painting, obviously approving of Burt's realism on the canvas, he asked as he lit a cigarette, "What do you think about modern art?"

"Which modern art?"

"Abstract art."

"Well," Burt said, and eased into a long diatribe about abstract expressionist painting then so emergent on the American scene. He talked derisively about Jackson Pollock. From there, his edge on, he rambled to his visitor some of his gripes about the "politics" of the art world in New York. Who knew whom. Who got shows.

Goldfus was a good listener. His eyes became sympathetic at the right places, he immediately conveyed a friendly interest in the problems of a painter thirty years younger than he. He sat down and leaned forward to listen, concerned.

"You?" Burt asked. "What do you think?"

"I have only vaguely heard of abstract expressionism. I haven't seen Jackson Pollock's work, yet. But I find most abstract art incoherent."

"Whom do you like?"

"Well, Levitan."

"Who?"

"Levitan. A late nineteenth-century Russian painter."

"Never heard of him."

"You would like him," Goldfus said. "You know, I think most contemporary art is headed down a blind alley."

"I do, too."

"And the worst part is the criticism. Most critics do not know anything. We need more knowledgeable criticism—don't you think so?—in all the arts."

Burt thought so. The two men sat talking for nearly an hour. Although they agreed about a great deal, Goldfus recognized that the younger painter knew more than he. He listened. He answered thoughtfully, not dogmatically, testing what he had to say. Guideposts were being set up between them, the terms of a friendship that would evolve through the next four years. The good feeling they had about one another was clear from the start. So, too, were the limitations. There seemed to be vast areas about which Goldfus would not speak, or could not

be asked to speak. Burt did not know just what they
were, but he noticed that his neighbor had a way of
brushing aside certain questions.

"Do you live in this neighborhood?" Goldfus asked.

"In Boro Park. I ride the subways. Do you?"

"Oh," he waved his arm in no particular direction,
"in a small room around here."

The vagueness was peculiar. But not really. Burt
thought that his friend was ashamed of grubby surroundings. Or jealous of his privacy—which Burt could well understand—and guarded it by being evasive rather than
rebuff the questioner directly. It did not matter much.

Goldfus could not be pressed. He would open himself
when he wanted to. And not until. Burt respected that.
He did not ask about Goldfus's work or what he had
done with his studio until the other man offered. A few
minutes later, Goldfus stood up again, stiffly, and said,
"Would you like to see my place?"

"Sure."

Goldfus picked up his jacket; Silverman found the shoes
he had left on the floor and they went together down the
narrow musty hallway with its frayed strips of no-color
linoleum. They passed a dirt-crusted hallway window and
Goldfus pushed open the door to studio 509. The room
was no larger than ten feet by fourteen. Its walls had
once been pale green, but the soot and fumes of Brooklyn
had erased the color. The wooden floor was painted porch
gray, the color rubbed through in the center.

Silverman looked around. A few sketches. The room
was lit by a single bare light bulb hanging in the center
of the ceiling; through the two windows on the far wall
could be seen the roof of the adjoining building and, beyond that, Cadman Plaza and a group of federal buildings, including a post office and United States courthouse.

"Most of these are still in progress," Goldfus said,
"but this one is finished."

Burt looked. The painting showed three men in baggy
clothes and crumpled hats, obviously Bowery bums; one
figure was seen from the rear, one faced out of the canvas. It was not very good. There was a gray wall behind
the three figures; the rest of the painting was done in
equally somber colors. Poor color sense, Silverman
thought. He was to see a great deal of Goldfus's paintings
and the same defects would crop up again. In the Bowery

bums canvas, the drawing was poor; some distortions in
the figures were meaningless, lines were elongated, the
bulk of each body extended outward, there was too
much overly literal detail, the composition was weak. The
subject was a cliché.

In spite of all that, not only in this painting, but in
most of his work, there was a great deal of feeling. It
was intense. Silverman felt that Goldfus could improve if
he had some technical advice. And he thought more about
the feeling in this painting than the amateurishness of its
execution. Some sympathy on the part of the artist for
those bums, some sense of pathos in it. What a peculiar
subject for him to choose, Silverman thought, but he did
not quite know why it was peculiar. Only later, when he
knew him better, would he realize that the sympathy
Goldfus expressed in the painting did not fit with what he
said about people like that. And he said a lot about them.

Goldfus was waiting, watching Silverman look at the
canvas. He did not say, "Well, what do you think?" but
his face did.

"It has some strong qualities," Burt said.

Goldfus came closer and looked as Burt was saying,
"But—why did you exaggerate that?" pointing to the way
the trousers and bodies of the men ballooned outward.

"I don't know."

"Do you think you would lose something if it were
closer to visual reality?"

"Um." Goldfus was nodding, listening, as Burt was
suggesting ways of improving the painting.

"Well, this is one of the first things I did."

"Okay. But I think you ought to think about . . ."

"Uh huh. Probably in the next one . . ."

When Silverman returned to his own studio and took
up his life again, it had been widened by a new friend.
Goldfus did not appear at his door every day, but gradually he seeped into the young painter's life. More than
either of them imagined. Goldfus became a confidante for
all the petty disturbances of man; he was privy to Silverman's gripes and shifts of mood, his troubles and triumphs
in his painting, his love life, his spirit. Goldfus's response
varied with what he considered the seriousness of the
gripe; he was jesting, cajoling, or empathetic but always
understanding. Sympathetic to a young man's striving, still

he did not make judgments about them. Which made him
a good friend.

As he became a friend, Goldfus was introduced to the
writers and artists who came often to visit Silverman's
studio. David Levine was living near the Ovington building, spending all of his time painting. He had just begun
to exhibit his work at the Davis Gallery. Levine came
often to visit Silverman's studio and later rented one of
his own in the building. Harvey Dinnerstein lived with
his wife near the Brownsville section of Brooklyn. Dinnerstein, a dedicated artist who had known Silverman since
their early years at Music and Art High School, was just
beginning to learn that survival as a painter in New York
meant taking on commercial jobs; he was working as an
illustrator for medical companies. Danny Schwartz lived
in Greenwich Village and did book jacket illustrations; he
was just beginning to paint. Sheldon Fink, likewise, had
just turned to painting after a successful career in adver-
tising. The two nonpainters in the group were Jules Feiffer and Ralph Ginzburg. Feiffer traveled daily from his
Lower East Side home to a filmstrip house where he
worked at cartoon animation. Ginzburg was an editor at
Look magazine.

Silverman, Levine, Dinnerstein, Schwartz, Fink, Feiffer, and Ginzburg: of similar outlook, young, well educated, Jewish, ambitious. None of them had yet been
successful at their careers, but all soon would be. Rarely
did they go to the popular artist hangouts in the city; they
worked. Although they came by Silverman's studio often,
they did not hang out there. They left a man in peace to
get his work done.

In varying degrees, each member of the group was involved in "unpopular" political activity. From signing pe-
titions to complete disaffection with their country's Cold
War policies, these artists were active and critical. In the
mid-fifties, the list of "unpopular" political activity was
beginning to extend to the reform wing of the Democratic
Party. Dossiers were being filled on all kinds of dissenting
young intellectuals and those members of the Ovington
group were sure to be in someone's dossier.

Into this scene came Rudolph Ivanovich Abel, KGB
colonel, *rezident* agent of the Soviet espionage *apparat,*
disguised as mild-mannered Emil Goldfus. For some reason
he had left the protective anonymity of the Upper West

Side for *la vie bohème* in Brooklyn. In his new surroundings, he would become known, engaged, and
vulnerable. Wearing the mask of Goldfus photographer-
become-painter, he had rented his studio in the Ovington
building and did not pretend to paint, but painted. He
lived among the group of people to whom he showed his
paintings, to whom he showed himself. Doing so, he
raised some questions about his own security.

The questions he raised among Silverman's friends lingered a while after he was introduced into the circle. He
told them all the story of having owned a photofinishing
business for years. Some believed the story, some thought
it odd, and some did not care. Although Silverman found
Goldfus a good friend, some of the others had no passionate reactions to him. Sometimes he stood—with his seedy
lack of location, his aura of a man forever transient—as
an example of what would happen to them if they failed.
Sometimes a discordant note would come into the thinking of these young men about the fellow in 509—no one
could put his finger on it; something did not fit.

"You know," Jules Feiffer told Silverman, "Emil gives
me the feeling of a guy who's been on the bum. No matter how much of a fat cat they get to be, they never lose
that look."

Which was strangely true. Rudolph Abel had, because
of the roles he played, lived like a bum, lonely and
homeless, picking up only acquaintances, leaving them as
the bum leaves a jungle camp to hop another freight. It
does leave a mark on a man, and Feiffer saw it, as Silverman had seen it for a moment when he looked at the
painting of Bowery bums. But they read it wrong.

Danny Schwartz visited Silverman's studio one day to
see what he was working on and to meet this Goldfus he
had heard about. Right from the start Danny thought
something did not jibe. Goldfus told his photofinisher
story; but Danny Schwartz had some experience with people in that business and he thought he knew the breed.
Emil was all wrong for that trade. He was too cultivated,
too intelligent, too worldly. His subtle, wry humor was
all wrong; his range of interests too wide. Schwartz left
the studio, puzzled.

"You know," he said when he got home, "the whole
thing sounds fishy. This guy isn't what he says or what
Burt takes him to be."

As each of Silverman's friends got to know him better, those early curiosities disappeared. They allowed Goldfus to be his vague and contradictory self. Involved in their own lives, living amid many inexplicable people, they simply took him in. They valued their own privacy; they accorded Goldfus his.

One spring night in 1954, Silverman stayed late in his studio with a girl friend whose portrait he was painting. The girl posed for hours. Then they stopped working, talked a little, and settled warmly and mutely on the studio couch. It was very late by then, long past the hour when anyone would have been in the building. They felt safely alone.

Suddenly there was a loud and decisive knock on the door. Silverman leaped from the couch.

"Who's there?"

A voice came muffled through the door.

"Who's there?" Silverman repeated, closer to the door, querulous.

"It's me, Emil. I'd like to borrow a cup of turpentine."

Silverman opened the door. He and the girl, laughing, feeling part of a living cliché, gave Goldfus the turpentine and closed the door behind him. Thereafter, Silverman, resolved, he would keep his friend well supplied.

The timing of the event was peculiar. Why Emil should have been in the studio at all after midnight puzzled the young painter. Something Silverman could not have known at the time explained it—Rudolph Abel stayed late in his studio twice a week to receive on his short-wave radio coded communications from Moscow. That spring night, when he was not yet accustomed to the rhythm of life at the Ovington Studios, he must have knocked at Silverman's door to find out for himself who was there so late and how safely he would be able to turn on the radio. The amorous scene behind Silverman's closed door must have reassured him.

Silverman, knowing none of this, asked Goldfus about the embarrassment a few days later and the answer was plausible enough. Goldfus said he had been painting late that night, saw the light under Silverman's door, and thought it possible to stop in for a bull session.

It was plausible. So, too, were the fragments of his life story that Goldfus presented from time to time:

He had gone to a special school for gifted children

when he was three years old. . . . He had been a student in Boston, where a Scottish aunt and uncle brought him up. . . He had traveled around the United States and knew the country well. . . . He had been in the Pacific Northwest and the lumber camps there. . . . He had worked as an accountant . . . an electrical engineer . . . a photofinisher. . . .

They were complicated people; they had a complicated friendship. Silverman often thought of Goldfus as astonishing, admirable, romantic. The age difference enhanced these feelings, for Goldfus was old enough to be Silverman's father and was often seen as such. As a father figure he was ideal. That extraordinary versatility. His indulgence. His generosity. Goldfus lent his friends, especially Silverman, paintbrushes, a slide projector, a typewriter, without a suggestion of when they were to be returned. He was known in the Ovington Studios for this generosity and, with it, his hospitality. Constantly, he invited people to his studio for a coffee break and provided "jungle coffee," as he called it, made by boiling coffee grounds directly in a small water-filled pan and letting the sediment settle to the bottom. It was delicious.

A friendship: tiffs, heated argument, moments of intimacy, confidence, wit, buffoonery. The relationship between Silverman and Goldfus was deeply serious, frivolous, giddy. They ate meals together, they drank jungle coffee together, they did not see one another for days. In short, each became part of the other man's life.

Emil Goldfus kept regular hours. He arrived at the Ovington building before half past ten in the morning and left, usually, by seven at night. Whatever he did as Rudolph Abel throughout 1954 and half of the next year, Goldfus spent hours painting. Silverman became his teacher. In Silverman's painting he found technical know-how that he wanted for himself. He liked the strength of Silverman's drawing and the control with which the younger man used paint to construct an image.

He came for advice about mediums in which to work, canvases, brushes. And he brought his paintings for criticism. Silverman's first impressions remained: Goldfus lacked awareness of color harmonies; he used painful combinations of brick red and blues or a dreary palette of grays and browns. The paintings had a dry, brittle cast that exacerbated the clumsiness of the drawing and composition. But Goldfus proved to be a determined, good student, and he learned what Silverman tried to teach him, quickly.

Silverman thought his pupil's progress phenomenal. This affable guy Goldfus had a core of determination that made him persist through what would seem insurmountable discouragement to other, similarly untrained people. Yet it fit the character of the man. His complaints about his own failings, and he often did voice them, or his unhidden sense of his own shortcomings, were always tinged by a feeling that he was confident he could overcome them. If he complained about sore feet or aching back or a sinus condition, and he frequently did, it was with wry amusement that he should have complained at all. His personal involvement with any task was, as Silverman saw it, always serious, yet he systematically seemed not to take himself seriously.

"There's an old simian proverb," Emil Goldfus would say, "that whatever one fool can do, another can."

So this fool improved. The paintings became more confident; Goldfus would sometimes catch an incisive character delineation in his figures. He started thinking in terms of paint and his intelligence and sensitivities started coming through. He would argue with his teacher about the use of color and the modern painters' experimentation with it. Goldfus said the best approach exploited those experiments while maintaining the best elements of the realist tradition. Silverman felt that color had become the sole content of painting and that many abstractionists let their experimentation with it become an end in itself. Goldfus wanted to maintain a tension between the two poles, to live in both worlds at once.

He painted portraits, many of himself, and still lifes. Often, he returned to the subject of the first painting Silverman had seen—Bowery bums. Goldfus spoke of bums bitterly, disapprovingly; he insisted that they were beyond redemption. That harsh judgment seemed out of character for a man who appeared so capable of understanding and so free of snobbery. And the judgments were incompatible with the way Goldfus painted those bums. The paintings showed compassion for the figure of the lonely old man beaten down by his world.

That sense of what one fool can do, another can, was soon applied to a new endeavor. Goldfus took up the guitar. Silverman had been playing for two years, mostly folk music. One evening, he brought the instrument to his studio and played during a break in his painting. Goldfus came in. He sat down and listened.

"May I try it?"

"Sure. Here."

Goldfus fiddled with the guitar; then he strummed it, but not haphazardly. He played a few bar chords.

"Hey, that's pretty good."

"Well, I have had a little experience with it." He played a few more chords.

Burt Silverman waited.

Goldfus played for a few minutes and then he said, "I spent some time in the Pacific Northwest."

He strummed.

"In the early twenties.

"I was young. I played in a lumberjack camp where I was working."

And he played for some minutes more before he went on laconically:

"Remember Big Bill Haywood? The Wobblies?

"We had our own backwoods combo, some of the lumberjacks and I, and we played at night after work. Marching tunes. Sousa. Army stuff."

Then he stopped and handed the guitar back to Silverman.

"Maybe I'll get one, too."

Goldfus left. The performance had been thoroughly believable. Emil appeared to his friend as a man with a taste for all human experience. Anything he said about his life would have seemed possible. This lumberjack story struck Silverman as rather romantic. He believed it.

Before long, Goldfus had bought himself a Goya, a Swedish guitar. He was at it every day, methodically. After a while he bought a tape recorder and ran it while he practiced; then replayed it, listened critically, and practiced again. He bought all of Andres Segovia's recordings the musical scores. He would sit listening to the record, following the technique. Only classical guitar music interested him; folk music not at all.

"That stuff is so banal," he told Silverman, "repetitious. And the lyrics are too sentimental."

Goldfus worked at his guitar and within six months was playing pieces by Bach and de Falla. Silverman and his friends were amazed and delighted. In spite of frequent gripes, discouragement, and frustration, saying his oafish hands could never do what they were told, he played wonderfully. And he looked wonderful when he played: sensitive and self-absorbed. Eventually, Silverman and his fellow artists drew him bending over the guitar. Goldfus refused to sit still otherwise; it was the only way to get him to pose.

As Goldfus improved his technique, he grew less tolerant of what Silverman did on the guitar. He listened, scowling slightly, and said, "You play the way I paint; too much feeling and not enough know-how."

The fifth floor of the Ovington building had become more home-like; initial impressions and puzzlements about Emil Goldfus had worn off. He had merged so completely into the life there that, when he wandered into Silverman's studio and found his friend and the others slumped in chairs or on the floor, their work shirts and old army pants still flecked with paint, he was able to walk right in, sit down, kick his shoes off, and join the party.

As he participated in those group talkfests, it became clear that Goldfus was intelligent, but his intelligence was different from theirs. Silverman's world, in spite of the fact that he was a painter, and contrary to popular cliché, was highly verbal. He and his friends were good talkers. Goldfus was not, really. Next to Jules Feiffer and Dave Levine, he seemed wooden; his expression lacked style. He had a sense of humor, but it was faintly square and corny. Silverman had grown up in an atmosphere in which ideas were expressed with wit and irony; he had trouble dealing with Goldfus. But he accepted this as a conditional limitation. The man had other qualities.

Goldfus was not an intellectual, but he had a remarkable technical mind. He was one of those people who finish *The New York Times* Sunday crossword puzzle immediately. And in ink. He read as easily about thermodynamics and calculus as he did detective stories. He could fix things. He could build things.

And talk to nearly anyone about anything. Silverman's younger brother Gordon, an electronics engineer, had come to the studio one day and drifted off to visit Goldfus. Silverman had followed soon after to find the two in the studio down the hall deep in discussion about physics.

The brother was impressed. To Silverman, that kind of
ability was admirable and it made up for Goldfus's not
quite fitting into the talk sessions into which the group
kept falling.

He would sit on the daybed in Silverman's studio, leaning against the wall, shoes thrown off, cigarette in hand.
He listened with a look of alternating intensity and
amusement. Sometimes a smile crossed his face, the smile
of an older man privy to youth's passions. Or an ironic
smile, as if he knew something they did not know.

Silverman and his friends talked about the politics of
the art world: who was being supported by whom; who
got exhibitions because of his connections; which critics
wrote about irrelevant art as though it were relevant because they were writing about their own friends. Those
young men are all older now and most of these vitupera-
tive outbursts are stilled. But, in the mid-fifties, they were
angry about what they called the "fraudulent" art being
"put over" on the public.

They discussed a group exhibition, some coherent presentation of the realist vision in painting, as an alternative
to Jackson Pollock. They made, remade, discarded the
plan, brought it up again the next time. Goldfus spoke
in generalities. He shared their antipathy for abstract expressionism, admired the work of these young men, and
felt enlisted in their cause. But he did not add materially
to their plans, and the group show was not to happen
until seven years later, when Emil Goldfus was long gone
from their lives.

Painting absorbed much of their energy and talking
time, rivaled only by two other subjects of pressing concern: politics and women. On both, Emil Goldfus offered
opinions.

Neither Silverman nor his friends were reluctant to talk
openly with anyone about what they felt were the incon-
sistencies of a fanatically anti-Communist society that still
claimed to be a democracy. "Fanaticism," Silverman
would say, paraphrasing Santayana, "is redoubling your
efforts while forgetting your aims." And it seemed that
the American government was doing just that: wire-
tapping, investigations, and general snooping into the political beliefs of private citizens. An aura of mistrust and
near paranoia enveloped both sides. "Good patriotic
Americans" were quick to call anyone suspicious, anyone

strange, a Communist. On the other side, fragile nerves
responded just as quickly to peculiar characters, but the
word that came to mind was not Communist, but "FBI
agent."

The people who came to the fifth floor studio in Brooklyn Heights breathed this atmosphere as much as anyone
else. Emil Goldfus would sit there listening as they talked
about it. From what he said on the subject, it was clear
that Goldfus was not even remotely part of political ac-
tivism. At worst, he seemed a disaffected Socialist whose
active political thinking had ground to a halt somewhere
around 1935. He knew most about Eugene Debs, the
Wobblies, and other political movements of the thirties.
Beyond that, he seemed unaware of what was happening in the world, or unconcerned. In the midst of heated
sessions at the studio, bombarded by the rage of his
younger friends about people who were being dragged to
testify before the House Un-American Activities Committee or at the extent to which McCarthyism had become
a way of life for most of the country—in the midst of
this storm, Goldfus would shrug his shoulders, a go-fight-
City-Hall shrug. He had long ago given up the battle. That
shrugging widened the generation gap between Goldfus
and the younger men. It seemed to define him quite
neatly.

Generally, he listened with that well-I'm-out-of-it look.
Only once in anyone's memory did he participate. He
engaged Shelley Fink at one of those sessions in a talk
about science. About scientific matters in general, Goldfus
was well informed. But this talk was political. Fink's
position put science in the service of revolutionary cultures. Goldfus insistently defended the independent role
science must play. "It has a life of its own," he argued.
"It should not change with political regimes." Goldfus
stuck to that line. He was clearly not a Marxist.

About women, he was less out of it. *That* struggle he
had not quite given up. Not as he had given up politics.
His attitude toward women was, to Silverman and his
friends, typical of the older generation: courtly, slightly
shy, distant. Sometimes he mocked women—especially
their inability to do anything that required manual dex-
terity—but often this was accompanied by a leer on
Goldfus's part as he speculated about the pushover, the
quick one, and the "hooker." This contradictory, ambiva-

lent attitude made him inconsistent in his talk. He swung
from sly quips about a contraceptive under the bed to a
stern view that sex was ultimately too much of a distrac-
tion.

Yet, in company, Goldfus enjoyed women, and they
him. He sometimes went with his younger friends to their
parties. The women thought him gallant, charming, old-
worldish. He was definitely accustomed to being in female company; quietly, he was a flirt. Women found him
sexy. Silverman thought he saw in his behavior, just behind the charm, a touch of irony in Goldfus's eyes. As
though he were satirizing himself and his own charm.

About women in his own life, Goldfus did not say
much. Everyone thought it a waste or a peculiarity that
he had no family. "A rational, unhedonistic guy like
that," said one of Silverman's friends, "doesn't seem the
bachelor type." Goldfus shrugged remarks like that off
with a gesture that meant, "Oh, it's not so terrible."

Like all the other molds Goldfus did not seem to fit,
the business of his being unmarried puzzled Silverman.
He asked him about it.

"Oh," Goldfus said, "women are always after something. Money. Or position. Never the guy himself."

There was a hint of a bitter story behind that answer,
but it evaporated. Goldfus smiled, shrugged, and that
ended it.

Once Goldfus told his friend that when he lived in
Boston, he had courted a young woman who played the
harp in a small orchestra.

"I learned the harp, too," he said, "so we would have
something in common.

"And," he said with a wink, "I tuned her harp for her.
I tuned it a special way and only when *I* had done it
would she play it."

Goldfus had once shown Silverman a photograph of a
woman. Silverman wondered why he had not paid much
attention to it at the time. The woman was nude in the
picture, but Goldfus had not made much of it; he showed
it indifferently. She was ordinary.

"Who is she?" Silverman had asked, though he was
not especially interested.

"Just a friend."

The door closed on Goldfus's personal life as quickly
as it had been opened. Silverman thought afterward that

his friend had offered the picture as a way of opening a discussion. But his own lack of interest had not let it happen.

One night Silverman was in the studio, working, when he heard a female voice coming from Goldfus's place. He remembered the picture. Maybe it was she. He mused on the entirely unknown love life of the relatively unknown Goldfus. And he thought, too, that he might take revenge for the night Emil had burst in upon him asking for turpentine. But he decided against it; and he never saw the woman, whoever she was.

Goldfus spent a lot of time in his studio all year, and access to it was never denied Silverman or his friends. Everyone dropped in freely, frequently, and saw the studio grow, like a pregnant woman, from week to week. As the studio cluttered, Emil's life there expanded. Any corner of it was interesting; nothing was puzzling, just multitudinous, the plenitude of objects reinforcing the image of a man of wide-ranging curiosity and talent.

On the left wall stood a tall chest and shelves, piled with paperback books, many of them detective stories. The lurid covers caught one's attention first, but there were other kinds of books: *The New Astronomy; A Study of Cyphers and Their Solution; Van Gogh; Murder on the Side; The Last Party; Elements of Symbolic Logic; World Famous Paintings; Science News; The Artist's Handbook; Number, The Language of Science; Degas; Silver for the Craftsman; Vuillard; Kaethe-Kollwitz; The Continental; The Journey of Simon Mckeever; Goya to Gauguin.* Spilling out onto the floor from the bookshelves were drawing pads, boxes of film, and cameras. It was often difficult to see the shelves.

Directly across from the door, between two windows, was a large worktable. On it, a Hallicrafters shortwave radio stood on end because a part had come loose and Emil, too lazy to fix it, left it in that position. All over the table was an array of drawing pads, and parts of camera lenses, cans of nails, books, pliers, small wrenches, cutting tools, etching needles and acid, odd bits of optical equipment, a magnifying lens, a coffee pot and electric burner. Above the table, the walls were covered with an accumulation of his paintings, an accumulation that spread to the adjacent wall until there was nearly no space left.

On the right wall, truncated because of the oblique slope of the building, was a smaller table, holding Emil's tape recorder, record player, records, the guitar, which he had taken up that spring, and electrical equipment.

Goldfus owned the kind of easel found in art schools, one with a single column, calibrated with metal stoppers to permit the cross-arm rest to slide up and down in any position. There was also a folding aluminum easel. Light reflectors had been strung around the room for extra illumination, for there was only the one dangling bulb. One of these reflectors was attached to the center shaft of the easel. Generally, Goldfus stood at the easel or sat in front of the large table to work, looking through the windows at the federal courthouse across the street. He wore army pants and an old shirt for working, hung his "good" clothes behind the door.

That room presented contradictory impressions; it was cramped and confused, although all the objects were usually neatly arrayed. Except for the overflow of books and leather briefcases on the floor, Goldfus seemed in control of his environment. Still, the tension existed, as it does in many artists' studios, between chaos and order, and that tension seemed precariously maintained.

As people came to know Goldfus better, they were exposed to his eccentricities. For one, he turned out to be the man of a million handkerchiefs. Goldfus suffered from sinus trouble. He was constantly blowing his nose and, consequently, used many handkerchiefs in a day. Strong white linen handkerchiefs. He would wash them himself, boil them thoroughly to be sure they were sterilized, and string them around the studio to dry. When a visitor came in, he often had to duck under the dripping handkerchiefs. One felt like a suburban housewife gossiping over the family clothesline. But it was somehow "right" that he would go to all that trouble when someone else with his problem would have taken to disposable tissues; it was distinctly old-fashioned of him, and kind of formal. It fit.

Those sinuses gave Goldfus a lot of trouble and he often complained about it. He complained, too, that his feet hurt, and his friends were sympathetic, for theirs ached, too, after long days standing at the easel. Once in a while his stomach bothered him. But these ailments were made little of, a pooh-that's-nothing wave of the hand. He was not thought of as an ill man, nor as an old man, for he was quite vigorous, nor as a moaner and groaner. Almost never did Goldfus seem disturbed by emotional problems. Once, when he did, Silverman was very much taken by surprise.

Emil came into Silverman's studio one afternoon, pushed his hat back disconsolately, sank into a chair, and lit a cigarette. Silverman was working at his easel. He looked up, but, sensing a difference in Goldfus's look, said nothing. Some few moments elapsed and finally Silverman said, "What's up, Emil?"

"Oh, nothing."

Another pause. Silverman kept working.

Emil smoked quietly. When he did speak, his voice was subdued. "You know, there are times when you need a good drink."

"Any time is a good time for drinking."

"But sometimes, like now, in the spring, it's especially good. I'd get drunk now, except that I don't even feel like that."

"This happen often?" Silverman was completely unused to this new role. And he did not quite know what to say.

"No. Sometimes, in the spring. . . . It gets rough sometimes."

Nothing else was said. The cigarette smoke was hanging there in the late afternoon, and Emil Goldfus suddenly flipped a fresh cigarette at his friend, smiled wryly, and growled in pretended roughness. "Here, you talk too much anyway."

A few moments later, he left. Silverman was disturbed. This rare display shook his image of Emil, for Silverman had come to regard him as someone without regrets, someone so accommodated to his place in life that he was not prey to fantasies about "what might have been." His self-possessed manner seemed to exclude moodiness. Seemed to. Silverman had speculated about Goldfus's life sometimes, about what it would be like to live the way he did. It depressed him to think too much about it.

So he chalked it up to spring fever. It was May 1955, and the days were getting hotter. Silverman forgot the scene, and Goldfus never spoke of it. In June the older man announced that he was running short of money and was going off to California to market a device he had developed. Silverman had seen part of the device, just a section of it, along with other bits and pieces of electronic equipment lying on the table in Goldfus's studio. It was supposed to be able to make multiple color prints from a single negative, simultaneously. Emil took Silverman into the studio and demonstrated the device again.

But why, wondered the young painter, go so far away?

Goldfus said he knew someone out in California who could dispose of it and secure a good arrangement on the rights.

It seemed plausible. Silverman looked again at the device; all he could make out was a large wooden frame with a series of metal parts vaguely resembling a large easel. He shrugged.

Just at the beginning of July, Emil was gone. He had not come in to say good-bye, but he had left a note under Silverman's door saying he would be back in a few months.

TWO

In Finland, a man was living quietly. A black-bread-and-vodka man. He had been in Lapland for a while working as a blacksmith. He moved to southern Finland, to Turku and Tampere where he built safes in a factory and did auto repair work. Every once in a while he met someone he could trust and paid him to stand witness to the fact that his name was Eugene Nikolai Maki and that he had lived in Finland since 1943.

Neither was true. His name was Reino Hayhanen. He was a citizen of the Soviet Union, employee of the KGB, who had just been given an assignment that would take him to the United States to be Rudolph Abel's assistant. Playing Eugene Maki was preparation for that work; Hayhanen was building his own legend.

There actually had been a Eugene Maki born in Idaho, the son of a New York-born mother and Finnish father who had become a naturalized citizen. When Eugene was ten years old, the family went to Finland on a visit and disappeared. Reino Hayhanen was near Maki's age. He had been born near a town called Pushkin about twenty-five miles from Leningrad. His father had been born in the same town. Theirs was a farming family, including two sons besides Reino and a daughter. When Reino was thirteen years old and had finished four years of elementary school, the family moved. His mother became a cook and his father a fireman in the new village, while Reino went to school for three more years. He did well. In 1936 he was admitted to a Pedagogical Institute in Leningrad and the usual entrance exams were bypassed because of his good grades.

The boy was getting ahead. He studied in the Finnish Department at the Institute until, in the winter of 1937, some Finnish teachers were arrested by the NKVD. The Finnish and Russian departments at the school were combined and education at the Institute continued in the

Russian language. Hayhanen had experienced something of the bizarre world in which he was to live. Dutifully, he became a member of the Komsomol and was graduated from the Pedagogical Institute *magna cum laude.*

A bright future, it seemed. Hayhanen was, at that point, excellently prepared for a career. He began teaching at an elementary school in Leningrad but was interrupted, after only a few months, by a call to the draft. Thus began, for the ambitious country boy, a brighter career. Drafted by the NKVD, he was sent for training to a special school at Leningrad. Thirty select students were put into a special group, all of them from the Leningrad District, all speaking both Finnish and Russian. Training, which lasted an entire month, included learning to handle a revolver and to interrogate war prisoners.

First step on a ladder: Hayhanen was assigned to the Karelian Isthmus, front of the Finnish-Russian War. But he was only an interpreter. His work consisted of translating intercepted Finnish documents into Russian and interpreting at the interrogations of Finnish prisoners of war.

He worked his way up, a step every few years. Not one for painstaking detail work, Hayhanen slowly moved into the more "active" side of NKVD work. He began interrogating prisoners; soon he was selecting and recruiting agents to send into Finland.

Right through the Second World War he continued, assuming more responsibility, gathering medals and promotions. Two small events, having nothing to do with his career, touched this man on the move: his father disappeared sometime during the war and Hayhanen was never able, although he put considerable effort into it, to trace him. The town his family had been born in was wiped off the surface of the earth as a "necessary consequence" of the expansion of Pushkin Airport.

Hayhanen, thrust into the mode of heroes—brother to Stephen Dedalus searching for the lost father and to Odysseus struggling to see the smoke of his own chimney again—was oblivious to his condition. He moved fervently on to the job of "relocating" anti-Soviet elements within the population. By 1948, he was a senior operational authorized agent and had achieved the rank of lieutenant, senior grade. He was then in charge of finding informers among the local population.

Hayhanen had learned the ropes. Off and on, for seven years, he had attended courses in all aspects of counter-intelligence organized by the NKVD. The courses were given during morning hours, before the lieutenant senior grade went out to his assignment; they were taught by department chiefs and secretaries of the Party. Attendance was obligatory; Hayhanen never missed a step. In addition to the technical training courses, once a month he attended meetings of his own particular department. "Production meetings," they were called, where the department's work was evaluated, unsuccessful "operators" were criticized, and successful ones praised.

He had gone as far as he would in counterintelligence; bigger things were in store. In 1948 Hayhanen was recalled to Moscow where for two and a half days he was told about a new assignment. He was transferred from the NKVD to the PGU, from counterintelligence to intelligence work, and sent to Estonia, a Finnish-speaking Republic of the USSR nestled between the Gulf of Finland, Latvia, and the Baltic Sea. For a year he lived in Estonia and learned everything the PGU thought he needed to know for his next assignment. He studied English and found an Estonian who had lived in the United States to give him conversation lessons. He was told which "agencies abroad" to work with; he was taught the fine arts of enciphering and deciphering, dead and live drops, purpose and development of a "legend," and how to photograph documents. In Tallinn, the capital, he learned to drive and repair automobiles proficiently, and in Valga he practiced photography. He was ready. Back in Moscow, he was given the "cover name" Eugene Maki and told to go to Finland to build his legend, which meant establishing that Maki had lived in that country since 1943. From Moscow, he traveled to Estonia and by boat to Porkkala (a Finnish territory then occupied by the Russians), and on to Helsinki. He crossed the Finnish border like a true romantic, in the trunk of a car driven by Major Vorobyev, who worked in the *Tass* office in Helsinki.

Legends are costly to build. For two years Hayhanen lived in Finland, first in Lapland for three months, then in the southern cities of Tampere and Turku. In Lapland, with a blacksmith; in the south, building safes and doing auto body repairs. "Just to show," Hayhanen explained brokenly later, "that I am earning money by working on some other place, but not on espionage work."

Two full years, the cost in time, to build his cover. For a man used to the active life, to giving orders and interrogating prisoners and hunting for informers, it was dull. But the time was necessary. A man may spend ten years working at a dull job, going every day to and from work, living in a home that is not his own, wasting time, it might seem. To the Center in Moscow none of it is wasted time; all of it brutally necessary. When that agent passes the immigration officials at a port of entry to his assigned country and there is no hitch, if he is not stopped, if he is home free and "planted," the time has paid off. Hayhanen understood this; he had been raised and nourished by the system. So he stayed. Two years.

Legends cost money, too. Hayhanen found several witnesses who would testify that they had known him in Finland as early as 1943 and that he was Eugene Maki. The witnesses were well paid. Whatever the cost of bribes and other miscellaneous expenses incurred on a project like this, Hayhanen did not mind. It was not his money. And the directors of the enterprise did not mind either. The expenses, like the time, were necessary.

There is another cost, one that rarely appears on the ledgers. It has no name; it is the cost to the man. He lives constantly in disguise. Whoever he is, if he is in fact anyone, he must forget. The price of admission to this theater is his self. The masquerade goes on and on, as it must, and something begins to corrode inside. It is indeed a lonely life, inside as well as outside. He makes whatever contacts he can from behind his mask; whatever communication he does accomplish is always to some extent a lie.

The weak man, who has no self to begin with and is relieved to be "given" a personality, will survive. So will the very strong, the man who retains a sense of self behind the mask, who makes the mask serve him. Hayhanen was caught in the middle, and eventually he paid the price. But while he was living in Finland, if he was feeling the strain it did not show. He did his job. He paid off his witnesses. He reported at intervals to his superiors.

By July 1951 they were ready to see how good an investment it had been; Hayhanen was instructed to go to the American consulate in Helsinki and apply for a passport.

He filled out an application form on July 3. Eugene
Maki, said the script, wanted to go home. Hayhanen produced a photostat of the Maki birth certificate. He provided all the necessary documents and details for the
forms: his mother, Lillian Luoma Maki, had been born
in New York City; his father, August Maki, had been
born in Oulu, Finland, and was a naturalized American
citizen; both parents were deceased; August Maki had
died in 1933; Lillian Luoma Maki in 1941. Attached to
the application form, Hayhanen included an "Affidavit to
Explain Protracted Foreign Residence," in which he explained how he had traveled to Estonia with his family
and lived there until 1941; after his mother's death, he
wrote, he had moved to Finland. He wrote in the names
of his witnesses and included an affidavit stating that he
had never served in the Finnish Army nor voted in Finland. The American vice-consul wrote his opinion of the
application and passed it on. The wheels turned.

There were no loopholes; the documents were verified.
If they were asked, the witnesses told their stories. Hayhanen was nearly Maki's age, obviously of Finnish de-
scent. It took a while, but eventually the wheels produced
a valid American passport. In the interim, Hayhanen
waited and worked at his jobs and kept out of trouble and
got married.

Indeed, he was already married, but he was married as
Reino Hayhanen and he was no longer Reino Hayhanen.
Eugene Maki wanted a wife.

Hannah Kurikka was twenty-seven years old when she
married the man whom she called Eugene Maki. She had
come to the city of Turku from a small village and Maki
was probably the best thing ever to fall into her life. Hannah had strong, earthy, blonde, apple-cheeked looks. The
men she later came across in the United States found her
extremely sexy, but Hannah proved to be a simple, domestic girl who liked to keep her house spotless and make
things grow in the garden. She married Hayhanen-Maki
to improve her life, glittery America dazzling poor peasant girls all over the world still.

The newlyweds lived in Turku for seven months, until
the passport came through. They parted. Whatever Hayhanen told his wife satisfied her; she asked few questions
about what he was up to and waited patiently to be sent
for from America.

In August, Hayhanen left his new wife and traveled to Moscow for further instructions. He took the train from Porkkala territory to Leningrad and then to Moscow. To cross the Finnish border he hid himself again in a car trunk. Safely, he arrived in Moscow. The weather was good in the capital at the end of August, a lot of warmth and sunshine that Reino Hayhanen did not get to enjoy. This trip was for business only. So Hayhanen reported, as he had been instructed to, to a private house somewhere in the city. He was met by a man called Stoyanov, whom he did not remember well, and two others. Vitali G. Pavlov was of medium height—about five feet nine inches tall—with a fleshy, sensuous look, especially around the lips. His face had the typical squareness of the Russian, with high cheekbones, pale eyes set deep in their sockets, and a peculiarly appropriate "soup-bowl" haircut that made him look official and forbidding. Pavlov was, in Hayhanen's words, "assistant boss of the American section of espionage work." The third man was Mikhail N. Svirin, rodentlike, with small eyes, thin lips, dark hair receding at the temples. Svirin was in Moscow on vacation from his "official" position with the Soviet delegation to the United Nations in New York.

Hayhanen's training in Moscow lasted three weeks and covered the conventional techniques of espionage. He learned once again how to make "soft" film—to remove the outer celluloid layer of ordinary or "hard" film, leaving it malleable enough to be folded and crushed and hidden in a small container. He went over, an infinite number of times, the microdot technique, the method of photographing a message and reducing the photograph to the size of a dot. Hayhanen had been practicing this for his entire career in Soviet intelligence, but he never did learn it well. In Moscow, those weeks of the waning summer, he practiced some more. He was shown how to use secret containers, places to hide those tiny messages. He handled hollowed-out bolts and coins and screws; he was shown how to secrete messages in matchbooks and the bindings of magazines. And he spent a lot of time on codes, enciphering and deciphering, learning his own special code. For practice, his mentors used nonsense messages. Endlessly Hayhanen turned *la plume de ma tante est sur le bureau de mon oncle* or its Russian counterpart into a series of numbers and back again.

There was one nagging question at the core of all this repetitive training. What was it for? A question Reino Hayhanen was not then or ever capable of asking, of his superiors or himself. He just did what he was told. He was a professional; he followed orders. Eventually, he was told what it was for. Or was he?

He was being sent, as he well knew, to the United States. For that assignment, his code name was now "Vik," a name to be used in communication with the Center, with his superiors anywhere he might be dealing with them, with his agents. What Hayhanen-Maki-Vik was to do in the United States was unclear.

The position had a name. Hayhanen was to be assistant to the illegal *rezident* already in place in New York. That was Rudolph Abel. Hayhanen was told that the *rezident* was to be called by the code name "Mark."

Pavlov gave Hayhanen instructions. He would settle in New York and contact "some illegal agents" who were sent by Soviet officials. He would receive five thousand dollars for cover work, four hundred dollars a month salary, one hundred dollars for trip expenses, and another salary in Russian currency to be paid to his relatives.

Pavlov handed him a piece of paper with that information written out. It had been okayed by higher KGB officials. Hayhanen read it. He signed two copies and returned the papers to Pavlov.

The mark of a truly professional operation, all this paper work. It fills the self-perpetuating need of a bureaucracy to give its employees something to do. A division chief in charge of contacts worked out the wording, a typist typed it, a reviser revised it, a typist typed it, a messenger brought it, Pavlov handed it to Hayhanen, Hayhanen gave it back to Pavlov, a messenger brought it back to the Center, an executive okayed it, a file clerk filed it.

You find the same sort of thing in every government bureau in Moscow, in every aspect of life in that city. Busy work everywhere, nine men doing the work of one. no one who is willing to accept responsibility for a decision, no answer to "Who is in charge here?" Ask a businessman who tries to sell a machine to a Russian factory; ask a traveler who wants to find out which ballet is being performed by the Bolshoi company that very night.

It is pure Soviet. Everyone knows it. And the extent to which this bureaucratic mentality permeates the business of espionage is extraordinary.

The plenitude of papers and copies, of hands along the chain of command, comforted Reino Hayhanen. It does many "secret" agents. It assures them that the organization exists. Since everything is written down in black and white, in triplicate, it is real. By an understandable jump in logic, all this "business" means the organization knows what it is doing.

So Hayhanen spent three weeks in Moscow making his microdots and practicing his code and feeling quite comfortable within the confines of the house he was kept in and within the confines of the KGB, trusting his trainers and learning the rules and thinking, all the while, how he could make the rules work for him.

Pavlov talked to him about the job ahead. He explained that "in espionage work we are all the time in war. But if real war will be for everyone or between several countries, that I don't have to move—to forget about espionage work. Even if they don't have any connections with me, so still I have to do my espionage work in the country where I was assigned. And . . . after war our country or our officials will ask from everyone what he did to win this war." So said Pavlov, according to Hayhanen.

Abstract, very remote, this patriotism for the future. Hayhanen, black-bread-and-vodka man, asked about the agents he was to have, what they were supposed to give him. It depends, he was told. He must check with his superiors about each agent; he must know where they work and who their friends are and, from that, what information they have access to.

That from Pavlov. Svirin was more helpful; Svirin stuck to the concrete. If the large picture was vague, the smaller one was full of details. Svirin had been living in New York and was to return there; he was Hayhanen's contact. Svirin told him at length about the city and the life there.

In that haven for spies, Hayhanen was to find an apartment or furnished room. Then to report his safe arrival. Then to set to work. Spies work according to a strict ritual. There are the codes and microdots and hollow containers, as Hayhanen had already assimilated. And there is the melodramatic side, the rest of what they do from day to day, the drops and signal areas and meeting places.

Drops are hiding places for messages which have been reduced to microdot and secreted in one of the hollow containers Hayhanen had been practicing with. Signal areas are for indicating that a message has been left in one of the drops. Hayhanen was assigned, there in Moscow, three drops and a signal area in New York City.

The drops and signal area were to be used only by Hayhanen and the consistently unnamed Russian officials with whom he was to communicate. Drop Number One, he was told, was in the Bronx, a hole in the wall on Jerome Avenue, between 165th and 167th streets. Drop Number Two was in Manhattan, a bridge over a footpath in Central Park, near 95th Street. Drop Number Three was in Fort Tryon Park, under a lamppost, which he would identify by the number on its base. The signal area was located in a subway station at 80th Street and Central Park West in Manhattan. The system was easy: he would use blue chalk; he would indicate by vertical lines that he had left a message in drops One, Two, or Three. He would wait. He would return the next day to see if the message had been picked up; a vertical line would tell him. The same procedure for messages left by Russian officials for him: lines on the wall would tell him where to go; a line of his own would acknowledge receipt.

Hayhanen could not speak English well; he could barely pronounce the words "New York," yet he commited all this information to memory. And his memory was good. He repeated it over and over; he practiced his cover story and did his enciphering and recited his drops. Before he left Moscow, the rank of major in the Soviet Army was bestowed upon him. It was the beginning of September, and Major Hayhanen was ready to move on.

He traveled back to Finland and for the sake of form stuck himself in a car trunk again. In Finland, he resumed the identity of Eugene Maki, kissed his wife Hannah hello and good-bye, made his way through to Sweden, then to England, and booked passage on the *Queen Mary*.

Mikhail Nikolaevich Svirin preceded Hayhanen. Svirin returned to New York in September with his wife Raissa

Vassilievna Svirina. He rented an apartment on the Upper West Side of Manhattan and assumed the post of first secretary on the embassy staff. The United Nations Chief of Protocol requested that Svirin be included on the UN list of members of permanent delegates entitled to diplomatic privileges. By December, it was done.

As Eugene Nikolai Maki, Hayhanen stepped off the *Queen Mary* on October 20, 1952. He made his way through the customs and immigration checkpoints, opening his valises for the watchful eyes of the authorities, holding his American passport out for the entry stamp. In his pocket, Hayhanen carried a small container; inside were photographs of his code. In case he forgot.

"Welcome to the United States," muttered the official.

Although he spoke English very poorly he made out all right. He was in a good location—just as they had said in Moscow—a city where foreigners move in and out all the time, where landlords and hotel clerks are not suspicious of strange accents and odd looks, where being a stranger is, in fact, normal. Reino Hayhanen was then thirty-two years old, about five feet eight inches tall; his complexion was fair, his eyes were gray-blue, he had a very husky, strong body. He was free. No one watched over him, no one restrained him. His pockets were full and his income was assured, and he was, in his heavily clever way, looking forward to having a good time.

First, a place to live. He checked in for the night at the Chesterfield Hotel, a transient place on East 50th Street. Then he moved to a furnished room and set out to see if he was followed. Ordinary paranoid citizens practice this daily: looking at reflections in shop windows, looking over the shoulder, walking down one side of the street and up the other. Hayhanen, had he been followed, would not have admitted it anyway for he was in this country to carve out a new life.

A week after his arrival he strolled into Central Park. It was beginning to turn cold and there were few lingerers. He went into the park at 79th Street, walked near the Tavern-on-the-Green restaurant, which had long since pulled in its garden tables, and came to the bridle path. Alongside was a sign. Hmm. He idled up to it. He pulled from his pocket a white thumbtack. Glances, furtively, left and right. Quickly, he did the deed; placed the white thumbtack in the white sign, gave one look around and left.

In Moscow Hayhanen had been told to signal his safe arrival this way.

Then he was on his own. Just looking around. He tried to get the "feel" of the place, but it was difficult. It was not the kind of life he was used to and he was thrown quite off-balance.

He gravitated toward the one thing he knew well: vodka. Hayhanen had always been a big drinker, had come from a society of big drinkers, and went instinctively to the drinking parts of the city, to the lower-class bars, the neighborhoods of working men, the beer drinkers. He spent time in bars and time looking around, but he was not neglecting his duty at all. It was his duty. When he had been in the city one month, Hayhanen found a furnished room on 43rd Street in Brooklyn, a suitably dowdy but otherwise characterless part of the world. He did what was required for setting up "cover," that is, establishing himself as Eugene Maki. He wrote for and received a photostatic copy of Maki's birth certificate, sent to him directly by the Department of Public Health, Boise, Idaho. He had a record of his marriage to Hannah transmitted from Finland and entered into the records of the Evangelical Lutheran Church in Brooklyn. Nor had he forgotten the drops. In November, he made his way to the Bronx and dropped into the prearranged spot on Jerome Avenue his first message. It confirmed the tack in the sign; Hayhanen reported that he had arrived safely, that no one was tailing him. And he asked for more money. Since he had been told in Moscow that money would be forthcoming when he needed it, Hayhanen did not hesitate. He had been on the job just a month, and he needed more. He wrote also, in that first message, that he was ready to open "cover" work. The answer came back shortly, again through the Jerome Avenue drop, that it was too soon to discuss such matters.

He was left on his own, with nothing to do but to be there. On the twenty-first day of each month he rode the BMT subway to the Prospect Park station, where he walked to the Lincoln Road exit. He wore, on each of these subway trips, a blue tie with red stripes. He smoked the same pipe each time. He was not by habit a smoker,

but he puffed away at the pipe as best he could; it was
part of his instructions.

When he got to Lincoln Road he stood around. Sometimes nothing happened. He stood, tried to puff casually
at the pipe, and went home. Once, in the spring of 1953,
after he had been making that subway trip for months,
someone showed up. Hayhanen recognized the man immediately, for they had met before, in Moscow.

When Svirin arrived, the two men went through the
subway turnstile, descended to the platform, and walked
toward the men's room. In the midst of stale disinfectant
mixed with urine, tiles smeared with graffiti, sallow subway lighting, rushing and trembling trains, they conducted
their business.

Hurriedly. An athletic, fair-complexioned man and a
"rodentlike" chap with small eyes, a prominent nose, dark
hair receding at the temples, eyeglasses. Something passed
between them. They left and walked out to the subway
platform, where they talked about the weather. They
spoke English, heavily accented. A train arrived and they
boarded it together, in silence. For ten minutes they rode
and then Svirin leaned over, said something quickly to
Hayhanen. At the next stop, Hayhanen got off, leaving
Svirin to ride on. He crossed the platform, caught a train
going in the opposite direction, and went home.

Until March of 1953, home for Reino Hayhanen alias
Eugene Nikolai Maki had been a furnished room at 816
43rd Street, Brooklyn. But Hannah had arrived to live
with the new husband she had not seen for six months,
and the couple moved. Throughout the spring they lived
at 176 South 4th Street, still in Brooklyn, a run-down
place where apartments were rented furnished by the
week or month. The Finnish couple attracted little attention there. It is a dreary neighborhood just a few streets
from the Williamsburg Bridge, a desert of run-down
buildings and new gas stations and ubiquitous candy
stores. But it was a convenient place for the Makis, not
only because of the assured anonymity of transient places,
but because it was close to transportation lines reaching
all over the city. That was important everywhere they
went. Hannah Maki did not know what her husband was
up to, but whatever it was, it involved a good deal of traveling.

As the year wore on and Eugene Maki plowed around

the city, going out to the "visual meetings" at Lincoln
Road, checking his drops all over the five boroughs of
New York, writing his messages and doing his job, and
being mostly on his own, drinking more and more, he began to crack a little. It was obvious to Hannah. After all,
this was not the life Hayhanen had imagined. Nor was it
the life Hannah had wanted. They quarreled. They made
up. He drank; she did not. They quarreled some more.
They moved to a new apartment, 932 Madison Street,
Brooklyn. The narrow three-story building was just off
Broadway in a neighborhood now almost entirely slum.
Out front was a high stoop, the concrete cracking and
rutted. Right at the bottom of the stoop was the Para-
mount Bar and Grill. The windows of the nine apartments
looking out onto Madison Street were draped with grimy
plastic curtains.

It was typical of Hayhanen—a place that, like all the
others, reflected his run-down spirit. The neighborhoods
he chose revealed who he was: the people were poor and
undistinctive and of such mixed ethnic backgrounds that
a sense of culture, of the transplanted cultures that went
into building each neighborhood was erased. The streets
were always dirty. There were subway lines and bus lines
all over the place. Way-station places. No one really lives
there, just gets off the train and catches a nap and waits
to get back on the train in the morning. Always, there
was a bar nearby.

Sometime in 1954 Hayhanen began to look for another
place to live. Not in Brooklyn this time, not in the city,
but in the country. Perhaps it was his own soul that, in
spite of itself, cried out for country air. Or Hannah's. It
would be nice to think that. More likely, souls did not
count in this move. Hayhanen lived under instructions. At
the Lincoln Road meeting, Svirin might have handed over
a new set of these: Hayhanen began to look for a place
where he might safely set up a radio transmitter. Brooklyn would not do.

He found what he was looking for in the New York
Daily News. A real estate advertisement, placed by a
company calling itself Westchester Lake, Incorporated,
showed a small cottage perched on a lakefront, thirty-six
miles from the New York City line. It was not the picture
that attracted Hayhanen—he was not one for idyllic
country homes on picture-book lakes—but the text:

First offering! Westchester Lake. A complete private
large lake; high above the Hudson; one hour from
N.Y.C. 5 minutes from r.r. sta. & city conveniences.
Low acreage tax rate. Free title policy. Acreage $890.
Easy terms.

Not that he understood the text. The location (away
from the city) and the price ($890) caught his eye. It
looked good, so he went up to have a look. The place was
right on the outskirts of Peekskill, New York, one of those
Hudson Valley towns that remain small in spite of their
expansion; one of those towns that boom with New York
people in the summer, manage to survive the winter, endure. Peekskill was the site of Paul Robeson's concert in
1949 that ended in a large-scale assault on Robeson's
friends by his antagonists, Peekskill's townies who came
with stones to express their anger at the "dirty-Nigger-
Commie" while the local police looked on. Peekskill is
known as a quiet place.

The plot of land that Hayhanen looked at was far from
the center of town, way out near the town line. He drove
with Hannah to the real estate office that had been
marked on a rough map in the newspaper ad. This turned
out to be a makeshift wooden shack on U.S. 9. Inside,
Hayhanen met Bertrum "Buddy" Kadis, who showed him
the land. The lakefront property was not to Hayhanen's
liking, probably because there were to be several cottages
along the shore and it looked too cozy. But Kadis had
another site, and it was better. It was on a dusty country
road called Dorislee Drive in honor of Kadis's sister, Doris
Lee Carr. The Drive, so-called, was a narrow unpaved
road extending no more than four city blocks up a long
hill above the Albany Post Road. There was only one
house then standing on it. A very isolated place. Hayhanen liked it.

Together, Kadis and his new customer went to the office to talk about terms. Kadis offered to sell the land adjacent to the only house then standing on Dorislee Drive.
He offered to put up the shell of a cottage on the plot of
land and to let Hayhanen do the rest himself. While they
were talking, Hannah, dressed in slacks and looking
rather voluptuous, leaned against the wall, comprehending nothing. Her husband filled out the application that
Kadis offered. He wrote that his name was Eugene

Nikolai Maki, his wife's name Hannah; his previous addresses were listed as 932 Madison Street, Brooklyn and
176 South 4th Street, Brooklyn. Under "previous employment," he wrote that he had worked as a shipper
with a plastics company in Brooklyn for four months and,
before that, as a vacuum cleaner salesman. Then he
handed the application across the table to Kadis.

Who laughed. When he read the line about a salesman,
Kadis had a hearty chuckle, for, with that very heavy accent and a noticeable stammer, his new customer did not
quite fit the image of a salesman of anything. Still, though
the employment details were impossible to believe, Kadis
did not mind. He cared little about Maki's background,
only his ability to pay for the land and the house. Kadis
kept looking at Hannah Maki, who struck him as extremely good-looking. Immediately the papers were
signed.

Hayhanen-Maki agreed to pay $1290 for the lot,
$1890 for the cottage, and Kadis agreed to begin con-
struction immediately. A down payment was made, the
balance to be paid in monthly installments. Hayhanen,
Hannah, and Kadis put their signatures on the document
and the couple left.

The only house standing on Dorislee Drive was owned
by Mr. and Mrs. Zoni. It was a large, comfortable house,
with a screened porch in the back, a gravel driveway, a
well-kept lawn. The Zonis used it as a weekend place and
spent their summers there. During the spring and summer
of 1954 they watched the cottage going up on the land
below theirs. It was a small cottage, no more than five
rooms, and it looked a little makeshift. When they began
to see a blue car parked outside the cottage, they went
over to say hello.

The new neighbors were odd people. Very strange,
very foreign. The man, who called himself Gene Maki,
spoke poor English with a very thick unplaceable accent.
He was unfriendly; he wanted no part of neighbors. His
wife Hannah could speak no English at all, and the Zonis
felt sorry for her, although they could not, at first, say
why. The Makis also looked peculiar. Although they were
both good-looking and had an outdoorsy, healthy aura
about them, they seemed to be going downhill. Gene more
than Hannah at first, but later, both. And their clothes!
Always ill-fitting, thought Mrs. Zoni, who noticed that

sort of thing more than her husband did. Gene Maki
sometimes wore an oversized overcoat that came to his
ankles. Hannah wore a frumpy dress, several sizes too
large for her, hanging from the waist and shoulders,
nearly to her ankles, too. When she was at home, Mrs.
Zoni thought, Hannah looked much better, wearing slacks
and a shirt and high leather boots. Then she assumed the
look that she must have had when she was a little
younger; one of those rosy, blonde "Scandinavian" athletic types that you see in travel posters.

The Makis kept to themselves. Gene Maki would
come and go in his Studebaker, leaving Hannah alone for
days on end. But Hannah did not mind. Mrs. Zoni
watched her from the window: Hannah, a sweet, domestic woman who liked country living, kept her house im-
maculate and spent a lot of time working in the yard. For
days, at the beginning, Hannah stayed out in the backyard in her slacks and boots, digging a barbecue pit. She
was a hard worker.

Maki, when he was there, was gruff, at odds with the
world, with Hannah, and with himself. His drinking
bothered everyone. He drank more than anyone around.
He drank vodka and not good country beer. He became
mean when he had too much, and the Zonis could hear
arguments in a strange language coming from the Makis'
cottage at night. Maki did not drink with the boys in the
local bar; he drank with Hannah who did not seem to
enjoy it, or he drank alone.

No one knew the Makis—although they had contact,
as they built their house, with men from the lumberyard,
electricians, contractors, a hotelkeeper, the driver of the
town taxi service. Mrs. Zoni, the next-door neighbor,
came closer than anyone. At first, she paid little attention.
But Mrs. Zoni was a curious lady, she kept her eye out.
When she came to stay for the summer there was more
time for doing that, and eventually she got to know Hannah Maki. Slightly.

People come to Peekskill from the grimy city for a few
summer months of rehabilitation. They lie around most of
the day in shorts. The men play golf; the women play
Mah-Jongg and canasta and, sometimes, bridge. Families
go off to swim in Sprout Lake during the day and to the
town's few movie houses at night. There is not much to
do. Visiting is the major social activity.

Often, in the afternoon, Mrs. Zoni would sit with friends and family on the porch or in the living room, and Hannah sometimes joined them. She listened to their gossip, to their boasts and complaints about their children and who-had-opened-his-own-office and who-had-married-whom and whose-children-would-soon-make-them-grandmothers. Hannah smiled and laughed when the women laughed and took it all in and did not understand a word.

The Zonis had a small collection of caged birds in the living room, mostly to please the children. Parakeets, canaries, nothing exotic, but Hannah loved to play with them. She would sit joyfully in the room as they were let out of their cages, fluttered around, and perched on her shoulder. Mrs. Zoni thought of her as The Bird Girl.

When she was not visiting Mrs. Zoni, Hannah cleaned her house and went to a bar with her husband if he was around. At the foot of Dorislee Drive, a long distance, was the Rock Cut Inn. The name of the place is painted on a Coca-Cola sign that hangs out in front of the gray clapboard building. It is not an inn at all; just a bar and sandwich place. Standing on the Albany Post Road where it catches a lot of the traffic heading toward the Bear Mountain Parkway and the Taconic Parkway, the Inn does a good business in the summertime and becomes a less lucrative but more friendly local hangout off-season. The Kornfelds, who own the place and have had it for a long time, usually close up for the winter.

Outside, there is a gas station, also run by the Kornfelds. At one end of the building is a large sign proclaiming "Foods," where Mrs. Kornfeld sells sandwiches through an open window. On the ground floor is the bar, a small place. At the back, away from the entrance, is the bar itself, with eight stools in front of it, a Zenith T.V. on the shelf above. The Kornfelds sell large boxes of candy from behind the bar. On special occasions, like Mother's Day, they do a good trade in candy.

Mrs. Kornfeld does the cooking for the take-out operation and the meals served in the bar. She works in a kitchen out to the left, where a large refrigerator holds the day's food and a good supply of cold beer. You can eat in the bar at one of the six formica tables scattered around. The specialty is meatballs.

Inevitably, there is a jukebox near the bar stools, with

most of the current hit songs and a few "country favorites." A pool table, too, with a new lamp suspended over it, gets a lot of use in the evenings. The clientele is mixed. There are the people whom the Kornfelds have known for years, the local truckers who pass by daily, the local residents who come in three or four times a week, the transients who are just driving by. About the people who have been coming to their place for years, the Kornfelds know a great deal.

Here Gene Maki would come with Hannah to eat and drink. He would walk down Dorislee Drive, usually in the evening, and sit with Hannah off in a corner at one of the formica tables, rarely speaking to anyone. When the Makis ate meals there, they would order tomato soup, which came from a can. Mostly, they drank—she, peach brandy, slowly; he, club soda and vodka, belting them down.

The Kornfelds, too, thought the Makis a strange pair. They liked and felt sorry for Hannah and thought Maki unpleasant. But, unlike everyone else, they were more consistently exposed to the strange things the man did. He was very odd about money, for example. No one knew what he did for a living and the Kornfelds would ask every once in a while, but got few answers. Whatever he did, he had a lot to spend. That intrigued the barkeepers. They said to one another that they never pried into other people's business, and they shook their heads. It was very mysterious. It must have been a shady business.

And it became shadier when Maki walked into the Rock Cut Inn one day and asked Jack Kornfeld to lend him fifty dollars. Kornfeld was surprised, for he had seen Maki consistently flashing twenty- and fifty-dollar bills. Kornfeld thought about making the loan, but it was a principle not to lend money to customers and not to extend credit. He was not about to make an exception for this Maki, whom he did not trust anyway. So he said no and a few days later Maki was in the bar slugging down his club soda and vodka and flipping through the twenty- and fifty-dollar bills in his wallet.

When he was not spending his bills in the Kornfelds' place or lounging in his cottage under the watchful eye of Mrs. Zoni, Maki disappeared. He left Hannah to keep house, told her he had to go to New York City on "business," and drove off in his Studebaker.

He would drive into the city, a short drive, and go about his job. Checking the drops, he went from Fort Tryon Park, where he picked up his salary under a lamppost, through the Bronx, stopped on Central Park West, checked Brooklyn, with his pockets bulging and his mind on the next bar.

At his last meeting with Svirin at Lincoln Road which had been the previous fall, the "visual meetings" at the BMT stop had been canceled and Hayhanen had been told that further instructions would be coming through the drops. So he drove to the city and checked the drops, and for six months there was no message. But, early in the summer of 1954, it came.

THREE

THE message said someone would like to meet him. It fixed the date in July or August at the RKO Keith's Theater in Flushing. Hayhanen was to come, as he had with Svirin, wearing his blue tie with red stripes and smoking his pipe.

He came. He stood in the men's room trying to puff on the pipe, being inconspicuous. Local teen-age toughs drifted in and out. Then Hayhanen was left alone, and a man came in.

The man was older than he, balding, lean, dressed in gray slacks, a sports shirt, tie, and jacket. He had on a straw hat with a light-colored hatband. The man came straight toward him. Hayhanen puffed. He waited for a password.

"Hello. Never mind about the passwords. I know you are the right man."

Hayhanen blanched.

Rudolph Abel carried himself stiffly. In contrast to Hayhanen, who was shorter and sloppier and more than a little scared, Abel looked stern and intimidating. Hayhanen felt that from the moment he spoke. The speech was clean and clipped; very good English. And no passwords? Hayhanen, child of the system, was thrown off-balance.

"Let's go outside."

They walked three or four blocks, but Hayhanen could not regain his composure. Abel, whom he knew as Mark, was his superior; he was cold, official, and awesome.

On the street, talking in English about nothing, Hayhanen stumbled over every word, could hardly stop stuttering or think of English words. At the corner of one street, they came to a coffee shop.

"Let's go in here," Abel said.

Hayhanen would have preferred a bar.

They ordered coffee and waited silently, looking one

another over. Neither liked what he saw. Abel saw immediately that Vik, as he knew the other man, was scattered, a loose package. Something about the sloppy way Vik dressed, the way he stood or the way he slouched in his seat, fiddling with the sugar on the table. And he disapproved immediately of the heavy Finnish accent. That was bad.

Vik was not exactly pleased either. He saw a hard man to please. A snob. An authoritarian. A man totally different from himself.

The coffee came. The waitress left and Vik waited for his new "boss" to speak.

Mark was annoyed. He had received a message long before that his assistant-to-be had arrived safely in New York. He was surprised, he said, that it took so long for instructions to come for him to meet the new man. Vik, relieved that it had taken so long, smiled. Or tried to smile.

Mark came right down to business. He explained that he had been in this country for several years, as if to establish his credentials. It was not necessary, for everything about Mark reeked of credentials. He was obviously a man who knew what he was doing. Vik, who needed a drink badly, listened attentively.

Mark asked if Vik had gotten cover work for himself yet. Vik said no. He wondered if Mark knew about the money he had received for that work. But Mark, if he knew, did not mention it. His mind was on immediate, practical things. The cover work was necessary, he said.

"We have to think about it. Because otherwise there will be difficulty with time. If you work eight hours a day, there won't be enough time for our work."

Vik agreed. Oh yes, to work somewhere eight hours a day would be very bad.

Mark said he would decide what kind of cover work would be most appropriate, most convincing for Vik to engage in. Vik offered no suggestions.

Before Mark left, he made some arrangements. First he changed the method of paying Vik's salary: Vik would no longer receive his money through the drops; Mark would give it to him directly. They would meet from then on once or twice a week. Mark would give him the first assignment soon and would communicate through the drops.

He stood up, said good night, and left.

Predictable, it had not been an auspicious encounter. Mark left the coffee shop and became Emil Goldfus, as he boarded the subway to Brooklyn. The next morning, he would appear as usual in his Ovington studio. For Rudolph Abel it had been a disturbing meeting. He was worried about what kind of assistant this Vik would turn out to be. He could not possibly be as bad as he seemed, Abel thought, for he had been chosen for this job very carefully and the Center knew what it was doing. Still, he could see that Vik needed to be instructed, as soon as possible, about a lot of things.

Vik became Eugene Maki again as he climbed into his Studebaker and drove north to Peekskill. He arrived home in time to stop at the Rock Cut Inn for a few and Hannah was asleep in the house on Dorislee Drive when he came in. For Reino Hayhanen, it had been an encounter that left him feeling fearful, resentful, and angry. He did not like that Mark. He did not like him at all.

As they began meeting weekly, Vik learned of three drops that Mark had. One was in the Symphony Theatre, the movie house at Broadway and 95th Street. The drop was on the right side of the balcony, second row from the rear, off the far right seat. Containers were placed under the carpet in the aisle next to the seat. At one time Mark had used the balcony to meet Russian officials, but he had discontinued that. Mark liked this location, he told Vik, because two people meeting there could leave by different exits.

Mark took Vik to Riverside Park, walked with him past mothers with baby carriages and old men dozing on benches and showed him two other drops. Off West 96th Street, along the West Side Drive, were two places in a railroad fence that were magnetic-container drops. One was on the side of a railing, the other not far away in a hole in the top railing. Mark stood off to the side watching while Vik went up to the railing and left a magnetic container sticking to it.

Abel checked his assistant constantly, giving him tests to see if he knew his trade. Often, Vik failed the test. His photography technique was not good enough. Abel told him to practice more. He looked over Vik's microdots and sent him home to do them again. Horrified that Vik had never learned Morse Code, the professor instructed him

to practice that, too. Over and over again, Abel insisted
that Vik find cover work. He decided that it had to be a
photographer's studio and shop in which Vik would work
on his own photography and sell equipment.

Early in the spring of 1955, Hayhanen found a place
for his cover. On the twenty-ninth of March he and his
wife signed as Eugene N. Maki and Hannah Maki a
three-year lease for an empty store with a four-room
apartment in the rear at 806 Bergen Street, Newark, New
Jersey. Which is nowhere. The street is full of television
repair shops, cleaning stores, candy stores, telegraph
poles, traffic lights, fire escapes, a drugstore, a bar, the
Number Eight bus. It is far from the center of Newark,
far from everything, totally anonymous. Like all the
other places Maki chose, it is easy to get to. That Number
Eight bus runs to downtown Newark; by automobile,
downtown Newark is ten minutes away; you can reach
several major highways easily from Bergen Street and it
will take half an hour to drive to Manhattan.

It was never a "good neighborhood." The street runs
north to south through the infamous Central Ward. It
looks like a lazy southern town, with few women visible
on the streets during the day and most of the men standing on the corner, sitting on wooden crates in front of the
Davis barbershop and drifting into Feller's Bar. In the
windows of all the dilapidated houses, young black men
in their undershirts, with two or three children tugging at
them, stare out at passersby. You feel the tension here.

In 1955, when the Maki couple lived there, Bergen
Street was a mixed neighborhood, poor white and poor
black. Nearly everyone who lived on the street then is
either dead now or has moved away. The Makis lasted
there a little over a year. They never really seemed to
move in. The street windows of what was to have been
the photography studio on the ground floor, easily peered
through from the sidewalk, were immediately covered
with Glass Wax. It was never removed.

Abel was pleased to hear that the shop had been
rented. He told Hayhanen to put photographic equipment
in the store as soon as possible. Hayhanen said he would.
Abel had sent a message to Russian officials telling them
the shop was being set up. The answer came back
quickly: it was agreed. Abel drew up some diagrams of
special tables that were good for photographic work. He

told Hayhanen that they could be built easily. Hayhanen bought the materials, made some tables, and reported to his superior. It looked as though they were in business.

Once or twice a week that spring, Mark and Vik met. Mark, preparing for a trip, insisted that Vik be adequately set up before he left. Vik complained that it was difficult to set up the semblance of a business that involved so much equipment when he did not have any. Although he had been paid considerable money for supplying himself with cover work, Vik pleaded poverty. Mark, avoiding a confrontation over the money and anxious to get on with it, offered to provide some of his own equipment.

Three times during the spring of 1955, Vik went to a place where Mark kept the tools of his trade. In May, he accompanied Mark to a large, dark building in Brooklyn, rode with him to the fifth floor of that building, where Mark had a storeroom. Mark gave him a shortwave radio. It was a radio Vik had seen before, just a week before his visit to the studio, when he and Mark had driven to the Croton Reservoir with it. They had stopped the car near the reservoir bridge; Mark had attached an antenna to the radio and tried to pick up something but could not. Then Mark took out a converter, attached it to the radio plug and tried plugging it into the car's cigarette lighter. Still, nothing came through. That was the radio Mark gave Vik out of the dark storeroom.

Again, in late May and early June, Vik came to the building. He knew its location by then, on the corner of Fulton and Clark streets. But at the last two visits, late at night, Mark would not let him come up to the storeroom. Vik waited downstairs just outside the lobby, and Mark brought some photographic equipment, including an Exakta camera, down to him.

At each meeting, Mark reminded Vik that he was going away for a while. It was important that Vik know about it, for Mark was going to Moscow and Vik would have to carry on without him. Mark told him again and again about the Moscow trip. He said he would be leaving sometime in June and that he did not know how long he would be there. He left instructions. Mark was very careful about instructions; he wanted to be sure that his assistant understood and he went over everything slowly, clearly, patronizingly. He was pedantic. Not trusting Vik to have learned anything, Mark put together an entire booklet showing how to make separation negatives and another about making matrix film. He told Vik to practice photography, particularly the process of making microdots. And he had a few personal instructions, too. He wanted Vik to get around more, to get to know more people and places in New York City. Not that he was interested in Vik's social life, rather Vik's accent. It was still, after three years in this country and considerable training, very heavy. Mark was worried that it might attract attention and told him to spend more time with native-born Americans.

When he left for Moscow, in July 1955, Abel was somewhat reassured. After all, Vik had indeed rented a place for himself and installed some of the equipment and constructed those photography tables and read the instructions. He had even indicated some initiative and found, entirely on his own, a signal area that was convenient to his Newark residence. It was a place for Russian officials to signal that there was a message waiting in one of the assigned drops. At the Market Street exit in Pennsylvania Station, Newark, there was an iron fence; beside it a flight of stairs leading to a lower level. The signal area was the first four upright posts at the corner of the fence opposite the train platform.

Abel was satisfied. He had been biding his time, hoping this "bumbling misfit" would work out or that his gross inadequacy was meant to be that way. Abel's faith in his government's intelligence service was unshakable, as it had to be, for his life depended upon that faith. It was the only security his job allowed. Thus he thought, or *had* to think, that Vik had been instructed to act as incompetent as he was acting, that there was some design to this behavior, that perhaps Vik was meant to attract attention. Or half of Abel thought that; the other half, the perfectionist-professor who could not bear to see people doing things badly, kept trying. All those instructions. Then he was gone for Moscow and Vik was on his own.

He drank enormously. At first it was Hayhanen who did the loud drinking and shouting neighbors heard at night, but Hannah joined him. They stayed home a lot and fought a lot and threw out great quantities of vodka bottles. Most of the neighbors thought Hannah exceptionally beautiful. They were sorry for the woman whose husband had taken to beating and humiliating her. The only way to account for her taking it, they thought, was that she was obviously dependent upon him to help her along in this country.

Abel was gone for nearly a year. Hayhanen functioned. As Eugene Maki, he paid his thirty-five dollars a month rent regularly, almost always in cash. He would take the money to the Star Credit Company at 62 Springfield Avenue in Newark and pay it to his landlord who also owned the Credit Company. Once, when Maki had come to pay this thirty-five dollars, he spoke to the landlord about buying a refrigerator from the company. But, he said, the price was too high. The landlord agreed, happily, to draw up a credit agreement, but Maki refused. Not because of the exorbitant interest rates usually charged in an operation like that, of which he was probably unaware, but because, he said, he did not want to sign the paper. He left. A few weeks later, Maki reappeared and bought the refrigerator, paying for it with cash.

One day he walked into the bakery on Bergen Street with Hannah, bought a loaf of bread, and proceeded to scatter the slices all over the floor. He ordered Hannah to her knees to pick the pieces up, and she did. But *his* pieces remained scattered. The screams coming from his place at night were terrible. No one was ever allowed inside the apartment, the bottles piled up in the hallway. People were suspicious of him: his car would stand unused for weeks and then disappear. No one knew where he got his money. He got into trouble driving dead drunk. He found the Bergen Street place too wet and cold and never made a move to open the photography studio. With Hannah and a large police dog he had acquired along the way, he moved in the winter of 1955 to 3rd Street and Orange Avenue, then back to Bergen Street for a while, then to Peekskill.

Just before he left Bergen Street for the last time, Maki got into a real mess. The Sixth Precinct of the Newark Police received what they called a "routine call 9-A for bodily injury situation." Lieutenants Gavarny and Kuehl went in a patrol car to a dilapidated storefront that had camera equipment all over the front room, including large copying cameras. The place was dusty. As they went through the front room into the rear ones, the policemen made their way through a litter of dusty parcels, beer bottles, vodka bottles, wine bottles. In the rear room there was a single mattress lying on the floor, no bed, a few chairs. They found what they took to be a Scandinavian couple, both drunk, speaking broken English. The man told them he had been trying to cut some string off a package and had accidentally cut himself. He had a deep knife cut on his leg. The patrolmen called on their car radio for a police patrol wagon—the situation was not severe enough for an ambulance. Then they left.

The patrol wagon took Maki to Martland Medical Center, where three stitches were taken in his leg. On Bergen Street, the neighbors, alerted by the noise, police, and ambulance, thought that Hannah Maki had finally lashed out at her husband. But he was soon back home, still keeping the windows covered in his storefront and telling the bus inspector who stood his post across the street that he was from "Illinois and Indiana." By the summer of 1956, he had moved back to Peekskill. On Bergen Street, he was unforgettable.

As he was in Peekskill, where people, by then accustomed to his irregular life, were shocked by the changes they saw. Gene Maki had put on a great deal of weight and developed a twitch. The signs of heavy drinking were obvious, but not new, for Maki had always been going downhill; but Hannah's deterioration was new and marked. She looked much older and she, too, showed signs of heavy drinking. When she sat next door on Mrs. Zoni's porch and tried to laugh with the ladies as she had done, Hannah could not keep her lip from trembling.

And their life together had grown more difficult than anyone remembered. They drank late into the night, but only rarely at the Inn. Usually they stayed home, and the neighbors would hear them arguing viciously. As the family crumbled, so did the family car. It was a curious metaphor. First, the blue Studebaker appeared on Dorislee Drive minus its rear fender. Maki said he had had a slight accident. Then the car disappeared, with Maki, for a while, and returned with a headlight gone. Then part of the front fender. At last Maki got into trouble with the New York State Police, who charged him with drunken driving and suspended his license. The Studebaker stood in front of the cottage, decrepit, undriven, and if the

Makis went out at all, they called the local taxi service and walked to the bottom of the road to meet it.

Nearly a year had gone by since Emil Goldfus left Brooklyn Heights to peddle his color-printing device in California. Burt Silverman was worried about his friend thinking that if anything had happened to him there would be no way to find out. Silverman realized how little he knew about Goldfus; none of his friends, no idea where he lived, no relatives. Harry MacMullen, the superintendent of the studio building, stopped Silverman in the hall and told him that the management was anxious about their missing tenant. The rent had been paid for a few months in advance, but Goldfus had been gone longer than that. MacMullen said the company would not carry Goldfus; if there was no word by the end of the month, he would be evicted.

The next afternoon, Silverman sat in his studio considering calling the Missing Persons Bureau. But he stopped; perhaps Goldfus wanted to be left alone. The telephone rang.

"Hello, Burt?"

A rich Scottish burr on the "r." He knew immediately. "This is Emil."

"You nut. Where the hell are you?"

A rush of talk; enormous relief on Silverman's part; an odd explanation from Goldfus. He said that when the business in California was done, he started back East through the southern part of the country. In Texas, he had a sudden heart attack and was hospitalized for four months. The news is disturbing, and why, Silverman asked, did he not write to anyone about it? Why didn't he let his friends know?

The answer was typically Emil. Oh, he said, he did not want to bother anyone with his foolish troubles. It wasn't really important.

When Goldfus returned to the studio, he elaborated a little about his heart attack. He told Silverman that there had been some petty thieving in the hospital ward, and he complained about the extravagant cost of medical care. He said that the medical facilities in Texas were awful and that is all he said. Burt asked him again why he had not written and Emil shrugged it off again. Obviously, he wanted to forget about it. Burt complied and did not press, although the story did seem strange, but he was long accustomed to his friend's reticence and what counted, really, was that Emil Goldfus was back.

Although Goldfus seemed undisturbed that his heart had given out, Silverman was preoccupied by it. He saw Emil as more vulnerable now; his isolation and older age were somehow exaggerated by the attack. Emil never complained; it was consistent with his style, with the attitude that all the "pissin' and moanin' " does not change anything. He worked within the framework of the possible. He was pragmatic, directly in confrontation with reality; without, it seemed, any cant or fantasy. One of those people who take pride in not having been sick a day in their lives. Emil refused to pamper himself or allow that he was ill. When the sinus condition he had had all along worsened, and Emil wandered around his studio with a nasal atomizer always ready, sniffing at it constantly, Silverman worried some more, for he knew that respiratory ailments were dangerous to those with heart trouble. And he knew it as intimately as one can, for his own father had died of heart failure, just six months after Emil moved into the building. If Silverman's anxiety over his friend came from those personal shadows, Emil caught none of it. He continued to be as active and engaged as he had always been; he was not worried.

Somehow, the circle at the Ovington building was drawing tighter. In the months after his return from that mysterious heart-attack trip, Emil was spending more time than before with Silverman and his friends. He seemed to be, almost imperceptibly, changing his role. At first it had been the ambiguous role of a friend who was old enough to be a father to any one of them. His reticence about himself and his projection of being removed from some of their young anxieties opened the door wide for fantasy. If none of the younger men actually voiced the fantasy, they were all faintly aware that they did consider Emil Goldfus a kind of father and felt about him that cauldron of feelings young men do about their own fathers. For Silverman, especially, the relationship reached deep into those feelings.

Over the years that they knew him, the faintly father-thing had become an unstated and rather safe way of relating to the man. But Emil could not be in so fixed a position for long. At times he stepped out of that role he had made, or the younger men had made for him, and became something else. In the months after his return, he dropped some of his distance from the others, acted the role of friend, and engaged more fully on a more equal plane in their lives.

He took a trip with Silverman one night to the Washington Market on the lower west side of Manhattan to take some photographs from which they both hoped to make paintings. Emil shared Burt's interest in street life, in men doing their work, in capturing on canvas those subtle gestures by which a figure reveals his whole life. That sensibility had shown up in Emil's work all along, but he did not talk much about it. Both men worked often from photographs, especially when it came to a subject for which a live model was not possible. So they set off on their joint enterprise on a fall evening, armed with several cameras, most of them belonging to Goldfus, and discussed, in advance, their "strategy."

Burt knew from experience that a "strategy" was needed, for it is difficult to explain that you are a painter and that the photographs will be used as studies for a painting. People are always suspicious of that; they want to know how come you are interested in *them* or what your gimmick is. Somehow, it makes things a lot easier if you simply say you are a photographer; people are less suspicious of photographers.

The two men decided in advance to pass themselves off as free-lance photographers, to say that they were working on a story about the Washington Market and let it go at that. They drove to Manhattan in Silverman's car and arrived at the market a little after ten when it is just coming to life.

It was the closet thing to Les Halles to be found in New York. The market was alive all through the night and the excitement that the place generated came in part from the knowledge that the rest of the city was asleep. Along those blocks near the Hudson River it was all noisy and sweaty and colorful. Produce trucks pulled up, undershirted men unloaded them; crates of fruits and sides of beef were lugged into the market stalls. Silverman and Goldfus wandered around with the cameras. They asked permission to take photographs and told their story about being free-lance photographers. Or one of them did. Emil, who enjoyed the idea of the masquerade more and more as the evening went on, let Burt do most of the talking. He was not good at projecting himself in social situations, he said. He was almost painfully shy. So Silverman told the photographer story and Goldfus hung back. Schoolboyishly, he giggled over the way they had put everyone on.

At four in the morning they had taken many rolls of pictures and were ready to go. They walked together to Silverman's car and Emil hung back. Silverman got in.

"Come on. I'll drive you home."

"No. Never mind. I can take the subway."

"Emil, it's four o'clock."

But Silverman, accustomed to that sort of thing, went on home. A few days later he discovered that an error in setting one of the camera speeds caused an entire roll of film to be underexposed. Oddly, the error had been Emil's. Although Burt considered his friend expert with cameras, the mistake was not only odd, but believable. It somehow added to Emil's credibility as a person that he would err where he ought to have been expert.

Emil made another photographing trip soon after that, with Burt's friend Harvey Dinnerstein. Dinnerstein planned to take some pictures in the Brownsville section of Brooklyn, again to incorporate some of the colorful street life in that neighborhood into his painting. Emil became involved because he lent Dinnerstein a camera, a cheap camera worth no more than twenty dollars, and invited himself along.

Emil was still self-conscious about taking pictures by himself. He was timid about approaching people to ask their permission and more timid about taking them without permission. Dinnerstein did most of the talking. They took most of their photographs together, but from different angles, and it was the subject of some discussion. Emil told Dinnerstein that his work, in his painting and from what he could see of his approach to photography, was very "frontal." Himself, he preferred taking things from an angle. He would stand off to the right or left of his subject and get a lot of oblique pictures. Emil said this gave the picture a feeling of perspective. Dinnerstein disagreed and his reaction to Emil's obvious feeling that this angling was more modern was simply that his friend misunderstood contemporary concepts. It rested there.

But the trip was productive and companionable. There were several good photographs of pushcart vendors and people slouching in doorways. Eventually, Emil painted some of the vendors. On the way back from Brownsville, Emil stopped at Dinnerstein's home for some coffee and left without reclaiming the camera he had lent. Dinnerstein forgot about it and Emil never pressed for its return.

There were other ways in which Goldfus's relationships changed after his long trip West. As a painter, he had always been the amateur in the group, whereas the others were, or hoped to be, professionals. Both he and they had often acted as if Emil were an apprentice, and Silverman, Levine, Schwartz, and Dinnerstein the teachers. But in the months after his return, Emil took a step in a different direction. He asked, in fact, to be allowed into the group on equal footing. After those photographing trips with Silverman and Dinnerstein, he began to sit in on some group sessions. They were mostly sketching sessions, in Silverman's studio, at which several of the young artists would hire a model, split the fee, and work for three hours. Emil joined the group, his first assumption of the role of a serious working artist.

The model arrived in the early afternoon and the four artists began to sketch her. She posed nude, in a variety of poses, and Silverman, Dinnerstein, Schwartz, and Goldfus worked silently. There was nothing remarkable about the model. She was a Negro woman, very voluptuous, with large breasts and good round buttocks, but still not especially attractive. It was the first time this particular woman had come to pose for the group and they were hard at work, thinking of her in terms of lines on the drawing pad. And Emil Goldfus, fiftyish, leaned toward Harvey Dinnerstein, who was sitting next to him. "Boy," he whispered, "I'd like to fuck her."

If Dinnerstein did not literally drop his sketching pencil, he did so in his mind. It was an extraordinary thing to say. First, because Dinnerstein did not think the woman attractive, the remark indicated an odd kind of taste. But, more, the idea of it was disturbing. It was a most sudden exposure of Goldfus's sexuality and that was something none of the younger men had really allowed into their conception of the man. It was like having your father nudge you in the ribs that way over some woman on the street.

Beyond the unexpectedness of its coming from Emil Goldfus, the line itself was intriguing. Perhaps he was trying hard to be "one of the boys," and the sudden crudeness was labored. But the feeling lingered that it might have been genuine and, if so, revealed something of him no one had seen.

Like another incident, as small as that one, but equally provocative. It happened, too, near the end of 1956 and it, too, revealed another face of the man, as well as the face of the times.

Late one night, Silverman came to the Ovington building. He had with him Helen Worthman, his girl friend. As they got out of the elevator at the fifth floor, they saw a light burning in Emil's studio and stopped to say hello. Emil was glad to have company. He put his brushes aside and brewed some coffee. Helen pointed to the Hallicrafters shortwave radio standing on end on the long work table. She asked if he could get European programs on it. Goldfus, nodding, got up and fiddled with the dial. It was a difficult manipulation because of the angle at which the radio stood. But it had to be in that tilted position, Emil told them, because it had a loose part and that was the only way it would play. He did not want to bother having it repaired. So he had to twist his arm to move the dial, and he turned it through several static-ridden bands until some music came through. Vaguely Strauss-like music. The three drank their coffee and listened to the music and when it ended a commentator came on the air and babbled a language the young couple could not recognize. It sounded Central European. As they were listening, the telephone rang in Silverman's studio, down the hall, and he went to answer it.

It was a friend who had tried to reach Silverman at home and was surprised to find him so late at the studio. Emil and Helen sauntered in while he was talking; the friend asked to whom the voices belonged.

"Oh, that's Helen and Emil."

Then joking, Silverman said, "We were just listening in on Moscow."

The friend laughed and Burt kept talking. When he had hung up, he turned to Emil, who said, "Don't ever say such a thing on the phone again. Even in jest."

And the look on Emil's face was harsh. He was not jesting; Emil was angry. And Burt was ashamed for, of course, Emil was right. At that time, in that place, you really did *not* say on the telephone that you had been lis-

tening to Moscow. Burt knew that it was a foolish and
perhaps compromising thing to say, for he knew that people as innocent of conspiracy as his cat were wary of the
telephone. So he took from Emil what he honestly considered a friendly and wise rebuke and never said it again.

Still Maki-Hayhanen-Vik managed to do his job, the
part of it that required him to travel to New York City
check for messages in the drops. That summer in
1956, soon after he had returned to Peekskill, he found
one. It read, "I would like to meet you in the same place
as before." He was not sure what it meant. The same
place as before, he thought, must be the Symphony Theatre, on Broadway and 95th Street, the site of his last
meeting with Mark before the Moscow trip. He went, at
the appointed time, to the Symphony Theatre and stood
around and looked around the balcony and checked the
men's room and did not see Mark. He left.

He sent a message through the drops: "I'll go and wait
for meeting with you in the same place where I met first
time Mark."

And he did. He returned to the RKO Keith's Theater
in Flushing where his first encounter with Mark had
taken place. In the smoking room, Mark was waiting.
Mark had indeed meant by "the same place as before"
the same place in which he had first met Vik.

The first thing Mark wanted to know about was the
cover work. Had Vik opened the studio? Vik said that he
had not because it was impossible to open over there, that
it was too wet, both in the storeroom and the other rooms.
Mark was not satisfied. He asked, then, about Vik's
photography and Vik had to answer that he had not
practiced much.

Little else was said. Mark reported briefly that he had
taken a plane to Paris and a train from there to Austria
and then to Moscow. But he had other travel plans on his
mind. He thought that Vik might as well go for a "vacation" to Moscow to "see his relatives."

The Makis stayed in Peekskill through the autumn and
into the winter. They drank and fought fiercely. Gene
Maki had his driver's license reinstated and was stopped
again. He barely passed the drunkometer test. He met
with Mark once or twice a week and was told that a message had been sent to Moscow that because the photo-

graphic shop had not been opened, there was time to
have a vacation. Mark presented it easily; Vik was terri-
fied. His instinct for self-preservation was not dulled. A
message came through one of the drops informing him
that Moscow permitted a vacation; as soon as possible he
was to apply for a United States passport and travel to
Europe as a tourist. This same message conveyed to
Reino Hayhanen the news that he had been promoted to
the rank of lieutenant colonel. Which must have been
meant to reassure him; to let him know that he was still
in good graces and that the vacation to Moscow would be
only that. It did not work.

Maki applied for a passport in November and, since he
already held a valid United States passport issued in Helsinki in 1952, it was only a matter of form to give him
another. It arrived in December.

On New Year's Eve, Maki took his wife to a party at
the Rock Cut Inn. It was loud and drunken and filled
with Peekskill's local population, working-class Irish and
Poles. Maki and Hannah sat off to the side. A man playing pool and getting progressively drunker asked Maki to
play. Maki stayed aloof. The pool player, goaded by the
foreigner's reticence, cursed him out across the pool table.
He hurled at Maki the worst epithet imaginable, one suggested by the stranger's thick Slavic accent and the local's
political orientation: he called Maki a Communist.

Negotiations for Maki's vacation in Moscow continued.
He received a message saying that he was to plan with
Mark how he would go and what he would tell his
friends, whoever they were, about his trip. Mark decided
to request that Maki make the whole trip by ship and
sent off the request, but an answer came quickly denying
it. Moscow preferred that Maki take a ship as far as Le
Havre, a train to Paris, another train to Germany, within
Germany to fly to West Berlin and then to Moscow. Mark
had wanted to send a parcel to his family in Russia
through Maki, but he thought it wise not to do so once
the final plans came through. He told Maki that he would
not be able to carry many parcels on a plane trip and
withdrew his request.

They also discussed alternate routes. He could go to
Mexico City, Mark instructed him, and wait in a specified bar for a Russian official who would arrive with further instructions. He handed Maki a birth certificate to

use in case it was impossible for him to use the United States passport. Mark said that the birth certificate would get him to Mexico and that from there he would be safe using the United States passport.

Maki took the certificate, in the name of Lauri Arnold Ermas, to Peekskill where he wrapped it in paper, stuck it in a cellophane bag, and buried it in the sand basement of his house. He said he "didn't like to use it."

Whatever hell it was to be with Maki while he lived through those months, Hannah began to show how she was taking it. Her temperament changed considerably and she who had been soft became brittle and had temper tantrums. One day she was out in the backyard watching some digging and leveling on the property. Maki had hired a local worker, Mike Spinelli, to level out a hilly section behind the house. Spinelli was at work with the steamroller. Hannah wanted to tell him something, something that had to do with the limits of her property. She tried, but because she was so angry and her English poor, Spinelli did not understand. He shouted at her; she shouted back and as she grew more agitated in her shattered English, Hannah grabbed a soda bottle lying in the yard and hurled it at him.

It is easy to forgive Hannah her outburst and easier still to see the chain of scapegoats in the Maki family. Gene Maki was clearly oppressed—by himself, by his inability to cope with his work, by what was to him a hostile environment, and especially by Mark, his superior, who treated him as if he were a fool. Whatever was bottled up in Maki was exacerbated by his relations with Mark and discharged upon Hannah, who endured.

The terror of the life that had evolved for her is unimaginable. Whatever she expected of Maki when she married him, she had not gotten it. However long she managed to blind herself to what her husband was up to, it was not forever. She began, feebly, to gesture in another direction.

Bertrum Kadis, the man who had sold the property to Maki, was driving his car through Peekskill one night when he saw Hannah heading for the railroad station. He stopped her and Hannah got into the car. Kadis convinced her to go home, and drove her back to the cottage on Dorislee Drive.

A few weeks later, she was visiting her next-door

neighbor Ruth Zoni and playing with the birds. Maki
came storming into the room.

"What the hell you do here? Come home."

"Keep your mouth shut," Hannah said. "You in enough
trouble already."

He did not keep his mouth shut then or in the months
that followed. Maki had been told what to say about his
trip. He told everyone in Peekskill, over and over again
so that they were tired of hearing about it, that he was
"gonna shoot pictures in Paris." He asked the Kornfelds
to keep an eye on Hannah while he was gone, to see that
she did not drink too much. But he had been talking
about it for months and did not seem any closer to leaving.

At the beginning of the new year, Mark said that it was
time. He instructed Maki to buy a ticket for the first ship
going to Europe and to send him the information through
a special drop created for only that purpose. The drop
was in a concrete staircase in Prospect Park, Brooklyn.
Maki managed to check with the steamship lines and discover that the *Queen Elizabeth* was to sail at the end of
January. He sent his message to Mark:

I bought a ticket to next ship—Queen Elisab. for
next Thursday—1.31. Today I could not come because
3 men are tailing me.

In the middle of February, Maki was still in the country; he was still living in Peekskill. He was summoned to
a meeting with Mark that took place in Prospect Park
near the drop site. At first Maki did not see Mark, for the
man was hiding behind bushes to check whether Maki
was being followed. He was not. Mark wanted an explanation. Maki explained. He said that he had been questioned by FBI agents and had not been able to leave on
the *Queen Elizabeth* because FBI agents took him off the
ship.

Mark insisted that Vik leave the country. He went,
again, over the established route: by ship to Le Havre,
train to Paris, train to Germany, plane to Berlin, then to
Moscow. Vik agreed to buy another ship ticket for the
first available sailing to Le Havre. Mark gave instructions
on what to do in Paris: to call telephone KLE 3341 and

convey, in code, the fact that he had arrived. Then a long lecture about how to use the Paris telephones, about how they were different from New York telephones.

Mark handed over two hundred dollars for trip expenses, extracted another promise from Vik that he would indeed go, and the two men parted.

FOUR

Burt Silverman began working on a portrait of his friend.
He had done some oil sketches of Emil before, but this
time he was moved to work on a full-scale portrait. Perhaps Emil's recent heart attack shocked Burt to a sudden
awareness of the older man's mortality, and he wanted to
preserve him, somehow. Whatever the motivation, Emil
did not like posing for the portrait. He had not minded
Burt's earlier sketches, for those had been of Emil reading
or playing the guitar and he had occupied himself while
Burt sketched. But posing formally irritated him and only
under constant nagging did he give way.

First, Burt did some small paint sketches to set the
mood for his evolving idea of the man. Apart from Emil's
striking features, he wanted to get something of that
searching, diligent intelligence, that competence and manual control of things. His studio, filled with all the bits and
pieces of technological civilization, yet still a painter's
studio surrounded by all the wonderful odds and ends of
his work-table, his glasses folded neatly in the pocket of
his white shirt, looking both serious and amused. In the
foreground was Emil's shortwave radio turned on end.

Once the pose and setting were accomplished, the
painting was not difficult. Emil complained and fussed
about the sittings, was impatient for it to be done, and
acted generally more difficult than at any time Burt knew
him. In spite of his irritability, he was a good model. The
bare bulb of the studio accentuated the sharp features—
the aquiline nose, prominent cheekbones, relatively severe mouth. The light made dark caverns for the eyes,
which nevertheless came through with a sympathetic look.
As he worked, Silverman found the face not only interesting, as it had always been, but more complicated than he
had thought. The face had at least two distinct moods:
that broad sweep of a forehead heightened by his bald-

ness made Emil Goldfus look mild and retiring at times and, at others, extremely intense and forbidding.

As the work went on, Emil said nothing about it beyond an initial murmured approval. But that was characteristic of him; he was reticent when it came to personal matters and his face on the canvas was, indeed, a personal matter. But he had a modesty that stemmed from embarrassment at being made too much of. As much concerned with approval and appreciation as anyone, he came across not as self-effacing but with a humorous self-deprecation, the kind that is really fishing-for-approval in reverse.

When it was done, Silverman searched for a title and decided to call it *The Amateur*. He had in mind the original meaning of the word: someone with a strong love of things. The painting was submitted for the annual exhibition of the National Academy of Design on Fifth Avenue in New York, a kind of holdout for "conservative" art, one of the few places left where one could get a "hearing" if one were a representational painter. It was accepted and hung in the Academy show throughout the following February.

It was a festive month for Silverman who had just become engaged to Helen Worthman. The Dinnersteins gave a surprise party for them and everyone from the Ovington building went—Feiffer, Levine, Schwartz, Fink, Ginzberg, Eugene Moses, a photographer, and Emil Goldfus, an old friend.

No one remembers much about the party except that the apartment was full of people and chaotic. Dinnerstein and his friends had painted murals in the style of Rubens, showing the loss of Silverman from the ranks of "eligibles" and groups of voluptuous nudes, Helen among them, with Silverman in the background as satyr. Goldfus arrived late, drank a little, and spoke to some of his friends. He left with Eugene Moses.

Moses was interested in antique camera equipment—Zeis folding cameras, old-fashioned Rolleis, the old tray system of photo processing. Only because he had that kind of hobby did Moses understand the photographic techniques Goldfus was talking about. Emil Goldfus knew a lot about technical things—lenses, focal lengths, and film sensitivities—but his information was at least ten years out-of-date. Moses thought it curious.

* * *

The engaged couple received a unique wedding present later that month from Goldfus, who seemed genuinely happy for his friend. He came into the studio one evening and presented a product of his work on the lathe, a rose-wood jewelry box with a hand-rubbed finish, silver hinges and clasp, and a silver medallion with a floral design on the top, which he had designed and etched himself. Inside, there was a small silver plaque, also leaf decorated, with an inscription: "To Helen and Burton from Emil." The workmanship was beautiful and the gift thoroughly touching, for it reflected quite clearly the man who had made it: richly conceived, warm, and just faintly archaic.

Dave Levine, Silverman's good friend, rented a studio in the building at the beginning of February 1957. He saw Goldfus almost daily. As he did Burt, Emil treated Dave Levine as a good friend, looked at his work and criticized it, brought his own in for inspection, lent art supplies when Dave needed them and never asked that they be returned. As Burt's, Dave's relationship with the older man was not simply professional. They went for walks together in Brooklyn Heights and they preferred to walk around the smaller streets behind the Ovington building, toward the new promenade. On one of those walks, Levine was surprised by a woman who came up to his friend Emil and said, "Don't I know you?" The woman insisted that she had known him twelve years before, in Chicago, a place Emil had never mentioned having lived in. Emil seemed embarrassed by the encounter and Levine was puzzled and the lady went her way.

Emil's work was no longer confined to the studio; his interests had expanded beyond the photography he had initially done and the painting in which he was still engaged. He had, in recent months, rented a storage room just down the hall on the fifth floor and had begun to use it for still another craft. Emil bought a lathe and in the storeroom, which was quickly crammed with more radio parts and lens parts and sketch pads and canvases and electronic objects none of the painters could identify or understand, began to turn out handmade jewelry. He worked in silver—producing small earrings, tie clasps, medallions—and in wood. From time to time he showed Dave and Burt the progress he was making; he was especially proud of some small rosewood jewelry boxes, beautifully crafted.

The studio, too, was stuffed with things. Dave Levine was free, as all of the people who came around were, to walk into Emil's place at any time without knocking. There were no secrets. Poking aimlessly around the room, often while Emil painted away at his easel, Dave came across some curious things. There were piles and piles of photographs and slides, which was not unusual, except that a great number of them showed parts of Bear Mountain State Park. Levine remarked upon that, for none of the views were especially interesting and the location was not known for its visual drama. Emil said nothing. And there was a tiny object wrapped in leather that turned out to be a small tripod with a slot into which a lens could be slipped. Dave could not make it out, but he never thought to ask Emil about it.

Reciprocally, Emil would wander into Dave's new studio, which had been put quickly into working order. He did not find there slides of Bear Mountain or small tripods wrapped in leather but, once a week, a collection of ladies from the neighborhood who came to be instructed in the art of sketching. Emil made a practice of arriving after the class had been in session for a while and treating the assembled ladies to his famous "jungle coffee." The ladies thought him charming.

Emil was not lavish, but he did give his younger friends gifts, inexpensive but personalized. At one point he presented Dave with a Japanese etcher's glass and, at another, following a long discussion about painters in Russia, during which Emil talked about Levitan whom he considered the Corot of Russian painting, a book of reproductions of the man's work. He also lent Levine a copy of Arnold Hauser's two-volume *Social History of Art*, in which the English Marxist art historian traces the sociological and psychological evolution of art from the Stone Age to the Film Age. The two volumes contain over a thousand pages written in a thoroughly German style, digestible only in small doses. Emil Goldfus had read the book thoroughly. Here and there, as he picked his way through the borrowed volumes, Dave Levine came upon underlined passages and marginal notes that read like a shorthand for his friend Emil's own social and philosophic thinking, a capsule of his hopes, fears, and idealism.

His longest marginal note was in a chapter dealing with
Homeric Greece. Writing about the emergence of the psychological naturalism of Euripides, Hauser noted how the
poet no longer used the Sophoclean motif of the "imma-
nence of justice in the course of the world." Hauser talked
about how life experience, for Euripides, was suddenly
seen from the human level of chance misfortunes, how
the playwright portrayed the capricious nature of worldly
fortune and translated mythological subjects to the level
ot the commonest problems of middle-class life. Emil's
note at that point shifted the focus away from Hauser's
literary and stylistic perceptions. He summarized Hauser
by saying:

> A reflection of the importance of chance (disasters,
> famine, floods, etc.) in commercial affairs. One day
> rich, the next reduced to poverty by fortuitous circum-
> stances, then by fortuitous circumstances elevated to
> richness, etc. etc. etc.

Emil's next concern was not with precariousness, but
craft. Hauser was at that point summarizing the art of
prehistory and primitive people. He said that the geomet-
ric style and formal stereotypes which evolve out of it
lead to a dilettantism that, in turn, reinforces the continued
simplification of forms. This happened, he said, because
the decorative abstract mode does not require anything
like the thorough training of naturalism. Next to this passage, Emil wrote, "c.f. modern art." This quip revealed
what the painters around Emil Goldfus had seen for
years, the intense concern he had for craft, training, and
technique. It showed up again in a stark question mark
next to a sentence of Hauser's dealing with the late
eighteenth- and early nineteenth-century Classicism and
Romanticism. Hauser quoted a juror of the French Academy who had taken issue with the importance of classic
precepts in painting, especially in the painting of David
and his school. "Talent," the Frenchman had written, "is
an expression of the heart, and far exceeds the significance of the hand." Next to the quotation, Emil Goldfus
wrote his question mark.

Emil was often drawn to Hauser's discussions of the
role of the artist as a human being in society. He noted a
passage describing modern art as an expression of the

lonely human being wherein art, as Hauser saw it, ceased to be a social activity and became the act of a single individual speaking to other single individuals. In the same vein, Emil marked for emphasis Hauser's statement that modern art owes a debt to Romanticism, from which it drew its exuberance, anarchy, violence, the "drunken stammering lyricism of our own time." Emil, like Hauser, disapproved.

In his notes in the book, as well as in his talk, Emil spoke of individualism that is not unbridled, not without respect for form, technique, and control. Yet he recognized the alternative, that freedom of expression is essential to the artist. In Hauser's book, he underlined a paragraph that described the Romantic artist: "Pre-Romanticism allowed deviation from the rules. Romanticism denies the validity of rules of any kind."

Emil picked up Hauser's anxiety about the repression or control of art in all authoritarian societies. He underlined Hauser's assertion that Fichte's dictum of "perfect freedom through perfect law" does not work and that it is wrong to assume that control will produce positive results. But Emil was still more suspicious of Bohemianism. He underscored Hauser's evaluation of the difference between Bohemianism in the 1830s, which the author considered exuberant, and the jaded tone of the late 1860s and 1870s when, Hauser said, "art no longer intoxicates, it only narcoticizes."

Through Hauser, Emil noted that doctrine and sterile abstract programs cannot automatically make for great art. He noted that often. Emil picked out a passage in which Hauser spoke of the Revolution in France, saying that revolution must change society first and that art will follow. In the margin, Emil wrote Karl Marx's dictum that art falls behind (society) just as often as it hastens in advance.

It was clear from the markings in the text that Emil, as a "technical man," was suspicious of the role of industry and business which, in Hauser's opinion, spurred enormous changes in the culture of Western Europe, breeding a hunger for novelty, a passion for innovation, for newness alone. This was toward the end of the book and there were only two notes that followed. Emil marked with approval Hauser's plea for the extension of the horizon of the mass of people so that Art might function without inhibition, so that it did not become the property of a minority, breeding a hothouse culture of esthetic exceptionalism.

The final note Emil wrote in the book was the most striking. He had drawn a heavy marginal line around a line of Dostoevsky's that Hauser quoted. "What can be more fantastic and unexpected for me," it read, "than reality?"

On March 2, 1957, Burton Silverman was married to Helen Worthman at the Hotel Bolivar, 82nd Street and Central Park West. Before the formalities, the couple held a cocktail party to which they invited the many people they knew whom they could not accommodate at the ceremony. Among those guests was Emil Goldfus who came from Brooklyn on the subway and ran into some of Silverman's friends on the way. Harvey and Lois Dinnerstein met him by accident in the subway station; a few stops later, Danny Schwartz and his wife Judy got on the train. The mood was merry, but Goldfus was not. He was complaining of sinus trouble. His difficulty in breathing got the best of him at one point, and before going on to Silverman's wedding, he searched out a drugstore and bought some antihistamines and a nasal atomizer. The younger couples were a little concerned for their friend, but he alternately said that his "condition" was indeed troublesome, and that really it was nothing, it would pass. He said that he had been thinking of going off to Arizona for a while, for a cure. That seemed a good idea.

The group arrived at the cocktail party and headed for the bar, which was kept under watch by the bride's mother. Drink in hand, Goldfus wandered among the guests, many of whom he knew. Since the wedding was an Orthodox Jewish one, the men were required to wear the traditional skullcaps. Goldfus dutifully placed one on his own head. Silverman saw him briefly at the beginning. He was, as always, a little shy and had come reluctantly, protesting when he was first asked that he was not one for large gatherings of people. Once there, he loosened some and went about the party (never far from his glass), the skullcap sliding crazily half off his head, looking like a Hassidic buck on a feast day. That angled yarmulke caused considerable comment. Some of the guests had jested about Emil's Jewishness before. They took it up again. Well, some thought, anyone who would wear a skullcap *that* way simply could not be Jewish. To others, the possibilities were more subtle: anyone who would wear one at such a rakish angle and get away with it must, of course, be Jewish.

Emil Goldfus did, in fact, look Jewish. That nose, primarily. It was quite large and prominent. And something about his manner. Not certainly, but possibly. His name bore out the possibility a little, for Goldfus might well be not only German in origin, but Jewish.

The speculation was good-natured there in the midst of the wedding festivities, and it was bantered back and forth for a while, then dropped. But it touched on something that had puzzled those people about Emil Goldfus all along and was not to be resolved.

The reception, begun at six, was scheduled to be over by eight. Toward eight, then, the room was emptying and the families of bride and bridegroom tried with utmost tact to get the lingerers to leave. Among those hanging on, oblivious to the schedule, was Emil. By that time, he had had quite a lot to drink and was tipsy. He talked with Silverman and was pressed by the soon-to-be mother-in-law to please leave. Politely. Emil refused. He complained that it had been such a great party, why couldn't he stay? The mother-in-law pressed more firmly. Skullcap askew, Emil left, the last to go.

The Silvermans, firmly married and ensconced in their new apartment, invited Emil Goldfus to dinner soon after their wedding. The evening was meant as an inauguration of the Silverman couple's dinner parties and a good-bye to Emil, for he had been talking quite consistently about the trouble his sinuses were causing him and the advice of his doctor that he go away for a cure. He had fixed a date of departure in April and the Silvermans, planning to leave on a European honeymoon, thought it would be some time before they saw him again.

Bearing a bottle of Liebfraumilch, Emil arrived punctually and the three sat down to a dinner Helen had concocted straight from a wedding-present cookbook. Emil tasted the dish, Welsh rarebit, and suggested to Helen that she ought to have cooked it slightly longer, with less water and a few more spices. Helen gulped, not in embarrassment, but surprise, for Emil had never shown himself to be especially interested in cooking, nor was it plausible

that this man, who dressed modestly and lived with a min-
imum of comfort and seemed interested in things other
than sensuous gratification, would really be a gourmet. But
there it was, still another facet of a seemingly simple personality, another door he slowly opened and then
slammed, another side of his life.

After dinner, the three moved to the other side of the
room for coffee and talk. Goldfus picked up a small balsa
wood "construction."

"What's this?"

"Something I'm doing for a design course," Helen said.

It looked like a small-scale model of an electric power
relay or a fragment of a bridge pylon, but it was neither.
It was merely an exercise in three-dimensional design, in-
corporating all the theories of spatial relationship, ab-
stractly.

"I don't like it," Goldfus said.

"It's meant to teach us structural principles."

"Well, it's not convincing that way. Or as an art form.
What you've got," he said, "is a sort of well-designed
nothing."

And they went from that to a general discussion of
how things are taught in this country. Emil was critical of
American universities, especially of the way each university had its own organization and requirements; he
thought that European universities allowed students to
move from one to the other without loss of credit or aca-
demic progress and that was better. His opinions on the
subject were strong, and Emil pursued his argument with
enthusiasm. He advocated a system whereby students
could move from one school to another with ease, allowing what he called a mobility of interest and full play for
intellectual investigation. Interestingly enough, the discussion, as it went on through the evening, was not only a
forum for Emil's strong ideas, but a way of taking the
sting out of his sharp reaction to Helen's design project by
generalizing his criticism. When he left, feelings were as
warm as they had always been and there was a twinge of
nostalgia on both sides. It was obviously a good-bye for
some time, for Emil did not know when he would return
from his sinus cure and the Silvermans planned to spend
the entire summer in Europe. Late in April, he called
once more and left.

*   *   *

On the day that Emil Goldfus paid the superintendent at the Ovington building two months rent for his studio and called Silverman to say he was leaving, a man called Martin Collins checked out of the Broadway Central Hotel in Lower Manhattan and left no forwarding address. Martin Collins was nobody. He was a reserve identity kept on hand for moments when Rudolph Abel could be neither himself nor Emil Goldfus nor Milton nor Mark. There was a certificate of birth in Abel's wallet that said Martin Collins had been born in New York City on July 2, 1897. Unlike the Emil Goldfus tale, there was no death at an early age to record for Collins. He never existed. The certificate was forged.

There are hotels in New York City, as there are in all large cities, inhabited by people waiting to die. They have different names; you find them in all parts of the city, but they are all the same. Furnished room hotels that take both transients and permanent residents, mostly permanent ones. The buildings are old and large and gray. As you come through the lobby there is a desk clerk in his shirt-sleeves, half asleep. He rents the rooms and runs the switchboard and sorts the mail and has learned to mind his own business. The hotel residents are sitting in that lobby on overstuffed chairs with shredding upholstery. They are old people reading newspapers in foreign languages. There are some drunks dozing in the dark corners, but most of the people are respectable, with no other place to go.

The elevator that takes you up is creaky and the operator has been at the job for twenty or thirty years. Each floor is like any other. The corridors are drab, the lights are dim, and the doors to each room exactly alike. Inside the room, you are cramped; there is no view from the window, only a back alley. The necessities are lined against the walls, like worn-out whores grown tired of saying, "Use me." There is a bed, often a double bed, a dresser in which the drawers stick, a desk, a lamp. Off to the side, if you are willing to pay extra for it, a minimal bathroom. If the window has curtains, they are plastic. If there are flowers in the room, they are plastic. It is not the end of the road, but it is one step away.

Into a series of these hotels, beginning in 1956, had come Rudolph Abel, registering under different names. For most of 1956 he lived in the Embassy Hotel at Broadway and 70th Street, a neighborhood he knew well. In September, he moved to the Ben Franklin Hotel, 222 West 77th Street; same neighborhood, same kind of place. On the card proffered for his signature when he arrived, he wrote "E. R. Goldfus," and on the reverse side, in the place marked "In Emergency Notify," the name of his friend, Burt Silverman. He stayed in the Ben Franklin until April 17, 1957. He was a good tenant, which meant he never bothered anyone, never asked for anything, and paid his rent every week. As if he were not there at all.

He moved in April and the move was a radical change from his life style of the past years. He went to the Broadway Central Hotel. He did not call himself Goldfus there, nor did he list his friend Silverman for notification in case of emergency. He became Collins, nobody. He checked into the hotel on April 19, saying that he planned to stay only two days. He listed his address as 3640 West Wilson, Chicago. Collins stayed until April 26. Two days later, he registered at another hotel, this time the Plaza in Daytona Beach, Florida. On the registration card, he signed Martin Collins, and gave his address as the Beekman Hotel, Broadway and 77th Street, New York.

Reino Hayhanen had sailed aboard the *Liberté* from New York on April 24. He had six full days of alcoholic thinking about his future. It did not make sense, however he thought about it. Hayhanen did not want to go home; his instinct for self-preservation was strong—on that count, he was no dunce. Whatever he anticipated at the end of his trip, he wanted none of it. What he really wanted was out. Not just out of the KGB, but out. Perhaps he had been trying all along to get himself caught, trying consciously or unconsciously. Still, he found himself on the Atlantic Ocean with a long trip to Moscow ahead.

The ship docked at Le Havre on schedule and Hayhanen arrived in Paris the next day. Appropriately, it was the first of May. He did as he had been told, telephoned the number Mark had given him, KLE 3341, and asked in Russian, as he had been told to ask, "Can I send through your office two parcels to the USSR without Mori Company?" The answer came back, in Russian, all a coded transaction, and a meeting had been arranged between Hayhanen and an official of the Russian Embassy. He rented a hotel room and went to the meeting, some-

where on the streets of Paris, wearing his same old blue
tie with red stripes, smoking his pipe in his own peculiar
fashion. As with his first encounter with Mark, Hayhanen
must have been absurdly obvious, for the official, like
Mark, recognized him immediately. They spoke in Russian and they walked to a bar for cognac and coffee.

The Russian gave Hayhanen two hundred dollars in
French and American currency for his onward journey.
Hayhanen, neglecting to say he had received his trip expenses from Mark before leaving the United States, took
the money and returned to his hotel room.

The next night, as arranged, he went to a visual meeting with the same Russian. He was, as they had agreed,
hatless and carrying a magazine in his hand; it meant that
he would leave the next day for West Germany and from
there by plane to West Berlin, East Berlin, Moscow. The
two men did not speak to each other, but the signal was
passed. Hayhanen went to the movies, back to his hotel,
and the next day to the American Embassy.

Somewhere along the line, and it is neither clear nor
public where, Reino Hayhanen decided to defect. To save
his skin, of course, not because he preferred the American way of life, but because he preferred to live. The decision to defect was not reasoned; it was the move of a
desperate man; it must have come to Hayhanen in one of
his many moments of fear and trembling. All he wanted
was out of the nightmare.

Hayhanen had a lot to say. He announced that he was
a Russian espionage officer with the rank of lieutenant
colonel and that he had some information to give American officials. He brought with him, as proof, one of the
hollow containers that he had used to conceal messages
left in drops. It was a Finnish five-mark coin that could
be pried open with a pin. A message, reduced in size,
could be hidden inside. He told about the drops and
everything else he knew and all of what he told was taken
down, painstakingly, inside the embassy and sent on home
for corroboration. A lot of it did check and on May 11,
less than three weeks after his departure aboard the *Liberté*, he was flown to New York City.

The man who wanted out of the nightmare was deeper
into it. There must have been, at the very first, a sense of
relief as he told his story in Paris; he must have felt, if
only for the first day, safe. After Mark's condescension,

Hayhanen was being taken seriously. He was protected, but not from himself. Although he did tell his story, he could not keep himself together, and he had regrets. On the plane from Paris, he tried to kick out all the windows. It was hard to keep him subdued, but the CIA men who accompanied him managed. Allen Dulles flew up to meet the plane and the interrogation began.

On May 12, the day after his return to New York, Reino Hayhanen gave written permission for a search of his house in Peekskill. At twelve twenty-five in the afternoon he wrote his signature on the paper put before him and drew a diagram of the Peekskill cottage, showing where he had buried a false birth certificate in the cellar. The permission authorized FBI agents Edward F. Gamber, John T. Mulhern, and George R. Masset to make the search. It was witnessed by Special Agents Lawrence McWilliams and Edward H. Moody.

Just after five o'clock that afternoon, Hannah Maki signed a paper saying she gave permission for her home to be searched. Hannah Maki had known nothing of her husband's plans and little of his life. She had received, since his departure for Paris, one communication which must have pleased her; Hayhanen had sent his wife a check for one hundred dollars, drawn on American Express, Paris. Jack Kornfeld at the Rock Cut Inn had cashed it for her. Then her home was searched and Hannah was left with a contingent of FBI men to guard her. She continued drinking heavily.

Hayhanen was kept in a hotel room in New York City where he was questioned continually. All day he talked to the FBI, and since they are scrupulous men the agents' notes taken during that period are dated. On May 12, 14, 15, 16, 17, 20, and 22, Hayhanen talked. He told his investigators everything he knew about his operation: Mark, the drops, the couriers he had known, the messages he had sent and received. When he was not talking, he was writing the story of his life in Russian, beginning with his birth in a village called Kaskisarri . . .

What a crowd there was around him. Six or seven FBI men at a time, no one knows how many from the CIA. For a man accustomed to being pretty much on his own, the hordes surrounding the defector oppressed and reassured him, alternately. He was not in good shape. He was frightened. He did not want to stay sober, but was forced to. He could give a great deal of information about Mark, for he had been to Mark's studio in Brooklyn three times. He could lead the FBI to the area of Clark and Fulton streets and eventually to the Ovington building. What he would not do is appear in public or testify in court. Hayhanen insisted on that, and although it was not immediately important, for Mark was still to be found, a courtroom lay dimly in the future.

On April 28, four days after his bumbling assistant had finally sailed for Paris on the *Liberté* and two days after he had paid the rent for two months in advance on his studio in Brooklyn Heights, Rudolph Abel arrived by train in Daytona Beach, Florida. He took a room at the Plaza Hotel and registered as Martin Collins, giving his permanent address as the Beekman Hotel, New York City. He stayed in Daytona until May 17; he painted a large oil seascape, then he returned to New York.

One wonders why. Reino Hayhanen defected to the Americans on May 4. Two weeks later Abel, who was safer in Florida than he could have been in New York and closer to an escape to Mexico, which he had once planned as an alternate route for Hayhanen, came back to the city in which he could be traced. Is it possible that the inefficiency of the Russian intelligence service extends so far as to leave Abel oblivious to Hayhanen's failure to reach Moscow, where he was certainly expected? It is conceivable that communications were that poor, but there is a better speculation about Abel's return and it had more to do with his mind than his network. Rudolph Abel trusted quite implicitly the service in which he held the rank of colonel. That trust had been indicated in his behavior before, and it remained steadfast. He accepted the *modus operandi* without question—the tedious and melodramatic system of drops and signals, the codes, the cover names, the multiple personalities. He accepted, too, the compartmentalization of the system. Agents generally knew little about one another that would be incriminating if one were caught. It was possible, then, that Abel did know of Hayhanen's "going over" and did not consider it a spontaneous act. He could well have thought that Hayhanen was meant to defect, that an attempt was being made by "his" side to "double" Hayhanen. If his instincts told him that he might be in personal danger, Abel ignored them well. He did not panic and he did not bolt. He returned to New York.

Another speculation. Abel did his job well. He was often called, later, by the press, a "hard-nosed professional." His job was more important than he was. If he knew he was in danger, if he knew that Hayhanen was capable of leading the Americans to him, he must have been highly motivated to return in spite of it. There may have been a job to do in New York City that was too important to set aside. Or there may have been things around that needed to be destroyed whatever the cost to himself.

He returned to New York and registered at the Hotel Latham, on 28th Street just off Fifth Avenue, as Martin Collins. He moved into room 839, for which he paid twenty-eight dollars a week, payable at the end of each week on Saturday. At first, he stayed away from the Ovington building. A few days after his arrival, on May 21, he visited Dr. Samuel Groopman, who had an office in the hotel. Dr. Groopman vaccinated him against smallpox and signed a health certificate. On May 23, he took the train to Brooklyn and went to his studio.

It might have been a scene from any gangster movie out there in Brooklyn Heights. Hayhanen had remembered the site of Mark's studio and led the FBI to it. The Ovington building was placed under surveillance and the agents scattered all over—in the Hotel Touraine, the tallest building around, two blocks down Fulton Street, with agents posted on the roof and in some rooms on upper floors. Across the street from the building entrance, in the park, agents on the benches. Inside the large post office building across Fulton, more agents. And a few just wandering around the neighborhood, looking inconspicuous. Although they had no assurance that Mark would return, they waited. The days are long when you have nothing to do on your shift but stare through binoculars at some windows or keep your eyes fixed on a doorway. You amuse yourself with odd things and you learn a lot about the lives of those on the periphery of your main target. So the agents in the Hotel Touraine had a good look, through their binoculars, at the windows facing them on the south side of the Ovington Studios. They learned little of interest in the Abel case, but a lot about the love life of one lady whose studio faced their lookout point.

The agents were so scrupulous in their watching that they could tell you the brand of cigarettes the lady smoked.

But on the night of May 23, their attention shifted elsewhere. Special Agent Neil Heiner was on the twelfth floor of the hotel when he saw the light go on in studio 505. It was a quarter to eleven. There was only one light in the studio, suspended on a cord from the ceiling with a shield around it. By that light, he saw a man's figure moving. He could not see the man's face clearly; all he could tell was that the man was middle-aged, bald, with a fringe of gray hair around the edges; wearing glasses. Just before midnight, Heiner saw the man put his hat on; then the light went out. It was that hat that came in for a good deal of attention in the weeks to follow: a dark straw summer hat with a bright white band. It made it easy to identify the wearer, even from a block away. Wearing that hat, Abel left the building and Heiner radioed to his colleagues.

Joseph C. McDonald, special agent of the FBI, was sitting on a park bench just across the street from the building. Just after midnight, he saw the man matching Heiner's description down to the dark straw hat with a two-inch-wide white band. Abel was carrying a coat over his arm as he came out the front entrance, made a right turn and walked along Fulton Street to Clinton, up Clinton to Montague and down to the BMT Borough Hall subway station, McDonald close behind him. The two men got into an elevator together and down the steps to the train platform. Abel walked all the way to the end of the platform, McDonald ten yards behind him. At the end, there was a crowd. McDonald stood among them and the straw-hatted man turned, walked right past him, and a train came in. The man boarded the next to the last car, McDonald the last. He could not see his man; the train pulled into a station and McDonald peered out of the closing doors. No, he had not gotten off. So McDonald changed his seat and rode with his eye on Abel to the City Hall stop, where they both got off.

The chase continued, Abel going up to Broadway, walking north on Broadway to the corner of Chambers Street, where he stood waiting. McDonald hid in a doorway. They waited. A New York City bus appeared a minute or two later, as if Abel knew the schedule, and he got on. McDonald hailed a cab and followed that bus. At

27th Street and Broadway, Abel got off and walked to
Fifth Avenue, one block along Fifth and turned the cor-
ner at 28th Street. McDonald lost him. When Special
Agent McDonald reached the corner of 28th Street and
Fifth Avenue, the street was empty. He made his report
and the watch began again.

The scene was repeated three weeks later, but this time
there was a different outcome. The cast of characters was
the same; their positions on stage just as they were on
May 23, the timing just a bit off. Agent Heiner, on the
twelfth floor of the Hotel Touraine, saw the light come on
in studio 505 of the Ovington building about ten o'clock
at night. The same man was in the room and he moved
about the same way as before. Just before he left, ten
minutes to midnight, he put the same hat on, a dark straw
hat with a bright white band. Heiner radioed again to his
colleagues. Agent Ronald B. Carlson in the post office on
the other side of Fulton Street watched the Ovington entrance and saw Abel leave. He stayed at his post office
post and radioed to the other agents scattered in the
neighborhood that the man had come out of the building
and turned east on Fulton Street. Heiner, his view of the
main entrance obstructed, saw the man walking down
Fulton. It was a warm night and Fulton Street was full of
people, but the hat stood out and acted as a beacon. The
hat passed just beneath Heiner's position; he watched
through his binoculars. Running up Tillary Street to Fulton was Agent Fred Sowick, who had been waiting in the
post office building. Sowick saw the hat walking along
Fulton and followed.

Together, the two men went again into the BMT subway station at Clinton and Montague streets. They rode
the Fourth Avenue line Manhattan-bound local train together to 28th Street and Fourth Avenue. It was a quarter
past twelve. Sowick left the train station and followed his
man as he walked west on 28th Street and turned into the
entrance of the Hotel Latham. He made his report and
the watch, now in a new location, continued.

One Friday night in June, Mr. and Mrs. Zoni were
driving up to their summer home on Dorislee Drive,
Peekskill. As they turned into the drive and off the highway, a deer stepped into the road. Mrs. Zoni screamed
"Don't hit him!" and her husband stopped the car and

turned the headlights off. Suddenly there was a thud; a
man had jumped onto their car and he was holding a
machine gun. The Zonis sat petrified in the front seat and
the man looked through the car window. "Oh, Mr. and
Mrs. Zoni," he said, and motioned with his gun. "Go
ahead." They went ahead, up the hill to their house right
next to Eugene Maki's cottage, right inside the house, and
right to the telephone. Mrs. Zoni dialed the state troopers.
She asked, not very coherently, who were the men on her
road with machine guns who knew about her and her husband? The trooper on the line said he would check and
within a few minutes the Zonis, trembling behind their
window shades, saw the flashing lights of the troopers'
car. The car left and Mrs. Zoni's telephone rang.

"It's perfectly all right, Mrs. Zoni," said someone from
the troopers' office, "you're being well protected."

For a while, no one in Peekskill knew what was up,
and around Dorislee Drive were wild rumors. But they
did not last long, for the truth was known. Eugene Maki,
their neighbor, had been exposed as a Soviet spy, been
returned from Paris, and, after a while, was kept in Peekskill. They had seen a lot of digging in the basement of
Maki's cottage and had thought, at first, that Hannah had
finally had enough and killed her husband. But the basement yielded no corpses, only empty vodka bottles and
beer cans. Eventually the Zonis learned that the men who
swarmed Dorislee Drive and hid out behind mounds of
sand in Maki's backyard watching the house were from
the Federal Bureau of Investigation. Soon Maki himself
was brought to Peekskill, ensconced in his cottage with
Hannah, surrounded by FBI men.

The special agents assigned to Reino Hayhanen and his
wife were to keep them happy and grill them. Neither job
was easy. Hannah made things difficult in her own way
by insisting that the agents stay out of her home, which
the agents allowed her to do. So Hayhanen and his wife
stuck out the early summer inside, a ring of agents around
them. Sometimes, Hannah would "allow" the men onto
the porch and there they would sit through the long afternoon, talking with her husband. Who was, to say the least,
difficult to talk to. About anything. Hayhanen drank constantly, he trembled, he was belligerent. Mrs. Zoni heard
one of the agents tell Hayhanen that if he drank another
can of beer, "I'll knock you out."

They did not knock him out; they pampered him. One Sunday morning, Hayhanen walked into the Rock Cut Inn and asked Jack Kornfeld to sell him a bottle. Kornfeld refused; it was too early and liquor sales at that hour were against the law. Behind Hayhanen materialized six men who showed Kornfeld their credentials. They told the proprietor to give Hayhanen whatever he wanted.

The wheels turned. Everything Hayhanen said was checked; the various arms of the Department of Justice reached, stretched out. The FBI had a lot, but they did not yet have Mark in person. A little after midnight on June 13, they had him; not in their possession, but in full view. Agents had discovered that the man whom they knew as Mark, who they knew had a studio in Brooklyn Heights as Emil Goldfus, was also living in the Hotel Latham in New York as Martin Collins.

The agents on the street reported to the agents at FBI headquarters; the information traveled to a supervisor and then to Washington, along links in the chain there. It passed through Sam Papich, liaison officer between the FBI and the Immigration and Naturalization Service. Papich took it to INS and left it in the lap of Mario Noto, deputy assistant commissioner for Special Investigations. Noto's job was to supervise any investigations falling within INS jurisdiction that dealt with subversives, criminals, drug addicts, and other "immoral classes of people." Which included Mark.

Noto had part of the story. He was told that a man was living in New York City who had entered the country illegally and was suspected of espionage. In the days that followed, more information flowed in; the story enlarged. Papich, still, was the bearer of the news. The FBI and INS had a list of all the aliases used by the man in New York; they knew that he had entered the country from Canada and engaged in espionage; and that he held a high rank in the Soviet espionage apparatus. Information concerning his true identity, Noto was told, had been established.

Noto took the news to his superior, Commissioner Joseph M. Swing. Noto, convinced that the INS had a good illegal-entry case, told the commissioner that he proposed to place the man under deportation proceedings. He told Commissioner Swing of the espionage involved; Swing had not heard of the matter before.

The result of investigations that had been going on since early May were sent to the Internal Security Division of the United States Attorney's office. The man in charge was William F. Tompkins who had come to the Department of Justice from the New Jersey legislature and made his name there prosecuting the rackets and crusading against narotics. Tompkins dispatched two attorneys from his division to talk to the witness, the only witness: Hayhanen.

The attorneys talked. Hayhanen, sullenly, listened. For two days, on June 18 and 19, Hayhanen refused—absolutely, categorically, vehemently. He said he would continue to tell his story, to give whatever information he had, but would not testify in public. He was afraid, he said, of reprisals against his mother, brothers, and sister, all of whom were living in the Soviet Union.

The matter went back to the Internal Security Division and someone made a decision. The available evidence was insufficient to secure a warrant or an indictment on espionage charges. Had the witness only been willing, the Division and the FBI were fully prepared as of June 19 and fully intended to arrest the man in New York and charge him with being a spy. But the witness was not willing and it could not be done.

Mario Noto, deputy assistant commissioner for Special Investigations, called Robert Schoenenberger, supervisory investigator, to his office at the Immigration and Naturalization Service in Washington, D.C. It was a very warm Thursday afternoon, June 20, 1957, just past three o'clock. Schoenenberger, a six-foot-tall man with a squarish face, aquiline nose, and very tight-lipped speech, was experienced at making Immigration arrests. His record included over one thousand such arrests in 1947 alone, and he was proud of that. Compiling that record had brought him in touch with some interesting aspects of humanity. He liked to talk about how some of his "cases" reacted to being arrested: one woman had torn off her clothing and hurled it at Schoenenberger as he tried to arrest her; another had stabbed him in the cheek with a nail file. The scar remained, formed a dimple on the right side of his face.

Schoenenberger had known for a few days about the alien-spy in New York. On Thursday afternoon, Noto told him he was to go up to New York to supervise the arrest. An INS agent who worked under Schoenenberger, Lennox Kanzler, was brought into the office and told about the arrest. Like the Soviet and American spy systems, the law enforcement agencies operate on the principle of telling agents only what they need to know. Mario Noto had most of the information; he passed some of it on to Schoenenberger, but not all of it. Reino Hayhanen, for example, talking away, was not part of the "edited" dossier that was being handed along the chain. So it was the first time Lennox Kanzler was hearing about the case, and he heard only that there was "some information that would possibly spell out a deportation case."

Noto, Schoenenberger, and Kanzler traveled to the FBI offices, where they met with Sam Papich and three or four FBI agents. It was late in the afternoon and the meeting lasted several hours. Noto had the papers drawn up and told Schoenenberger and Kanzler to contact the New York office of the FBI when they arrived.

Noto had called the New York office of the INS and asked that they ready themselves and send someone to meet the Washington men who would arrive at Newark Airport at half-past eight that evening. Ed Farley had been sent to meet the incoming plane. He arrived with plenty of time to spare and had to wait two hours. At half-past ten, the two men from Washington arrived, bearing the documents required to make the arrest: a warrant and show cause order drawn up in Washington, naming Emil Goldfus alias Martin Collins, wanting only the signature of the man with jurisdiction in New York. Schoenenberger carried also a detailed report on the activities of Goldfus-Collins, which had been prepared by the FBI in Washington.

At midnight, there were five men in the offices of INS on Columbus Avenue in New York: Schoenenberger, Kanzler, Farley, Edward Boyle, an investigator from the New York office, and John L. Murff, acting district director. Boyle knew nothing of the "mission" he had been assigned to until Schoenenberger drew forth the warrant and show cause order, to which Murff put his signature. Half an hour later, the assembled company met as had been arranged from Washington with special agents of the New York FBI office. The arrest was mapped out and gone over for two hours, and finally, there in FBI headquarters, everyone went to sleep.

Very early the next morning everyone was up and, many cars full, heading toward the Hotel Latham on East 28th Street. All of the men were, of course, accustomed to long nights on duty with little or no sleep and only a few felt tired. Schoenenberger and Kanzler left at six-thirty in an FBI automobile; two special agents went with them. Farley and Boyle traveled together in another car. It was early and already the day was warm. With no traffic impediments, the cars reached the Latham in less than thirty minutes.

Where the FBI was ready. Agents had been "staked out" there since the day before, occupying room 841. There were, in all, eight agents scattered around the eighth floor, hanging around the corridor, wandering in and out of room 841, smoking cigarettes, watching the time.

FIVE

ON June 21, 1957 in a room in the Hotel Latham it was stifling, so hot that the man on the double bed slept naked. Around him, in that twenty-eight-dollar-a-week room, no more than ten feet wide and thirteen feet long, clutter. The clothes closet door was ajar; the chest of drawers, desk, luggage rack strewn with books, paints, last night's clothing. A gray Hallicrafters shortwave radio stood silent on the night table.

At seven o'clock in the morning, INS Supervisor Schoenenberger and Investigator Kanzler were cruising in the streets. Farley and Boyle, INS agents, went up to the eighth floor of the hotel and waited in room 841. FBI Special Agents Gamber and Blasco were in the corridor. Gamber knocked on the door of 839.

Something sleepy came from inside: "Just a minute" or "Wait a minute." The door opened; Gamber pushed it wider and went in. Rudolph Abel, groggy and naked, blinked. Blasco followed his partner in, leaving the door open behind him. The two agents handed their identification cards to the nervous Abel who took them, turned them over, handed them back.

Then there were three. Special Agent Joseph Phelan joined the group.

"Put something on."

Abel reached for a pair of undershorts.

"Sit on the bed."

He sat.

"Are you certain you know who we are and which governmental agency we are with?"

"Yes."

"The FBI has jurisdiction in matters pertaining to the security of the United States. We want to talk to you concerning a matter involving the internal security of the United States."

Abel was silent.

The questioning began, ceremonial, conventional, wooden. Abel played his part sullenly.

"What is your name?"

"Martin Collins."

"Date of birth?"

"June 15. July 15."

"What?"

The spy, in his undershorts, looked up.

"Could I have my false teeth?" he muttered. "They are in the bathroom."

Phelan, who had been leaning against the bathroom door, went to get them. A slight interruption. Teeth in place, the play continued.

"Date of birth?"

"July 15, 1897."

Why had he originally said "June 15, July 15," they wanted to know.

No reply.

"Where were you born?"

"New York City."

"Where do you live?"

"Here."

"How long have you resided in the Hotel Latham?"

Abel looked as though he were giving the question some thought. No answer.

"Where did you reside prior to the Hotel Latham?"

Silence.

"Your mother's name?"

"Martha Collins."

"Her maiden name?"

He hesitated. "Rollins."

"Are you employed?"

"No."

"When were you last employed?"

"Some time ago."

He was asked for details. No answer.

"Father's name?"

Silence.

And so on, into the second act: Gamber spoke.

"Colonel, we have received information concerning your involvement in espionage."

It was the first time Blasco, special agent, heard that the man they were talking to was a colonel.

Abel did not say a word.

He was told that if he did not "cooperate," he would be under arrest before he left the room.

Silence.

The agents had their instructions. If Abel "cooperated" about his background and activities in the United States, they were to call their immediate supervisor in the New York office and tell him of the degree of "cooperation" being exhibited. If he failed to do so, they were to summon the men next door, INS Agents Farley and Boyle, to arrest him.

He was, obviously, failing to cooperate. Twenty-three minutes gone, and the colonel was silent. He thought, when he talked about it later, that the scene had been played much faster. He thought that the FBI men had pushed their way into his hotel room and barraged him for five minutes and then someone said to "bring in the others." He thought, too, that when the "others," came in, there was an army of them. Rather cinematic; actually, it was done in a lower key.

Blasco and Gamber went off to confer in whispers in the corner. Finally, they decided to move and sent Phelan to get the INS men. He did not have far to go. Farley and Boyle were waiting in the hall.

They came forward onto center stage, armed, prepared for resistance, although it was not necessary. The situation was "obviously secure," according to the INS men; the FBI had "pacified" it. As Farley and Boyle moved into the room Blasco had to move back, away from the bed; with Special Agent Gamber, he lounged near the doorway. The INS men shuffled forward.

"What is your name?" Boyle asked Abel who was sitting on the bed, elbows on his knees, chin in his hands.

"Martin Collins."

Boyle and Farley showed their identification cards.

"We are placing you under arrest."

Boyle took from his pocket the warrant for arrest of alien that had been signed by Acting District Director of the Immigration Service John L. Murff and dated the previous day, June 20.

"Whereas," he read, "from evidence submitted to me, it appears that the alien Martin Collins alias Emil R. Goldfus who entered this country at an unknown point from Canada during 1949, is within the United States in violation of the immigration laws thereof, and is therefore liable to being taken into custody as authorized by section 242 of the Immigration and Nationality Act . . ."

Abel listened silently.

"You are entitled," Boyle said when he came to the end of the document, "to consult a lawyer. It is also your constitutional right to remain silent."

Boyle endorsed the warrant as having been served. It was 7:35 A.M.

Through the open door came two more men, Schoenenberger and Kanzler. Schoenenberger was there to supervise, Kanzler to assist in the next act: the search.

Boyle told Emil Goldfus alias Martin Collins that he would be taken to INS headquarters and that it was best that he take his belongings with him. Farley searched the man in his undershorts and Boyle went to the closet just to the right of the entrance to the room. Lingering at the entrance were the three FBI agents, out of the spotlight. In the closet, Boyle rummaged around the clothes and valises, looking for documents of nationality and weapons. From one of the valises he drew a wallet and, from that, three slips of paper.

The first, typewritten, said: " 'Balmora,' Avenida Oberon. 3 p.m. Display left of entrance. I. 'Is this an interesting picture?' L. 'Yes. Do you wish to see it, Mr. Brandt?' L. smokes a pipe and has red book in left hand."

On the second piece of paper, also typewritten, were two addresses: "Mr. Vladinec, P.O. Box 348. M-w. K-9 USSR. Sign 'Arthur.' W. Merkulow, Poste Restante, M-a, USSR (Russia). Sign 'Jack.' "

And the third, this one handwritten, said: "In Mex: Signal 'T' on pole opposite # 191 Chihnaahva (Chihvahaa) St. (Fonolia Roma), using side of pole towards roadway. Sat or Sun, Tues, Thur. Met on Mon, Wed, Fri at 3 P.M. movie 'Balmora.' "

In the same wallet Boyle found a clothing store bill made out to Emil Goldfus. He turned to the man he called Martin Collins, whom he had just arrested.

"Who's that?"

"That's me."

The search went on. At first Abel had run to the bathroom for sips of water, back and forth, often; he had complained that his dentures did not sit right, he had difficulty talking. His Adam's apple kept bobbing constantly and that, to the practiced eye of the INS agents, was a sure sign of anxiety. But, as a half hour passed, he regained his composure. His clothes were searched and piled on top of the dresser. Everything was taken from the closet and from his suitcases and from the drawers of the bureau. Spread on the bed was all the clutter, laid out; there the man lay exposed.

He was almost a drugstore himself: foot powder, a thermometer, aspirin, athlete's foot powder, athlete's foot lotion, Sucrets, Band-aids, Ace bandage, Ar-Ex Chap Cream. And a well-groomed fellow, too: Old Spice Shaving Lotion, Old Spice Cologne, Stopette deodorant. He had in his wardrobe a gray tweed jacket from John Wanamaker, a gray jacket from John David, five pairs of gray Daks pants, three ties, three shirts, checked pajamas, a sweatshirt, two pairs of undershorts, and three T-shirts. A decent wardrobe, good quality, but short on underwear. He also had eleven pairs of white socks (for the athlete's foot ailment) and thirty-three white handkerchiefs, which the INS men bemusedly noted on their list. There were three pairs of reading glasses and one pair of sunglasses. Rudolph Abel was prepared to look after himself.

The rest was an odd miscellany of keys, hotel bills, painted canvases, including a self-portrait, sketchbooks, film, lenses, cameras, laundry bills, stationery, envelopes, stamps, greeting cards, pipe cleaners, an alarm clock, pencils, charcoal, and paint brushes.

An ordinary assortment; what you would expect of an artist-photographer until you came across two birth certificates (one for Emil Robert Goldfus, one for Martin Collins) and a certificate of vaccination against smallpox recently issued to Martin Collins. Put them together with a photograph of a man with the name "Morris" written on the back and one of a woman with "Shirley" written on it; a bankbook from the East River Savings Bank showing a balance of $1386.22 in the account of Emil Goldfus; twenty-five twenty-dollar bills, ten fifty-dollar bills, and a brown paper wrapper holding four thousand dollars in twenties—not so ordinary.

Those pieces of his life lay there on the bed, a puzzle. No one in the room could quite put them together, but then, it was not their job to do so. That came later. The job of the INS agents was to arrest Goldfus-Collins and bring him, along with his possessions, to their headquarters.

Farley asked which suit he wanted to wear. A gray one.
The suit was thoroughly searched, for the second time,
and handed over. Abel requested an undershirt and that,
too, was searched. He dressed. An INS agent was sent
downstairs for the hotel bill.

Then the packing began. Suitcases were laid open and
the contents on the bed thrown into them. There were
some things scattered around the room still and Abel began picking them up, putting some in the suitcases, and
throwing others away into a wastepaper basket. He said
he did not need to take the jars of paint lined up on the
windowsill. Into the wastebasket he flung some books
(*Nights of Love and Laughter, The Ribald Reader, A
Time to Love and a Time to Die, Paintings from the São
Paulo Museum*), an empty tin of Sucrets, a box, half
empty, of Sheik prophylactics, Neo-Synephrine nosedrops,
a piece of garnet paper and rubbing block, four pencils.

The INS men were doing most of the packing. Abel
watched his things being thrown into the largest suitcase
and objected. He asked to repack it himself and Schoenenberger, who was in charge, said all right. Slowly Abel
refolded the clothes, placing each piece carefully inside.
Kanzler interrupted to ask what Abel wanted done about
his hotel room. Rhetorical question.

Abel answered. "Will you tell me where I'm going?"

"Immigration office at 70 Columbus Avenue."

"Well, I guess I might as well check out of the hotel."

The agent who had gone for the bill returned.

Abel took twenty-one dollars from the bed, where piles
of his money were lying, and handed it over. The agent
took the money down to the desk and Abel kept working on his suitcase, folding, refolding, packing. He asked
to transfer some things from a camera case to the bag.
Schoenenberger said it was okay. Abel was repacking
some Winston cigarette packs that had spilled from a car-
ton. He stopped.

"Should I take them?"

Schoenenberger answered, "Yes."

"Will I have access to them?"

A nod.

He put the cigarettes in, closed the suitcase. It was just
half past eight in the morning. Out came the handcuffs
and Colonel Abel left the Hotel Latham handcuffed to
Agent Boyle's left arm. With Schoenenberger, Farley,

Boyle, and Kanzler, he went down to the 27th Street entrance of the hotel and out to a waiting car. As they came onto the street, a woman was passing. She looked at the men and gasped when she saw the handcuffs. Boyle wondered who she took to be the prisoner, for Rudolph Abel hardly looked criminal. If I didn't have a tie on, Boyle thought . . .

Upstairs, there were still the special agents of the FBI, standing in the vacant hotel room and waiting in the corridor. They watched the prisoner leave. Special Agent James P. Kehoe went to the room of the hotel's manager, Nathan Wilson. Wilson had been somewhat informed of what was going on in room 839 of his hotel and had known that FBI agents were in the room next door. He did not quite know what it was all about, but suddenly it was over. Wilson signed permission for the special agents to search and seize any property in room 839.

Three agents went through everything. Although the prisoner had taken nearly everything with him in the INS car, the men of the FBI spent three hours in the room. The hours were profitable ones, for the wastebasket held a treasure. When they finished turning over the magazines and trash that lay on the dresser, the agents came to the wastebasket, filled to the brim. They looked through *Nights of Love and Laughter, The Ribald Reader, A Time to Love and a Time to Die.* Then they came across a discarded pencil, which turned out to be hollow. Inside were some microfilms. Also, a block of wood in a casing that he thought to be sandpaper caught an agent's eye and that block, along with the hollow pencil, clearly suspicious objects, were sent off to the FBI laboratory.

Downstairs Boyle and his charge got into the back seat of the INS sedan; Farley, Kanzler, and Schoenenberger rode up front. They went straight up Fifth Avenue, turned right at 59th Street, drove across town to 62nd and Columbus. Hundreds swathed in the little disturbances of man—making traffic lights, finding parking spaces, thinking about punching time clocks—passed that car early Friday morning. They were not noticing. Nor was the colonel, sitting upright inside, noticing them.

Boyle saw Abel inch his left arm along the front of his body.

"Hold it," he shouted. "What are you going for?"

Abel had a tie clip in his hand. Boyle, with his free

arm, flipped it up to the front seat and asked the other
three to have a look at it.

"See if there's anything in that."

Schoenenberger, Farley, and Kanzler each looked to
see if they could take it apart. They could not.

"No, nothing," Schoenenberger said, and gave it back
to Boyle.

Just before nine, they arrived at INS headquarters.
Abel was in the building for seven hours; he was finger-
printed, photographed, questioned, and searched. The
INS agents asked him again and again to cooperate. Abel
refused. The agents pored over his sketchbooks, his paintings, his thirty-three white handkerchiefs. Abel watched
them. The agents were impressed: Abel could talk on any
topic; he was thin and stooped, but he bore himself with
extraordinary, untouchable dignity; he was scholarly. As
he talked and refused to answer questions, the colonel
doodled on some pieces of paper that had been put in
front of him. One of the agents picked the paper up,
could not make it out, and said, "What's that?"

"Logarithm tables," said Abel.

In the late afternoon, he was moved. Traveling in another INS car with two investigators, Seeley and Judge,
who were to be with him for a while, Colonel Abel was
taken to Newark Airport, through New York City traffic
jams on an impossible summer Friday. There at the airport, a DC-3 was waiting. The colonel wondered why
there were no reporters around for, if nothing else, his
fantasies of being captured were accompanied by the pop-
ping of flashbulbs. The airport was full of weekend trav-
elers and no working press; the three men were the only
passengers aboard the DC-3. Soon after take-off, the
handcuffs were finally removed and the colonel, sitting
back in his chair, relaxed and asked his inevitable question: "Where are we going?"

"I don't know," Seeley said.

About eleven at night, the plane came in for a landing
and the prisoner, watching from the window, said they
must be in Alabama. He had calculated the plane's course
by the stars and estimated the distance from Newark by
its speed. They were in the Mobile, Alabama airport,
where the plane was refueled. An hour and a half later,
they took off again. Colonel Abel fell asleep on a couch
inside the plane and when he awoke, they had landed

again. They were in Brownsville, Texas; it was half-past four in the morning, still dark. Two cars were waiting to carry the prisoner and his INS companions across sixty miles of flat Texas countryside to the Alien Detention Facility, McAllen, Texas.

The place is in the middle of farm country, mostly citrus fruits and vegetables, and close to the Mexican border. Tourists on their way to Mexico pass through the city of McAllen, and those coming the other way, usually farm workers who are not coming legally, often find themselves in the Detention Facility. The camp population was about three hundred when the colonel arrived, mostly Mexican. The colonel did not get to see his fellow prisoners.

He slept for a few hours and had a good breakfast. Seeley and Judge arrived to question him at nine o'clock. They asked about his aliases, his addresses, his bank accounts, his entry into this country, and his spy activities. To most of the questions Colonel Abel said, "I'm not answering."

They took a break for lunch, returned, and did the script again. This time, the colonel did answer two questions. Asked about the storeroom he had rented near his studio in the Ovington building, miles away in Brooklyn, Abel told his investigators that he shared it with Dave Levine, a painter, and Dr. Jacobs, "who has laboratories in the building."

"How did you find the studio?"

"Quite by accident. While passing by the building, I saw this sign on the door. I was looking for a reasonably priced place, and there it was in Brooklyn. It had a notice on the door saying they had a studio for rent, so I went in."

That was Saturday. He was questioned again on Sunday and Monday, sometimes by the same INS team of Seeley and Judge, sometimes by two FBI men who had flown in from New York, Gamber and Blasco. Monday morning, the INS men gave him a pamphlet describing the laws that govern an alien in this country. He studied it until lunch time, and then he told his story.

He said that his real name was Rudolph Ivanovich Abel; that he was a Russian citizen and that he had entered the United States illegally. He explained how he came to do that: once upon a time, Rudolph Abel found a large sum of American money in a ruined blockhouse in Russia; he took the money to Denmark, where he bought himself a forged American passport; with that he came to Canada in 1948 and crossed the border to the United States. It was an old story; it was not believed by the INS. In the days after he made that statement, the colonel became more and more panicky.

Every night of his spy life, the colonel bedded down with the knowledge that there might be that knock at the door in the morning. That much, he accepted. That much is part of the thrill of it all and part of the job. But the colonel did not know, in June 1957, what kind of knock it had been. He did not know how much "they" really knew about him and how much "they" could use against him. So he reached for the only escape open: he admitted to being an illegal alien and hoped that the penalty under law, deportation, would be invoked. And fast.

Monday afternoon, Abel ate his lunch while Seeley and Judge reported the blockhouse story. Gamber and Blasco came in for a few minutes to ask about it and then Abel thought about a lawyer. He told Immigration officials that he did not know any lawyers except someone called Abt or Apt in New York. First he thought of writing to Abt or Apt but he changed his mind, saying that the man would probably not fly out to Texas. Instead, he went through a classified directory with the names of all the attorneys in the area and chose the firm of Stofford, Atlas and Spilman.

Someone called the firm and that afternoon Morris Atlas came out to talk with his client. He returned the next afternoon and conferred again. Abel had been told that he had a right to an immediate hearing on the deportation charge. Yes, he wanted that. Mr. Atlas requested it for him, and the hearing was set for June 27.

The hearing was at ten in the morning before James A. Winters, special inquiry officer. Abel was questioned by Vincent A. Schiano and represented by Morris Atlas and an assistant from the firm, Robert Schwartz. Asked to give his true and correct name, he responded, "Rudolph Ivanovich Abel."

"Have you also been known as Martin Collins or Emil R. Goldfus?"

"I have."

"Now, this order to show cause and notice of hearing indicates that you have requested that a prompt hearing

be held in your case and that you have waived your right
to any additional time; is that correct, and is that your de-
sire?"

"Yes, sir."

It certainly was.

"Mr. Goldfus, the order to show cause and notice of
hearing alleges first you are not a citizen or national of
the United States. Do you admit or do you deny that allegation?"

"I admit it."

"The second allegation, you are a native of Russia and
a national of the Union of Soviet Socialist Republics. Do
you admit that allegation is true or do you deny it?"

"I admit it."

"The third allegation, you last entered the United States
at an unknown point across the boundary from Canada
in 1949. Do you admit or do you deny that allegation?"

"I do not deny that allegation, but I will correct it by
saying that it was in 1948."

At the end of the hearing, Rudolph Abel was asked by
the special inquiry officer, "Do you admit your deportability in this charge?"

"I would say," he answered, "I accept deportation."

A month later Abel was still in his cell in McAllen.
The only official charge against him was that made by the
Immigration and Naturalization Service. He had made his
statement; he had had his hearing; he had asked to be
deported to the Soviet Union. And nothing had happened.
No more hearing; no deportation. At the beginning of the
month he was given a copy of a search warrant for his
Brooklyn studio with a list of items seized by the FBI.
However he had steeled himself all those years in the
KGB, the shadow of discovery was no longer a shadow.
Abel looked at the list and saw that evidence was being
collected against him. He wrote a letter to David Levine:

Dear Dave:

I am writing this to you in the hope that you will see
your way to help me in the disposal of whatever remains of mine in 252 Fulton Street.

The power of attorney is sufficient authority for you
to dispose of things the way you see fit to do so. I have
no specific desires except that you go through my paintings and preserve those you think worth keeping until

—if ever—I may be able to get them again. I have no objections to having you keep and use any materials you may find useful for yourself or the other friends of mine.

If you find it possible to sell anything, I would like you to pay yourself a sum that would repay you for your trouble. Should you decide to take this responsibility on yourself—or refuse it (in which case maybe you could suggest somebody else who would do it) I would appreciate an early reply to my lawyers Stofford, Atlas and Spilman, P.O. Box 1128, McAllen, Texas, Att. of Mr. Schwartz. My best regards to all of you.

Sincerely yours,
Emil R. Goldfus

July 24, 1957

Enclosed is $35. Please pay Mac for the next month's rent of the studio. This will give you time to do the job.

Abel's request that Levine dispose of his remaining possessions at the Ovington Studios included what had been left in the storeroom they shared, which had not yet been searched by the FBI. If Abel's professional motive in writing that letter was to hint that Levine clear out the storeroom, it was also personal. Trapped, Abel reached for a connection. He never made it. He was beginning to panic at McAllen and he tried once again for the only way out. He wrote to John M. Bailey, supervisor of the Alien Detention Facility:

Dear Sir:

I have been advised by the Embassy of the USSR in Washington that they do not recognize as Soviet citizens persons who merely claim such citizenship.

As I have stated to officials of the U.S. Immigration Service, my name is Rudolph Ivanovich Abel, born in Moscow USSR in 1902, July 2. My father, Ivan Ivanovitch Abel, deceased. My mother, Lubov Karneeva, deceased. Education—elementary and secondary schools in Moscow from 1910 to 1920. I have worked as a translator and as a teacher of English in secondary schools in Moscow.

In view of the statement of the USSR Embassy, I

request the Immigration Service to contact the USSR
Embassy officially, giving all the information on this
matter.

He signed the letter "E. R. Goldfus" and, in parenthesis,
"R. I. Abel."

It did not work. It never could have, for no one in the
Department of Justice had a moment's thought of deport-
ing Rudolph Ivanovich Abel. Most likely, the official request to the Embassy of the USSR was never made. There
was no cause to do so, for a grand jury was about to be
called in New York and would soon indict Colonel Abel
for espionage.

Immediately after Colonel Abel's arrest, the FBI had
gone to work. Everything taken from the hotel or left behind was examined. It was incredible, the agents said, that
a professional spy, a man who had been so careful, had
left so much incriminating evidence around. It looked incriminating at first, but the more the FBI investigated
leads provided by Abel's possessions, the more they realized that there was nothing linking him with anyone else.
Still, they pushed on. The Bureau sent its agents out to
look for anyone who had known Colonel Abel under his
various aliases. Everyone was a potential accomplice.

Among the things taken from Abel's hotel room was a
key with the number 1077 imprinted on it and a small
white tag attached. On the tag the number 2508 was
written. The FBI laboratory traced the key to a safe-
deposit box, number 2508, at the Manufacturer's Trust
Company, 1511 Third Avenue, New York. But the box
was not listed in the name of Abel or Goldfus or Collins.
It belonged to Paul Owen, a young painter-sculptor. Inside was fifteen thousand dollars in cash.

"Milt asked me to rent it for him in my name. So I
did. And I turned the keys over to him. I never opened
it."

"Weren't you suspicious?"

"No."

"Why not?"

"I don't know. People do weird things."

Owen does not like the FBI. He thinks their operation
ludicrous and their tactics just like the "enemy's." The
Bureau, he says, refuses to see that. For them, every-

thing is black and white. Owen sees the gray. His favorite word in connection with the FBI is "entrapment." If even half of what he says is true, they gave him quite a time.

The first time they came to question him, the two agents at his door announced they would burn him in the electric chair. They were convinced that Rudolph Abel had tried to recruit him. They suggested, heavily, that there had been some homosexual hanky-panky between the two. Owen laughed. Not long.

They came often to question him. Owen thought them stupid; he laughed at them, cursed at them, put them down, blew up. They were buffoons to him. He had one agent he did not like removed from the case. At one session an agent said to him, "Want to see how impostors try to make out they are FBI agents? Want to see a phony FBI identification?" He handed it to Owen who knew what they wanted. He pressed his fingers hard on the plastic case, leaving good clear prints, and gave it back. And smirked.

They questioned him about everything. What his Milton did, where they ate together, what they ate, whether he ever saw any "un-American types" lurking around or reading the *Daily Worker*. Once they asked why he was smoking so much and Owen again smirked, "I listen to your radio program and I know I'm supposed to be scared."

And they followed him. Owen was taking summer courses at Columbia University and he would arrive there with a "tail." He would go into a classroom and the "tail" would lounge around outside the door, pick him up again as he left. His teachers were questioned; his girl friend was questioned. It was not funny. If you are a young liberal and you do not like the FBI to begin with and a man you have known well turns up a Russian spy, you are not quite amused. Owen, who probably knew more about Abel than the people in Brooklyn Heights did, and may well have been more "involved" than they were, found himself flung into a nightmare. He coped with it by laughing.

When he knew he was being followed, which was most of the time, Owen walked long hours through the city in the summer heat, his only pleasure knowing that the FBI men behind him were suffering as much as he. On one of those walks, he saw a few blocks behind him what was obviously an FBI agent, wearing a red-black-check sports jacket. It made him visible for quite a distance. After some streets of tracking Owen along the concrete the agent removed his jacket, and Owen, over his shoulder, saw two men appear "from nowhere," argue with the jacketless man and disappear. The man behind him, next time Owen looked, again had the red-black checks on his sweating back.

A detail of FBI agents was sent to Brooklyn Heights to discover what they could about the life and times of Emil Goldfus, painter. The first man they talked to was the superintendent, Harry MacMullen, who proved very useful.

A week after Abel's arrest, MacMullen signed an affidavit for the FBI. The agents who took that affidavit from him attached it to one from Edward A. Boyle, one of the INS agents who arrested Rudolph Abel, and from Joseph Phelan, special agent, who had questioned the man before he was arrested. Those three affidavits were used to convince a district judge in Brooklyn that there was sufficient cause for him to issue a warrant authorizing the FBI to search Goldfus's studio in the building. What MacMullen contributed to this presentation was simple: he told, in his statement, how he had first seen the man he knew as Goldfus in December 1953 when he rented the studio. He said that Goldfus had paid for that studio until the end of April 1957 when he left for a sinus cure. He also said, and this is what the FBI needed his statement for, that he had often visited that studio and seen in it a shortwave radio; MacMullen had seen a photograph of the Hallicrafters radio seized in the hotel room and identified it as *not* being the one in the studio.

The judge issued the warrant immediately. It instructed any special agent of the FBI to search the studio for specific property listed there: "a Hallicrafters shortwave radio and related radio equipment; camera equipment including microfilm and microdot equipment; . . . items which are suitable to be fashioned into 'containers' for secreting and transmitting of microfilm, microdot and other secret messages; and tools with which to fashion such 'containers' and microfilm, microdot and other messages, including coded communications, which material is fitted and intended to be used in furtherance of a conspiracy to violate the provisions of 18 USC 793, 794 and 951."

Buried in the legalese of that search warrant and the numbers of the United States statutes that there was a suspected "conspiracy to violate" is a tilt in the way things had been going. A big tilt. Those first two statute numbers refer to espionage laws. Rudolph Abel had been arrested just a week before this warrant was issued, on the authority of the Immigration and Naturalization Service. He was charged, when arrested, with being an alien illegally in the United States. On that charge, he was being held at the McAllen Alien Detention Facility in Texas. The shift from "illegal alien" to "conspiracy to commit espionage" is enormous. The first carried a maximum penalty of deportation; the second, depending on the circumstances, of death. Not only the severity of this change in what Abel was accused of is important; its legality is. Evidence collected while an arrest was being made on the immigration warrant was used, a week later, to obtain permission to search the studio for evidence that would be used in prosecuting the criminal charge.

The constitutionality of the government's switch would come up later. At the end of June 1957 it was important for another reason. Abel had not been arrested for espionage because he would have been entitled to a speedy hearing on that charge and the government had no case. Reino Hayhanen had refused to testify in court and there was scanty evidence without him. By the time the search warrant was issued Hayhanen had changed his mind.

The government was careful. No one wanted to slip, and Tompkins said he made sure nothing would be "haywire" and provide the basis for an appeal. A search cannot be made before the day for which the warrant is issued; this one was sworn out for June 28, 1957. Tompkins and two FBI agents got up at the crack of dawn that morning, making sure the sun was up and it was indeed daytime. The studio was searched at half past six in the morning, and what turned up clearly belonged to the man arrested in the Hotel Latham. All of Abel's possessions bore his mark; again, the studio yielded an extraordinary variety of things. Some of the things were useful to the government and helped build a case against him; the rest only serve as pieces in the puzzle. The things in the studio that were not used as evidence are still evidence. They tell who he was.

Like the books. He had on the shelves *The New Astronomy, Cryptanalysis: A Study of Cyphers and Their Solution, Murder on the Side, Elements of Symbolic Logic, World Famous Paintings, Number, The Language of Science, The Artist's Handbook, Silver for the Craftsman, Vuillard, History by V. Gordon Childe, Goya to Gaugin, The Last Party.*

Mystery stories and advanced science. Likewise the objects taken from the studio reflected the versatility of the man who had lived there. Sketchbooks and canvases, camera equipment, most of it German, a tape recorder and tapes of someone playing the guitar, maps of Bear Mountain State Park, the Loop in Chicago, Los Angeles, New Jersey, and Baltimore, a Hallicrafters radio that had stood in the studio and another in a brown leather carrying case, empty Sucrets boxes filled with nails, filmstrips, cuff links, taps, rivets, and washers. A watchmaker's eyepiece. Musical scores. A thank-you note from Mr. and Mrs. Burton Silverman; an invitation card from the president of the National Academy of Design. Winston cigarettes, pipe tobacco, magnifying glasses, bankbooks, a note pad with the telephone number of Columbia University written on it, color slides of country scenes, flashlight batteries, hollowed-out nails, nuts, bolts, and coins.

The FBI agents took what they had come for and departed. They deposited their evidence at the FBI laboratory for investigation and returned to Brooklyn Heights to question some of the people who had known Goldfus in his studio.

"Excuse me, Mr. Silverman, we're from the Federal Bureau of Investigation."

Silverman had just come from his job at the *New York Post.* It was late Friday afternoon and he had ridden the subway, emerged into the humid air, and hurried home. At the front door, just inside the cool hallway, were two men looking like insurance salesmen.

"Would you mind answering a few questions?"

Who does not mind? Who does not ever mind, but especially in 1957, if you are political and you know that your politics are considered radical, when the FBI wants to ask you some questions—do you not mind? Do you not think: Oh, oh, what are they after? Are you not conspiratorial: it is a frame-up; I am innocent.

Silverman, bewildered, fumbled.

"Here?"

"No. Upstairs. Or right out there in our car."

They showed their official identification cards; they spoke in their official monotone.

"Just a few minutes."

In the car, a green Chevrolet parked at the curb, Silverman sat in the back seat with one agent on either side. Two more had been waiting in the front.

"What *is* this?"

"Do you know this man?"

He looked at the photograph.

"Hell, yes. That's Emil. Emil Goldfus. What's happened to him?"

"When did you last see him?"

"About two months ago. Is he hurt? What's happened?"

"Do you know where he lived?"

"No."

"Who are his friends?"

"Did you ever see this man?"

Another photograph was handed to the back seat—this time a fuzzy print of a fat man in a white shirt.

"Did you ever see anyone visit him?"

"Did you ever see a fat man who fell asleep while he was talking?"

"Oh, come on."

"Levine said he didn't know this man, either."

What? What? No, none of those things. No fat men; no one who slept while he was talking. What are they after? Me? One of my friends? Why are they using Emil? What has he got to do with it? Burt went through the list of offenses that involve the FBI, but none fit. A con man? Impossible. Kidnapping?

"Did he ever give you anything to keep for him?"

"No. I mean, yes. I borrowed things from him all the time. I have to think what I might have of his now. Yes, his guitar. What the hell is this all about?"

"I'm sorry, Mr. Silverman. We can only say this is a question of the highest national security."

Now, there's a phrase that rolls around in the mind. Highest national security. Another hunt for "subversives." Another Rosenberg case. But *who* are they after and why don't they say and why this hocus-pocus about Emil who is no radical in anyone's terms?

"Look," Silverman said, "I can't go on answering questions in the dark this way. Either tell me what's going on or I leave."

They could not say. They repeated "highest national security" and told him to talk of it to no one. The interview was over.

Puzzle pieces; parts of a whole. For Silverman and his friends the summer was scattered with peculiar things about Emil Goldfus. He had left the city at the end of April and no one had heard from him, yet his presence was in the air. Dave Levine felt it, too. Goldfus had left the key to his studio with Levine and suggested that when he had time he might like to go through the collection of slides there. Levine had. Pile after pile were views of Bear Mountain State Park, boring views. Among the slides, Levine had come across something obviously an optical device, a small thing with three feet to stand on and two lenses. He had set it up and put something under it. The blowup was larger than anything Levine had ever seen. What, he wondered, would Emil be using a thing like that for? And then he had put it back where he found it. Puzzling.

A week or two later, Levine opened the door to Goldfus's studio and found it looking ransacked. Conspicuously gone was the Hallicrafters radio that had stood, tilted, at the end of the table. What else was missing? Levine thought of calling the police immediately to report robbery, or of finding Mac, the superintendent, who might know what had happened. But Mac was gone for the weekend.

Levine returned the next day, Saturday, for a second look. It was still in a clutter unlike the way Emil kept his things. But this time something had been added to the clutter: just to the side of where the radio had stood, on the long table, held down by two soup cans, was a notice. It said that pursuant to public law something-or-other some items had been taken from the studio. And there was a list that included, among other things, nuts and bolts and screwheads. Who had taken those things? What were they for? What public law? All Levine knew was that the studio had not been robbed. He was puzzled, and so were his friends, but there was nothing to be done about it.

Then the FBI came to visit. Their questions were vague. They refused to say what they wanted. Something was obviously amiss with Emil Goldfus, but what? There was always the possibility that Goldfus had been hurt or had had another heart attack—but why the FBI then?—and the possibility, as Silverman thought, that Goldfus was an excuse and the questions were really meant for one of them.

By the time the letter Abel had written to Levine from McAllen arrived in Brooklyn, Levine was not there. He had gone with his family to Connecticut. The letter was forwarded. It took some days to reach him and not until the beginning of August did Levine read it. Peculiar letter. Why did Emil write to him and not to Burt? Why did Emil have a lawyer? How did the letter fit the strange events of the past months? The tone was equally disturbing: that mixture of personal and official language did not sound like Emil Goldfus. And the pessimistic undercurrent—"until, if ever, I may be able to get them again" —was unsettling.

Levine wavered. Not knowing whether he wanted to take on the power of attorney Goldfus had asked of him, Levine finally called his lawyer and made an appointment for the following week. It was Wednesday, August 7, when he took the train to town from Connecticut with the letter from Emil Goldfus in his pocket.

SIX

REINO Hayhanen was kept in Peekskill until he was needed. The Department of Justice provided him with two baby sitters: Anthony J. Palermo had worked for United States counterintelligence in Munich before going to work for the Internal Security Division where Palermo had been feeling that he had somewhere missed his calling. Until the Abel case. "When this fell into my lap," he said, "bang—Munich all over again and right here in my own backyard, in Brooklyn." Palermo had been assigned to the case in June. Thinking he was going to New York for the weekend, he packed a small bag and stayed four months. New York-Peekskill-Brooklyn; it blurred. The second government attorney working with Hayhanen was James J. Featherstone. Featherstone's job was to prepare the witness for his grand jury appearance. He too did a lot of traveling that summer.

Peekskill had been almost pleasant for all of them. Warm days on the porch of Hayhanen's cottage, he sipping vodka and cream of tomato soup; Hannah staying inside most of the time. Featherstone and Palermo questioned him continually and tried to make sense of his answers. They gave him an IQ test and he scored high. He talked about whatever he wanted to talk about. How he arrived in New York and stayed at the Hotel Chesterfield in the Times Square area; how he had money in his pocket and started cutting up. Contrary to Moscow's instructions. How he bought a car. Contrary to Moscow's instructions. How he brought Hannah here. Contrary to Moscow's instructions. He was proud of himself and he related an infinite number of times how clever he was in getting the false birth certificate that made a United States passport easy. He boasted that he had been "champion drinker in KGB." He said, too, that he liked to drive and had been enjoying his contrary-to-Moscow's-instructions car until Mark found out that he had one.

After that, the pleasure of the car was gone, for Mark made him into a chauffeur, which he did not like.

From Peekskill Hayhanen was taken to the offices of United States Attorney Moore in the federal courthouse on Fulton Street, Brooklyn. William F. Tompkins had come up from Washington. "A case of this dimension," he said, "could not very well be run from down there." They convened in Moore's office—Hayhanen, Tompkins, Palermo, and Featherstone—to work out the testimony. Which meant getting Hayhanen's story coherent. Everything about it had been checked and rechecked and no one doubted its authenticity. The problem was keeping Hayhanen together, for he was willing but reluctant, and getting him to tell the story straight, in English.

At one of the first interviews in Moore's office, Hayhanen rambled about a Czechoslovakian pilot who had brought his MIG down in Turkey, defected, and got a lot of money for it. Moore was tipping back in his chair, listening. Tompkins, catching the point of Hayhanen's ramble, told him, "You'll get just what every other witness gets—five dollars a day. No more."

Moore nearly fell out of his chair.

Hayhanen started. Well, one more ploy that did not work. Tompkins was not letting him get away with it. Eventually, because of this "straight" way of dealing with one another, Tompkins considered himself the only man Hayhanen would trust. The United States attorney was in a position to say to him, several years later, "Gene, I'm the best friend you have in this world and you know it."

Hayhanen's mind was not on his best friend, but his worst enemy: the English language. He had inordinate trouble and the attorneys working with him found his poor English more frustrating than his vacillating and difficult temperament. It was James Featherstone's job to explain to Hayhanen what a grand jury hearing was and to get him ready for it. Featherstone thought Hayhanen at least as intelligent as Abel. The language trouble made him seem stupid. Tompkins agreed. One of the words Hayhanen, ironically, did not really understand was "espionage." To him, espionage meant stealing secret information. Hayhanen was able to say and write, with aplomb, that he had never been engaged in espionage. In fact, in his definition, he had not: no bribing of physicists in atomic plants, no clandestine photographing of se-

cret documents. Featherstone understood that Hayhanen
thought of himself simply as a secret service officer and
that, as a spy, in our sense, he was interested in everything, in any kind of information he could get, even what
may be innocuous. Unclassified information was as important to him as anything else.

Working on Hayhanen's testimony for the grand jury,
they went over the list of drops Hayhanen could provide,
their exact location, their method of operation. In spite of
his soggy mind, Hayhanen had a good memory and could
recall almost any place he had been to in New York
City. That had been demonstrated earlier when he led
the FBI to the Ovington building. In July, as he had just
after his defection, Hayhanen could recite the exact location of each drop. Even to experienced attorneys in the
Internal Security Division of the Department of Justice,
the drop stories seemed ridiculous. But they also seemed
true. Featherstone asked Hayhanen during one of those
sessions, how come the chalk marks he used at various
signal areas did not attract attention. It was simple: people thought the marks had been made by the children playing, Hayhanen said, and they were never noticeable.

As they worked with Hayhanen, the attorneys could
not help but think on the weakness of Soviet intelligence,
sending as its agent this man with what the United States
security people called classic "vices": the vice of drink,
the vice of women, and lack of love for the work he was
doing. His linguistic weakness showed similar holes in the
system. But maybe, Palermo said, it was still an effective
system. Both Hayhanen and Abel were here, undetected
for a long time, and they would have remained so. As
Palermo went over the testimony and shaped the government's case, he kept coming back in his own mind to
the "most shocking thing in the case—the failure of our
own counterintelligence." The more he listened to Hayhanen, the clearer it became that we were extremely
lucky to get Colonel Abel and that we had done so only
because he was handed over to us by Reino Hayhanen.

At the height of the summer, the grand jury heard
all about Rudolph Ivanovich Abel, colonel, KGB. They
heard mostly from Reino Hayhanen. He repeated what
he knew and what he would repeat later at Abel's trial.
Then they heard the testimony of a young man who had
known Abel under a different name.

Paul Owen testified before the grand jury dressed neatly in coat and tie, which was not his style. It was his lawyer's idea; the lawyer had insisted on an "All-American-boy" image. Owen answered to that, "Shit, cut it out," and by the time he left the jury room, his shins were black and blue from the lawyer's kicks under the table. Paul testified for an entire day.

There were thirty people in the room. Only thirty. It still felt like three hundred. And the questions came from all sides.

"What about the safe-deposit box?"

"Why did you rent it for him?"

"What was the money for?"

Paul said that fifteen thousand was more money than he had ever seen. He did not know what it was for. He rented the box because his friend asked him to.

"Did you ever borrow money from him?"

"No."

"Did he give you money?"

"No."

The jury had before it a slip of paper with names and figures: "Owen-100; Harv-100; Box-20; Rnt-100; Tk-75." What did it mean?

Owen did not know.

Had he ever seen anyone reading the *Daily Worker* while he and Abel were together?

Had he ever seen any "foreign" types lurking around?

Owen said, "You don't remember things like that."

"But you're an 'A' student at Columbia."

"Yes, but I don't need a good memory for the things I study."

"How could you get such good grades with a poor memory?"

"Students with memories for things like exams just forget everything the next day, anyway."

"Do you remember anyone reading the *Daily Worker?* Any suspicious foreign types lurking around?"

The questioner was a high school teacher.

Owen felt the jury trying to implicate his girl friend who lived with him, an attractive and slender girl in her early twenties, a good-looking Irish redhead from Pennsylvania. They were trying to prove some kind of conspiracy: Abel had once taken a trip with Paul and the girl to the girl's hometown, where they stopped in to visit her parents. Obviously, to the jury, a diabolical link.

Paul was shaking. He left the hearing and was put into an empty room, where he sat by himself for a few minutes. The door opened. Someone he had never seen before came in, said nothing, took a long look, and walked out. Paul Owen was told he could go home.

Came the indictment. It charged Rudolph Ivanovich Abel, also known as Mark and Martin Collins and Emil R. Goldfus, with conspiring to do three different things. One: to transmit to the USSR information relating to the national defense of the United States of America, particularly to arms, equipment, and disposition of this country's armed forces and its atomic energy program; two: to gather that information; three: to remain in the country without registering as a foreign agent.

The last count is the most innocuous. To the layman, it makes no sense anyway that a foreign agent would let the secretary of state know where he is and what he is up to. Still, the law has applications. The penalty provided for failing to register is, at maximum, five years in prison.

The first two counts are more ominous. A man convicted of conspiring to collect the information specified is subject to ten years in prison. If he keeps that information stuffed in his mattress, ten years is all. But if he conspires to transmit information about our national defense to a foreign nation—any foreign nation; even one with which we are legally at peace—he may be put to death. The law is known as the "Rosenberg Law," and Abel's was the first case of an alien being tried under its provisions.

The indictment in, Reino Hayhanen still in one piece, Abel sweating it out in McAllen, the government rushed to trial. Most of what they had was bound up in the corroding body of an alcoholic defector and no one knew how long he would endure nor how long he would cooperate. The indictment was handed down on Wednesday, August 7; an order of removal of the marshal of the Southern District of Texas, the "word" to bring Abel back, filed the same day. Then William Tompkins held a press conference, passed out copies of the indictment, and answered reporters' questions. The afternoon papers had the story. In spades.

INDICT RED COLONEL HERE AS SPY. . . .
BROOKLYN GRAND JURY INDICTS SO-
VIET COLONEL AS SPY CHIEF. . . . UN-
MASK BROOKLYN "ARTIST" AS TOP SPY
FOR RED ARMY. . . .

The news came from the text of the grand jury indictment and Tompkins's remarks. Right there, in those first
stories, was the tone of the way the press would handle
Abel's case. His rank of colonel was of prime importance.
It meant, of course, that we had bagged a very big cheese.
It was a great coup. We congratulated ourselves. Abel
was called the "head of a Soviet spy ring," the "highest-
ranking espionage agent ever caught in this country," the
man who "headed the Soviet espionage network in the
United States." No one, not the newsmen nor the faceless
"federal officials" who give out remarks like that to the
press, really knew what the colonel had been up to; but,
it goes, if he were a *colonel,* it must have been something
big.

Second in dramatic impact, as it came out in the papers, was that the colonel might die. There was great bal-
lyhoo about it. Every story listed the charges in the grand
jury indictment and pointed out, actually underlined, that
the "spy charges [could] upon conviction, mean death."

The rest was not yet interesting copy. The first stories
were filled with the low-keyed trivia of the indictment:
the list of aliases ("he lived in Brooklyn under the name
Emil Goldfus . . . he had registered at the Hotel Latham
as Martin Collins . . . he was known to members of the
ring as Mark"); the names of his coconspirators, which
meant nothing to anyone, just then; and some vagaries
about the "secrets vital to the national defense" he had
been scooping up in our midst.

Yet there were distortions in those first stories, some
serious and some not. The charges on which Colonel Abel
had been indicted and for which he would be tried were
charges of conspiring to do certain things. Which meant,
at that point, that someone had *said* he "plotted" with
Colonel Abel. The someone, of course, Reino Hayhanen,
not receiving much mention that day. The press brought
it out as if the colonel had actually *done* a lot: "A federal grand jury in Brooklyn indicted Abel, charging that
from 1948 to this year he had obtained and transmitted

to Russia vital information about national defense secrets. . . . Abel was held on charges of transporting photographs, photo negatives, maps, and notes on U.S. defenses." In fact, he was charged only with conspiring to do those things. Which makes a difference. He could, indeed, be convicted of the conspiracy charges without ever having accomplished a thing, without having put a finger on information about national defense secrets.

But it seemed, from the stories, that the colonel had gotten to us. It seemed, too, that if he had directed *the* Soviet espionage network in the United States, it was the only one and, with his apprehension, it had been put out of business. We were now not only to be congratulated on the vigilance of those "agents," not quite specified, who had captured this threat to our security, but we were now to feel quite safe, for *the* network was finished.

The arrest was handled by the press with necessary pussyfooting. The public was told that this Master Spy had been put under arrest six weeks before, but it was unclear why it was not brought out until early August. Necessarily unclear. The story, as you got it then through public channels, runs like this: Rudolph Abel had been arrested by the Immigration and Naturalization Service on June 21 because he was an alien who entered and lived illegally in this country; no one could say how INS found out about this delinquency; after his arrest, the FBI somehow materialized and examined both the possessions of this alien and the things he left behind. Astonishingly, they found evidence of espionage. Then there is a gap in the story. Why did not the FBI then, in its capacity as a law enforcement agency, arrest the man as a spy? No answer. Meanwhile, in accord with the provisions of the Constitution, the alien was granted a speedy hearing, in McAllen, Texas, under immigration law. The hearing resulted in an order for his deportation. But, according to Mr. Tompkins, chief of Internal Security, the "disposition of the case will now depend on the outcome of the criminal charges. . . . Today's indictment on the spy charge will block his departure."

The other distortion was metaphysical. It did not matter much for the record, but did for the people who knew Rudolph Abel. It had to do with masks. The colonel was said to have been "unmasked," to have been "posing as a Brooklyn artist." The "real" Abel, according to this logic, was a hard-nosed master spy; Emil Goldfus was a fake.

Helen Silverman was on her way to meet Burt to have lunch and finish off some errands for their August 12 trip to Europe. Helen was riding the subway and looking aimlessly, in that subway-rider's way, at the man opposite her, who was reading a newspaper. She looked at the man, she looked out the window, she looked at the floor, and she saw part of the headline: TOP SPY CAUGHT. . . . The man turned his paper and Helen saw BROOKLYN in the headline. She could see nothing else.

At the Rector Street station she got off the train and hurried upstairs. Burt was waiting.

"Did you see the papers?"

"Me? Why should I, I work for one."

"No joke. Look."

And she dragged him to a newsstand. There were all the day's papers, folded and laid out, and it was all there. Burt could see the headlines; under the fold was a photograph, but he had not yet seen that.

Burt picked up the newspaper. He thought of his friends and he remembered the FBI men's questions, and he had a sense that he knew the "Brooklyn artist," that someone suspected of being "subversive" was being framed by the government. Who? Dave? Jules? Harvey?

They were flashes and fragments. They lasted only until he turned the paper and saw his friend Emil.

There are no words for the feeling. Think of yourself and your friends; think of the headlines and the photograph and you may know. You may not. Shock is too mild; so is disbelief. Everything about Emil coalesced for a moment and fell apart again. It made sense: his strange disappearance; the FBI interview; the letter to Dave; the admonition about saying "Moscow" on the telephone; the disarray of the studio. It fit. It did not fit. First a whole picture, then pieces: Emil in his undershorts fixing a leaking radiator; the shortwave radio turned on end because a tube was loose; Emil in the studio with his shoes off, smoking; Emil laughing; Emil listening; Emil with his camera, his paintbrush, his books; Emil the first day in the elevator; Emil and the turpentine; voices in the studio, silent moods, the heart attack, the Liebfraumilch;

Emil at the wedding; "I'd like to fuck her"; the guitar; Emil who was out of it; Emil who said, "Whatever one fool can do, another can"; Emil, his friend.

Dave Levine had taken the train from Connecticut. He was bringing to his attorney the letter Emil Goldfus had mailed from Texas, for he did not know what to do about it. He got off the train in New York City and, on his way to the attorney's office, stopped to buy a newspaper. He did not believe it, not any of it. As he stared at the stories and the photographs of Emil, he was sure that the man was not guilty and that, for some reason, the government was trying to frame him. Dave arrived at the office with a new kind of legal advice to request.

Gordon Silverman, Burt's brother, had just rented an apartment on the West Side of Manhattan. He was out walking with his wife-to-be, Rosalyn, exploring the new neighborhood. They went past a candy store newsstand at Broadway and 103rd Street and Gordon saw the *New York Post* laid out with a large picture of Emil Goldfus on the front page.

"Just a minute. Who is that man?"

"Of course," Rosalyn said, "it's Emil."

The headline was covered; all they saw was the photograph. Well, why not, Gordon thought. Perhaps Emil had won an award in mathematics or engineering. It was perfectly plausible that Emil Goldfus had discovered something or had finally made his mark with an important invention.

Gordon turned the newspaper over and stared at the headline.

Everyone who worked at the Ovington Studios, or knew someone who did or knew someone who knew someone, behaved oddly after Colonel Abel's first public exposure. There was widespread aversion to anything involving spies, Russia, or the FBI. None of Dave Levine's weekly sketching-class ladies appeared that week. Levine had a stock of Christmas cards that he and Shelley Fink had designed stored in the storeroom at the Ovington building. Just after Emil-Abel's arrest was announced in the newspapers, Levine and Fink worried about having those boxes of cards rifled by the FBI. Their concern was practical; not political. Nothing was hidden in the Christmas cards; the artists did not want them dirtied. Trying not to attract attention, they began packing the cards. They went to the home of Neil Estern, a sculptor friend, and borrowed his car from his wife. They got in, started the car, drove slowly down the street, unobtrusive, and the car stalled. Levine looked at Fink. Fink looked nervously for agents hidden behind hedges. And Neil Estern, coming home, saw that his car was gone from the driveway. There, down the street it was with two men inside. "Stop," he screamed, "stop," loudly, as he ran down the street, "that's my car."

And then, a few days later, Burt Silverman and his wife ran into a friend on Remsen Street near the studio building. They were talking about Emil-Abel on a street filled with midafternoon shoppers.

"Wait a minute," the friend said. "Wait." Silverman startled, asked, "What is it?"

"Keep talking. Just keep talking. Don't stop. Talk about the weather. Talk about anything. Just keep talking."

So Silverman said it was a beautiful day and just then a man walked by. A clean-cut, close-cropped man. Silverman went on with the lovely day.

"You see that guy?" the friend asked.

"What guy?"

"That guy. The one who just walked past us?"

"Him? What about him?"

"Listen. He was an agent. And he had a tape recorder hidden in the front of his shirt."

They were distressing days for the young artists who had known Emil Goldfus. All of them were in an awkward position. All had, in varying degrees, unpopular politics: in 1957 the only kind of politics that would have been popular were I-Like-Ike ones; even Stevenson supporters were suspect in some places. You could call most of the Brooklyn Heights group "left-wing" if you wanted to. Or you could push it further. And not one could guess how far the government might be interested in pushing a description of their political positions. The exposure of their friend Goldfus as, according to the news reports, "chief of the Soviet espionage network in the United States," was personally traumatic for each of

them; it shattered their complacent sense of who Emil
Goldfus was; it replaced that sense with another; it replaced the reality of Goldfus with what was no more than
an illusion to them—Colonel Rudolph Abel.

With no way to gauge the situation. It occurred to all
of them that Goldfus, whom they had nearly ignored
when it came to political activity and social ideas, might
become the focus of a new crusade that would exploit
them. They worried about how easy it was to connect
people with one another; how the unique consequences
of living in New York meant that through someone you
might have met someone else and thus be implicated in
almost anything. It was not a hypothetical fear: picking
up one spy is one thing, making a "ring" is quite another.
And the papers were full of talk about Colonel Abel's
ring, only no one knew who was in it. Think, they said
to one another, of what has been done in terms of keying
up the country against Communists; think how easy it
would be to make the people in the studio building look
like part of Abel's "ring."

Chance meetings in the street took on a conspiratorial
tone although nothing was conspired. The presence of
FBI agents all over the place and the very real possibility
of wiretaps charged each conversation with novelistic melodrama. Silverman and his friends stood outside themselves, listening in, guarding against anything that might
be made to sound incriminating. Everyone thought to protect himself; everyone had reason to do so.

In the end, the fear was exaggerated and their behavior mistaken. No one was "after" any one of them; no
one had any intention of implicating Silverman or his
friends in Colonel Abel's espionage or of "making anything" of their political lives. Still, that first week was, understandably, a crisis-laden one for a group of serious artists in Brooklyn Heights.

One Saturday afternoon, soon after Abel's story appeared in the news, Burt's wife Helen heard the front
doorbell ring. She called down from their fourth-floor
apartment, "Who is it?"

Up from the ground floor came an unfamiliar voice:
"Is Burt home?"

"No."

There was a long pause.

Helen leaned over the banister and saw the man standing four floors below, someone she had never seen before. Neither spoke. Then the man said, "Well, I'd like to show him some pictures."

"Who are you?"

"Well," he said, in a very loud stage whisper, "I'm from the FBI."

"He's not home right now."

"Well," in the same stage whisper, "I'll come back."

That same week, two special agents went to talk with Silverman's friends, Harvey Dinnerstein and Dave Levine. They had come to talk before and been refused. This time, once the story was out and the agents were willing to make clear that they were interested in information about Emil Goldfus-Rudolph Abel, people were willing to talk with them.

But, what kind of information were they looking for? It is difficult to tell. What could anyone have known? Anything, it seems. Like the men who work in intelligence, these agents of counterintelligence operate on the principle that any fact may become valuable even if it does not seem so at first. They asked about everything and their questions revealed how little they knew about Abel's case. Or, how clever they were at playing dumb.

They began with a set speech: the FBI is protecting the security of the nation. We look into many cases. Some of the information we get is nonsense, just as the German Americans during the Second World War were said by their neighbors to have shortwave sets sending messages to the enemy. The FBI looked into this and it was nonsense. But the FBI has to investigate those charges.

Then the questions:

"By what name did you know the man?"

"When did you meet him?"

"Do you know where he lived?"

"Did he know much about photography?"

"Did he have any friends that you know?"

"Did he ever express interest in the opposite sex?"

"Did he ever speak about his family, or his past?"

"Did he have expensive camera equipment, art supplies, expensive clothes?"

"Did he ever discuss politics with you?"

"Did he ever express any opinion about the Korean War?"

"Did he ever ask you to deposit money for him, or register at a bank?"

"Did your wife ever see him when you were not around?"

"Did he ever philosophize?"

"How many cameras did he have?"

"How often did you see him?"

Routine questions. Routine answers. Goldfus's life in the studio was nondescript. He had rarely been seen coming or going at odd hours; his shortwave radio was a commercial set on which you could listen to the BBC. No one knew where he lived; no one knew any of his friends.

Sometimes, in the course of these FBI interviews, something of what a remarkable man Emil was would come up. The FBI asked Harvey Dinnerstein if he had any pictures of Goldfus.

"Yes. He posed for a portrait painting and some photographs."

"Strange," said the agent, "that such a man would permit himself to be painted."

"How long did he pose?"

"One sitting."

"So quickly? I didn't know you could do a painting so quickly."

Dinnerstein offered that Emil Goldfus was a man of many talents—among them playing the guitar well.

"Did he play in any group?"

"No."

"Did he favor any particular type of music or musician?"

"I think he expressed an admiration for Segovia."

"Would you mind spelling that?"

Burt and Helen Silverman were scheduled to leave for Europe on August 12, five days after the first stories about Rudolph Abel appeared. In those full, short days before their departure they received little public attention and endured no stress because of their close connection with this Master Spy. On one of those days a *New York Times* reporter called to verify that the Spy had attended their wedding; the *Times* discovered that because one item on the list of things impounded by the government in Emil Goldfus's studio was a thank-you note from the Silvermans for the rose-wood box he had given them as a wedding present.

As they packed for their trip the Silvermans found a typewriter and slide projector, borrowed from Goldfus. Everyone had been asked by the FBI if they had anything of Abel's; Silverman remembered the agents' request that he let them know if he did come across something. He wavered. Really, the projector and typewriter were innocuous. They could have no relevance to espionage, could they? Maybe he ought to forget about them. He was reluctant to help build a case against Emil Goldfus. On the other hand, Silverman thought, they *did* belong to Abel and were technically his. Perhaps they were convertible to cash. Abel might need the money. And then, what if those things did play a role in this weird business? Silverman decided to call the Bureau and tell them.

It was not odd that Silverman had forgotten the things Emil had lent him. So pervasive and unconditional was Emil's friendship that nothing was ever thought of as being "on loan." Nearly everyone had something he had borrowed and nearly everyone forgot that he had.

Burt made the call. The special agent was nonchalant. "Well, hold on to those things. We'll pick them up another time, if necessary."

"But," Silverman said, "we're going abroad. I told you that already."

"Oh, well, it doesn't matter. Just keep them."

It seemed to rest there. But an hour later the telephone rang and it was the FBI saying a man would be by to collect the typewriter and projector. The men came. They took the typewriter and projector and handed over a receipt which said that Burt Silverman had turned the two items over to two FBI agents and each kept a copy of the receipt. On the paper also was the serial number one of the men had copied from the undistinctive Remington portable. The agents were about to leave when Burt stopped them.

"Are you sure I won't be needed for more questions? I'm leaving in two days for Europe."

"Oh, are you? No, that's okay."

"I'll be gone for three and a half months. Are you sure?"

"Where will you be going?"

"To Europe. You know, the Grand Tour."

"Does anyone have your itinerary?"

Silverman had given a complete itinerary to two other
agents some days before. In his mind at that frustrating
moment flashed a cynical thought: doesn't anyone talk to
anyone else in this outfit?

"Well, generally. But we'll be staying places without
any fixed schedule or reservations."

"Okay. Well, have a good trip."

They left and the Silvermans were bewildered. Why
was it that the presence of any object connected with
Rudolph Abel—about which some teams of agents had
been so insistently inquiring—did not immediately arouse
the Bureau's interest? But it seemed to be the end of the
episode. The Silverman's returned to their packing and,
two days later, sailed for Europe.

The more time Silverman had to think about it, the
more disturbing Emil's "story" was. Not only disturbing
in that the press had presented to him a man he had
never known and said that it was the same man who had
been his friend. Mostly, it was the precipitous break with
Emil that disturbed him. Emil was dead; Rudolph Abel
was alive. The names slipped back and forth: Emil-Abel.
No train station good-byes, no transitions, just jump cuts
all over the place. Pure Godard.

The FBI was still talking to Dave Levine about the
storeroom space he shared with Goldfus. They had taken
an affidavit from Levine in which he stated that some of
the things in the storeroom belonged to Rudolph Abel,
alias Emil Goldfus. With the affidavit, the FBI got a warrant to search the storeroom. They arrived on August 16
and Dave Levine went with them. He was pointing out
which things were his, which Emil's. The agents opened
cartons, went through everything, and kept a detailed list.
Levine was relieved to have moved the Christmas cards.
In the midst of the search came a soft knock at the door.

There were two agents in the storeroom, one a "heavy"
and the other smaller and more sympathetic. When the
knock came, the "heavy" turned fast, his hand close to
his gun. He was a big man; he flung the door open.

Standing there was a man in his late fifties, Franz
Felix, a painter. Goldfus had let him keep some posses-
sions, including his clothing, in the storeroom because
Felix could no longer afford his own studio.

Franz Felix was five feet four inches high. The FBI
agent stood well over six feet.

"What the hell," he said, hand resting on his gun, "do you want?"

"I've come," whimpered Franz Felix, "for my pants."

Colonel Rudolph Abel was extradited from Texas and flown to New York. On Thursday, August 9, at 11:20 P.M. he arrived at Newark Airport in the company of several United States marshals on a commercial flight from Houston. The press was there. Abel said little. Marshal Neil Mathews reported that he and the prisoner had had a long and interesting talk. Photographers took their pictures. Fifteen minutes later, a cavalcade pulled away and the colonel was escorted to the federal detention center in Manhattan, on West Street. The press could write only about his physical appearance for all Colonel Abel said was that he wanted to consult a lawyer. The stories the next morning described him as being in good spirits and full control, looking tired, wearing his "uniform": gray slacks, gray sports jacket, open shirt, and, on his head, a battered dark straw hat with a large white band.

The next morning he was brought before Judge Matthew T. Abruzzo in Brooklyn and arraigned. The press was there. So were an uncountable number of security guards, United States marshals, FBI agents, Immigration agents, police. The charges handed down by the grand jury were read to him; Judge Abruzzo asked how the suspect pleaded. Abel asked for time to get himself a lawyer and to put off the plea until then. Judge Abruzzo set another date, the following Tuesday, and entered a plea of "Not Guilty." Abel went back to West Street.

There was an "Abel story" in the news every day. That week, the Senate approved a Civil Rights Act seventy-two to eighteen; *Confidential* Magazine was on trial in Los Angeles charged with hiring prostitutes to ensnare stars for "scoops"; Oliver Hardy, of Laurel & Hardy, died. Robert F. Kennedy was playing recordings of wire-tapped conversations showing that Johnny Dio was "in close relationship" with "high officials of the Teamsters' Union," notably Jimmy Hoffa; a nuclear device was exploded over a Nevada desert while pacifists prayed thirty miles away and the Gallup poll concluded that Carey Estes Kefauver was first in the hearts of his fellow Democrats for the 1960 presidential nomination: 29 percent of Gallup's sample wanted Kefauver; running just behind him was Massachusetts's Senator John Kennedy with 23 percent, and Texas's Lyndon Johnson with a limp 8 percent. But Colonel Abel was the big story.

First, the colonel needed a lawyer. He had said before Judge Abruzzo in court that he did not know how long it would take him to get one, for "I have no experience in these matters." Then he had gone back to the West Street jail and asked to be put in touch with John Abt, who had defended many alleged Communists prosecuted under the Smith Act, gulped, quite audibly, for the press. He did not think he would have time to take the Abel case and, although he did visit the colonel on West Street for one brief session, refused.

The colonel appeared in court twice that week. On Tuesday, as scheduled, he told Judge Abruzzo that he had not yet found himself a lawyer. The press was there. Abel was reported as looking better rested and less unkempt than at his first court scene. Also, although no one said so directly, quite aware of what he was in for, quite knowledgeable about the operation of the law. Colonel Abel took a hand in his own defense. A rather sure hand. He began, that Tuesday in court, by asking for a copy of the grand jury indictment. Abruzzo gave it to him. And the defendant told the judge that he understood that if he was unable to find his own lawyer, the Bar Association could be asked to provide one. Yes, Judge Abruzzo said, such a request could be made. Abel went back to West Street and was in court for the third time on Friday.

Just a week after Abel had been returned from Texas, Judge Abruzzo said that sufficient time had elapsed; he would appoint the lawyer himself. The trial was set for September 16, to be held in the Brooklyn Federal Court before Judge Mortimer W. Byers.

When there was no "hard-core" news to report, the papers were filled with color stories, background stories, and editorials. It was the most sensational event of the Cold War and the best piece of propaganda our side would ever muster. To repeat: the captured man was a colonel in the Russian secret police; he had been spying on us for years and that proved that we had been right all along about the Russians: they were out to destroy us. Abel was proof of it and proof, too, that we would not be destroyed. If we were vigilant, we would win. All the terrible strains of the vigilance we had practiced since at

least 1950 were paying off. We had met the enemy and
he was ours. "I have no intention of dropping this case,"
said Chief of Internal Security Tompkins. "I have no de-
sire to make anything easy for Soviet spies."

Abel's story allowed the whole business of Communists-
in-our-midst to sputter across the country again. The equa-
tion is easy: the Russian is a spy; anyone who is
pro-Russia ideologically is a spy, too. Everyone was happy
those days, for it had been proven that there really were
spies and subversives under every mattress. Anticommunism, vindicated, with a clean bill of health: we
were not paranoid. The menace was real.

The press coverage of Abel's arrest and then of his
trial were self-congratulatory in other ways. Readers were
reminded of the efficiency of the federal agencies. Every
day there was a story about how the FBI was going
through Abel's possessions for "clues." There were no stories about how all the clues led nowhere. Each time the
story of how Colonel Abel came to be arrested was repeated, the role of the "federal authorities" grew. Tompkins told a reporter from the *Daily News* that "smashing
of the ring came about through a tip to federal authorities.
The FBI swung into action immediately." You could read
a description of how the colonel did not know, at the
time of his arrest, how exposed he was, and of how he
tried to get himself deported: "had he suspected at the
time of his arrest how thoroughly both FBI and Immigration agents had penetrated his masquerade as a nondescript New York artist and photographer, he might
have felt differently."

The press came up with stories like this from the *World
Telegram*:

> As it was, prolonged investigation by the G-men of his
> activities in supplying Moscow with American defense
> secrets had paved the way for his apprehension. In the
> beginning, it was strictly an FBI case. But long before
> he was picked up in a New York hotel room by Immi-
> gration agents, both divisions of the Justice Department
> had learned a lot. . . . Indeed, it was at the request of
> the FBI that the arrest finally was made on June
> 21. . . . The G-men had picked up one of the master
> spy's colleagues.

And this, from the *New York Herald Tribune,* which enjoyed a reputation for good reporting:

SPY HUNTERS HAD EYE ON ABEL A YEAR
ARREST MADE AT THEIR REQUEST
By Richard C. Wald

The immigration authorities' arrest of alleged master spy Rudolph Ivanovich Abel was made at the specific request of "several government agencies," it was revealed yesterday by Lt. Gen. Joseph M. Swing, Commissioner of Immigration.

"We were well aware of what he was when we picked him up," Gen. Swing said. "Our idea at the time was to hold him as long as we could."

Gen. Swing indicated that Abel would not have been arrested by immigration officials on June 21 if American counter-intelligence had not requested it. The commissioner said he could not comment, however, on which agencies provided the information or asked for the arrest. Conceivably, the immigration officials were called in as a device to arrest Abel while preserving as much secrecy as possible concerning how much the government knew about his activities for Russia. The agencies, probably the Federal Bureau of Investigation and the Central Intelligence Agency, had followed Abel for a year and undoubtedly knew whether he planned to skip the country. They might have wanted a chance to search his effects thoroughly without tipping their hand.

There were two things wrong with this story: if the federal agencies were so efficient, omniscient, and thorough, how had Colonel Abel operated his alleged "spy ring" here for nine years, undetected? No one was saying. Nor was anyone saying how those agencies got their first "information" about the colonel, which was presented as such a coup. In other words, it is not very clear that Reino Hayhanen, who had in his own head the only "clues" about Rudolph Abel that anyone would ever find, had of his own free will, you might say, turned Abel in. This bragging about the role of the FBI in tracking the colonel down and ordering his arrest was, of course, the first response of the government's public relations men to the story. It did not last long. In fact, it proved embarrassing. The "case" of Colonel Abel, as it was to emerge once a team of defense lawyers had been commissioned, would hinge on those points: how much was known about Rudolph Abel when he was arrested by Immigration authorities, what "request" had come from the FBI, and what the intention really was of arresting the man on immigration charges. That would come later and would go to the Supreme Court of the United States. Unfortunately, in early August, no one had yet noticed the implications of those new stories.

The story of Colonel Abel's activities and capture was presented as one of those so-fantastic-you-wouldn't-believe-it-if-you-read-it stories. It was. Mildred Murphy of *The New York Times* called the plot "more devious and intricate than the nightly procession of espionage conspiracies flashed across TV screens." It was. There was no need to fictionalize about this one. Out came, day after day, the icons of modern espionage. There were photographs of hollowed-out bolts and coins and pencils used for hiding messages, stories of fake birth certificates and multiple identities and code names, shortwave radios and unbelievably complicated numerical codes, microdotting techniques and the system of dead and live drops, odd meetings at night in the parks of New York City. The people of New York read it all with rapture, for they had been oddly touched by history: it had all happened under their noses.

What you learned about the craft of intelligence was elaborate, but wrong. You learned that it was the "Enemy's" craft. *The New York Times* printed stories of other spy rings that had been "exposed" and a historical rundown of the KGB. It was, of course, terribly one-sided. Although reporters knew enough to liken the KGB to the CIA, they went no further. There was no indication at all that we operated the same way or that we, too, had intelligence networks set up around the world. It was the pre-U-2 era and no one spoke of the American craft of intelligence; comparing KGB with CIA only made it more mysterious. Reading the parade of stories in the press, you could only think of Abel's spy career as somehow very exciting and important. That, too, was wrong.

Behind all the news, you sensed that there were real men in the story—men with dimension, with hate and love and doubts and fears, histories and hopes, but you could not find them in the press. Naturally not, for the media do not deal, except in Newspeak, with personalities. You missed a sense of humanity in this bizarre story, but you could not quite blame the press for it; they were simply doing a job. So the job turned everyone into a caricature—each with a bit of truth.

William F. Tompkins, chief of Internal Security, wore the mantle of "Prosecutor." He posed for the press in the Brooklyn courthouse, pointing to the studio building in which the spy had lived, bemused that it could be seen so clearly from the courtroom window. Tompkins was sure and unruffled. He was, of course, none of those things. He was tired; for the case had been quickly built once Hayhanen agreed to testify and everyone for the government had worked extraordinarily long hours on it. He said to the press that everyone knew what they were doing and he said in private that "you can't afford to lose a case like this in front of the whole world." It was typical of most of the lawyers who came into the case: they presented a public face of just routinely doing a job, and privately they loved every minute of it and found it often the most interesting thing to have come along in their entire careers. "This case," Tompkins told his friends, "is a lawyer's dream." You would expect the Prosecutor, the man who stood for government at the trial, to feel negatively about the defendant, the enemy. Tompkins found the colonel "fascinating, brilliant, with a good sense of humor," and, obviously, likable.

Reino Hayhanen's name appeared daily but little was known about him. He was the "mystery man" who had "defected to the West" and would be the government's chief witness at Abel's trial. He was hidden somewhere in the country and there was fear the Russians might try to get to him. Nothing more.

And Rudolph Ivanovich Abel, dimmest of all the characters. Who was he? In the press, he was the Enemy, Soviet Spy, Mastermind, Chief of a Spy Ring—a stereotype —clever beyond bounds, ruthless, calculating, a lesson in what we were up against. The propaganda value of making Colonel Rudolph Abel larger than life was enormous. So an unnamed "expert" surveyed the paintings Abel had left in his studio and pronounced, according to The New York Times, that "they showed what is known as socialist realism" and "reflected little that would contradict strict

communist tenets regarding creative art." The paintings
were "very typical of most Russian art—quite documentary," the anonymous critic said, and "he is a social realist, extremely interested in the neighborhood around
him. . . . While he does not reveal a great deal of imagination, he certainly is a good observer." The *Times* did
not bother to ask its unnamed critic if he might not say the
same things, perhaps according room for talent and imagination, about the other painters at the Ovington Studios.
The critic would have found that American realists like
Moses and Raphael Soyer, Edward Hopper, Ben Shahn
showed the same interest in life in the neighborhood, the
same focus on what the *Times* critic called "prosaic
stances" of the figures, what might be called from another point of view the ordinary moments of life observed. Nor did the *Times* bother to define the term "socialist realism" which, according to Lenin's requirement
of the "partyness of literature and art," enlists both writer
and artist in the "ideological remaking and education of
toilers in the spirit of Socialism." But the *Times* did not
explain or elaborate; the critic had no way of knowing
the extent to which Abel's approach to painting had been
touched by, not the Soviet dictates, but the attitudes of
the American realist painters around whom he worked.
Picturing his artistic life as coherent with his assumed political attitudes made the colonel seem consistent, made
it seem that the parts fit easily together and the whole
was comprehensible.

The press made much of the spy's "double life" in the
same way. Everything about his existence in Brooklyn
Heights was paraded before the public as the carefully
contrived masquerade of a man whose "real" life was sinister. It was a "contrived cover"; the colonel, according
to a long, "in-depth" story about his "cover existence"
published in August by *Life* magazine, "dealt with the
innocents, among whom he lived and schemed, with a kind
of gentle effrontery." He had two shortwave radios in his
studio, the press consistently reported, and left readers to
draw their own conclusions. In fact, both Hallicrafters radios were available at neighborhood radio shops and were
used to *receive* transmissions and not to send messages to
Soviet Russia. The larger radio had stood on the colonel's worktable and Burt Silverman had given it a prominent place in his portrait of the man. Still, the radios

seemed sinister. So did his knowledge of electronics; so did the fact that he often "sat alone" at a bar on the corner near his studio; and the fact that, according to the building superintendent Harry MacMullen, prominently displayed in the huge assortment of pictures published by *Life,* "Abel always paid his rent on time, but [the] last payment for July was brought by a stranger." Of course it seems mysterious; *Life* magazine did not tell its readers that the colonel was securely in custody of the United States government in July and that if any "stranger" did show up with the rent, he was probably a special agent of the FBI. Which, in a way, *is* odd.

You would read those stories through the summer and fall of 1957 looking for the face of the man. You saw him in his dark straw hat or with his balding head shining under camera lights. His face was "stern," "composed," or "grim." You tried to get closer. He was described as "hatchet-faced," "looking more like a Bowery panhandler than chief of the biggest spy ring ever to operate in this country," "commonplace," "shabby," "bird-faced." You could get no closer. Abel, captive, never became real. Still he played a role and wore a mask. Still you, real in the world outside his jail cell, peered quizzically and wondered who he really was. Puzzle pieces. Parts of a whole. You tried to put it together and it never worked. Hungry for a sense of what was behind the masquerade of Colonel Rudolph Abel, you stayed hungry.

SEVEN

CLOSE to the end of August, Colonel Abel—caught, indicted, arraigned, deposited in the West Street jail—waited to be tried. The Department of Justice was prepared and anxious to move fast. The cast, on the prosecution side, had been assembled for months: Tompkins, Featherstone, Palermo. They were ready. Still, there was no one for the defense. Judge Abruzzo turned to the Brooklyn Bar Association for advice and the Association chose someone almost immediately. Many had come forward to offer their services and been rejected by Judge Abruzzo or the Brooklyn Bar. Some with good reputations as criminal lawyers had been approached and had declined, largely on the grounds that it would be unfavorable to their own political ambitions or their private business interests. To be Colonel Rudolph Abel's defense lawyer was quite a double-edged thing: it would bring a man to immediate national prominence, but it might, at the same time, compromise them. The Bar Association was careful. The man who defended Abel would have to be well above suspicion—no tousled liberals would do. He would have to perform adequately. He would represent American justice on trial before the world. Everyone in the case, from the beginning, understood that.

They found the perfect man: James B. Donovan. Donovan had attended Harvard Law School and been, during World War II, an intelligence officer in the United States Navy and a member of the OSS. He had made his mark on the staff of the late Robert H. Jackson at the Nuremberg Trials and gone into private practice. Most of his legal work had been in the field of insurance law, but Judge Abruzzo, who assigned him to the defense, brushed that aside. What mattered most was Donovan's respectability.

The headline in *The New York Times* on August 21 was:

EX-NAVY OFFICER TO DEFEND ABEL. JAMES B. DONOVAN CHOSEN BY BROOKLYN BAR—HELPED PROSECUTE TOP NAZIS.

Donovan met with his client that afternoon. From the first, he admired Abel, felt considerable sympathy with him, and thought him to be exactly what the government claimed he was. The two men had a great deal in common: both were professional intelligence officers; both accepted the underpinnings of the Cold War, the need for intelligence operations on both sides, the rules of the game. Abel trusted his country's secret service *apparat* and believed wholeheartedly that he was on the "right" side. Donovan felt the same way about the United States. Both men had a sense of humor and a keener sense of both adventure and melodrama. Each had his own kind of cool; each enjoyed playing roles. Beyond that, they shared an interest in art and respected, consistently, the lines that circumscribed their relationship. They got along well.

Donovan knew that he could not handle the defense by himself. He was working against all the resources of the United States government: the CIA, the FBI, the United States Attorney's office, and INS. What he needed was an assistant or two well versed in criminal procedure. Help came from a list of lawyers who had worked for the United States Attorney's office in the Southern District of New York. It had been a fertile period for that office and most of the able young men there have since gone on to be judges, deans of law schools, deputy mayor and commissioner for investigations in New York City.

Arnold Guy Fraiman, whose name was first on the list submitted to Donovan, had come to the United States Attorney's office from Columbia University Law School, worked in the criminal division there, and left to join the law firm of former Governor Thomas E. Dewey. Fraiman had been reading the news stories about Rudolph Abel with relish. "Wouldn't it be great," he thought, "to be involved in a case like that?" But he was not then involved and he went on with his litigation work at the Dewey firm until he received a call from Donovan.

It came, he said, like a bolt out of the blue. Fraiman met Donovan late one August afternoon and went with him to the Brooklyn Bar Association. The case was discussed; Fraiman accepted; the public was informed on August 30. The law firm lent Fraiman as a public service.

Around Labor Day, the third man joined the defense. Thomas E. Debevoise had been, like Fraiman, in the United States Attorney's office of the Southern District. After two not uneventful years there—the attempted assassination of President Truman and the shoot-out in the House of Representatives—Debevoise had moved to Vermont where he intended to practice. He, too, had been reading about the Master Spy case and was intrigued by it. Debevoise was chosen, agreed, left Vermont for New York, and before any work was done on Abel's case had a strange dream: he saw himself traveling to the courthouse in Brooklyn, entering an office, and saying he wanted copies of the warrants used to search Emil Goldfus's Brooklyn Heights studio and storeroom. Debevoise woke from the dream perplexed and went off for his first work session with Donovan and Fraiman.

While the public was waiting to see what would become of the Master Spy and what would be revealed at his trial, the defense lawyers went over the evidence. They examined the facts of the arrest, everything that had happened between June 21, the day of that arrest, and August 7, when a federal grand jury indicted Colonel Abel. And they found what they were looking for. Special agents of the FBI had taken the evidence picked up at the Hotel Latham on an Immigration warrant and gone before a federal judge to obtain warrants allowing them to search the storeroom and studio in the Ovington building for evidence of espionage. What the FBI found in the studio and storeroom—along with what was taken from the hotel and coupled with the testimony of a mysterious defector—was the sum of the government's case against Colonel Abel. The defense attacked that evidence. They claimed that the studio evidence was illegal to the extent that what was taken from the Hotel Latham was, in legal terms, "suspect." Debevoise was sent to the Brooklyn courthouse for copies of the search warrants and the defense drew up a motion to suppress. They moved to have everything taken from the hotel declared inadmissible at the trial. The notice directed the government to return and suppress as evidence all property seized on June 21 at the Hotel Latham on the ground that it was "illegally seized without warrant, contrary to the provisions of the Fourth and Fifth Amendments to the Constitution of the United States."

In his affidavit supporting the motion to suppress, Donovan explained the facts of the case and the legal reasoning underlying his motion:

From June 21st to August 7th, Abel was treated by the Department of Justice, as a matter of law, as an alien illegally in the United States. Actually, however, it is evident that the Department believed that he had committed the capital crime of Russian espionage and this was the principal interest of the Government in the man. Such undoubtedly was considered to be in our national interest. Any person familiar with counter-espionage realizes that a defecting enemy agent can be of far greater value than one of our own operating agents. Not only is there the opportunity for our Government to obtain complete information on the enemy's espionage apparatus but it can lead to such specifics as the names and locations of other enemy agents, the breaking of enemy ciphers, etc. Moreover, there can be the possibility of using such a man as a "double agent" who, although believed by his original principals to be still working on their behalf, in reality is serving the other side.

However, the Constitution and laws of the United States are clear on the procedures which must be followed in order to arrest an individual and to search and seize property in his possession. In the instant case, for example, absent an indictment, the FBI having reason to believe that a Russian spy was in Room 839 at the Hotel Latham, would obtain a warrant for his arrest from a U.S. Commissioner or federal judge, charging him with espionage. In the event the man was arrested in Room 839, the law is clear that the agents could search the room and seize anything which could be considered as the instruments or means of committing espionage, the crime charged. The prisoner would then be taken before the nearest available U.S. Commissioner or federal judge "without unnecessary delay," where he would be entitled to consult counsel. He would then be remanded to a federal prison. In the event that the agents wished to search Room 839, in the absence of its occupant, they could

have obtained a search warrant by complying with equally
clear and precise procedure.

Sometime prior to June 21, 1957 the Department of
Justice, believing Abel to be a spy, had to make a decision
with respect to him. The FBI possesses the dual functions
of a law enforcement agency and of a counter-espionage
arm of our national intelligence forces. The decision had
to be made as to whether:

(a) As law enforcement officers they should arrest
Abel on charges of espionage, conduct any lawful search
and seizure, and follow all other procedures established
under the Constitution and laws of the United States; or

(b) As counter-espionage agents, fulfilling a national
intelligence function, they should seize Abel, conceal his
detention from his co-conspirators for the longest possible time, and meanwhile seek to induce him to come
over to our side.

The election between the two alternate courses of action was made. While that election may have been pro-
spectively in the best interests of the United States, it did
not succeed. The Government thereafter cannot pretend
that such an election was not made, or attempt to pay
lip service to due process of law.

Donovan's affidavit ended with a statement of principle:

Abel is an alien charged with the capital offense of
Soviet espionage. It may seem anomalous that our constitutional guarantees protect such a man. The un-
thinking may view America's conscientious adherence
to the principles of a free society as altruism so scrupulous that self-destruction must result. Yet our principles are engraved in the history and the law of this
land. If the free world is not faithful to its own moral
code, there remains no society for which others may
hunger.

Among themselves, counsels for the defense disagreed
about why the government had proceeded the way it had.
Tom Debevoise thought the government had been bargain-
ing for time, hoping to turn the colonel into a "double
agent." Fraiman said that part of it was not significant

—that the government simply did not have a case at first and needed to secure time to get more evidence.

It was not only the government that needed time; the defense was, in those first September weeks, enormously pressed. They conferred late into many nights with little idea of the scope of the case or the motion they were about to make. They used whatever they could to support that motion. Thus, the defense submitted, as an exhibit in support of the motion to suppress, a news story. It was the one the *Herald Tribune* had printed, in the days just after Colonel Abel's arrest was made public, on page one under the headline: *Spy Hunters Had Eye on Abel a Year, Arrest Made at Their Request.* The story quoted Lieutenant General Joseph M. Swing, then commissioner of Immigration, who had said that "The immigration authorities' arrest of alleged master spy Rudolph Ivanovich Abel was made at the specific request of 'several government agencies.'" The story went on to tell the tale of American counterintelligence displaying its customary vigilance. The agencies, which the writer speculated must have been the FBI and CIA, had known about Abel for a year before he was arrested and had asked the Immigration people to arrest him. Debevoise and Fraiman, working on the papers for the motion, felt the story was not really valid. But they needed it. It was submitted as Exhibit A, annexed to the affidavit of Arnold Guy Fraiman, in support of the motion.

Colonel Abel's lawyers had no idea how effective their motion would be. Donovan thought that "if it had been any other man and any other time, this case wouldn't have gotten past the circuit court." The government's case, he said, was "a thin case at best; their proof was thin." Debevoise was less sure. "Even if the motion to suppress were granted," he said, "they would still have had enough to win their case." Just with the testimony of the defector, Debevoise thought the government was in a strong position. Fraiman thought the jury would convict Colonel Abel. "The question," to him, "is the appeal."

Notice of the motion to suppress was filed on September 13. Since the arrest had been made in the county of New York and not Brooklyn, the motion would be argued in the Foley Square courthouse, Manhattan.

There is no immediate feedback in legal process. You draw up your papers and submit them and wait; you are

assigned a date on which to argue your motion in court
and you wait; you make your case and, often, wait some
more for the decision. While Donovan, Fraiman, and Debevoise were filing papers back and forth on the search-
and-seizure issue, waiting to argue the motion, they were
also worrying over two other problems. Under a Supreme Court ruling called the *Jencks Decision*, defense
counsel was entitled to have a look at any statements of
witnesses whose testimony prosecution would offer in
court. Since Donovan knew little about the man being
billed as the government's "star witness," aside from what
he could gather on his own, it was possible that he would
ask for Hayhanen's statements taken down by the FBI.
Donovan wanted to have a look at that witness. When he
received from the government, as required by law, a list
of prosecution witnesses—names and addresses— one
name was missing. The mystery man. Donovan exercised
the right to have the names and addresses of *all* the witnesses. Anyone not listed could be disqualified. The government, of course, complied and offered a compromise:
they would make the witness available to Donovan. They
named a day and Donovan agreed to meet with one of
the prosecution attorneys on that day.

And all along the government was pressing to go to
trial. The defense could not understand why. "I mean,"
Arnold Fraiman said, "we don't object to our client sitting in jail." The government did. They objected because
Reino Hayhanen, witness for the prosecution, not yet
known to press, public, or defense lawyers, might not
hold out. No one could tell how long he would endure
or keep his promise to appear in court. The "star witness"
was a lot of trouble and the government wanted to be
done with him quickly.

On the appointed day, September 28, at the appointed
hour, early in the afternoon, James Donovan and Arnold
Fraiman were driven out of New York City by James J.
Featherstone of the Department of Justice. Watching
them, you might have been puzzled by the extraordinary
behavior that small band of men exhibited. Featherstone,
driving, kept looking into his rearview mirror. No one
spoke much. Fraiman, the youngest of the band, was the
least informed about what they were all up to. So Fraiman kept his eyes open and surmised, as the car traveled
up the West Side of Manhattan and north through West-

chester County along the Saw Mill River Parkway, that they were going to interview one of the government witnesses who was for the time being a resident of Sing Sing.

It made sense. It was wrong. The car turned off the highway at Elmsford and went a short way through the countryside. They arrived. They were at the Muffin Man, which turned out to be no more than an ordinary wayside diner. Into it marched Featherstone, leaving Fraiman and Donovan behind in the car. They waited. Out came Featherstone, asking them to go inside and wait.

Waitresses at the Muffin Man are used to serving truck drivers and summer people and their neighbors. They are not used to bands of men looking exactly alike in their crew cuts and suits and hats, whispering over their coffee and making surreptitious telephone calls. Which is what happened at the Muffin Man on a country road in September 1957.

Donovan knew what was happening. And why. "I really could not blame them," he said later. "Hayhanen was a marked man; the KGB surely had put a price on his head and he was the government's key witness. Without him, their case would be in bad shape."

They drank their coffee and Featherstone continued to confer in whispers with the suited, faceless men. Fraiman thought the whole idea was senseless. After the coffee and the cigarettes, Featherstone shepherded them outside again and into another car, this one driven by a "heavy." They went off down the road in the bright afternoon sun and swung around. They came back and whizzed right through the Muffin Man parking lot again. Across the road, down another, slowing down at a gas station, and then suddenly backing up a few feet into the parking lot of a motel.

It was the Saw Mill River Motel right on the Saw Mill River Parkway, just below the Hawthorne Circle, plainly visible from the highway and easily accessible along that highway from New York City. Still, the twisting and turning had been necessary, for, as Donovan explained, Hayhanen had a price on his head. The Saw Mill River Motel is a clean, innocuous place, very respectable; the only cops-and-robbers touches to the scene provided by these participants. Hayhanen was in a room in the rear, on the second floor. Outside was a wrought iron balcony and all around, guards.

The room was dark, the blinds drawn, the television set going, Hayhanen in shirt-sleeves, his hands shaking. Fraiman kept thinking how unhealthy it was to be inside with the television set on a beautiful afternoon. In all, they were in the room with Reino Hayhanen, alias Eugene Maki, alias Vik, for less than ten minutes.

Hayhanen had changed since his defection. All those days waiting it out in Peekskill, waiting for Mark to be arrested; feeling about that arrest, when it was finally done, both relief and terror; all that drinking, wavering, and answering questions. Some men would waste under that pressure, but Hayhanen had puffed up. He had gained at least fifty pounds. And, although Donovan could not know it then, Hayhanen was in disguise. His naturally light skin and fair hair, his typically Finnish looks had been altered: his hair and eyebrows were dyed jet black; he had grown a mustache and that, too, was dyed.

Donovan and Hayhanen, face to face, acted their rehearsed roles. Hayhanen said, "I have right not to talk with you." "I will not talk until trial." "I talk no more." "You wasting your time here." The result was what the script called for: nothing. Still, the rules had been observed and Donovan had seen the government's witness. On the drive back to New York City, he made a sketch of Hayhanen (it looked more like King Farouk), which he would use in his detective work about the defector's predefection life in the United States. Later, Donovan would present the sketch to Rudolph Abel for approval and, much later, to Prosecutor Tompkins for a keepsake.

The hearing on Donovan's motion presented a preview of the government's case and a painful opportunity for Rudolph Abel to hear the story of his arrest told five times over. Four members of the Immigration and Naturalization Service were called to testify; one special agent of the Federal Bureau of Investigation. There were no surprises, no sudden revelations, for the stories of the five men had been painstakingly taken down in sworn affidavits before the hearing began. It was clear to everyone that if Judge Byers denied the motion and allowed the government to present its evidence, the case would be appealed. A great deal of the questioning and the line of argument was *pro forma*, necessary because it had to go into the record. It was a curiously impersonal production; the men who spoke did so from behind their masks as employees of the government and their lines were delivered in monotones. Still, it was important. The issue emerged clearly—were the procedures followed by the FBI and the Immigration Service unconstitutional?

For a curtain-raiser you had a look at some of the evidence. Together, defense and prosecution lawyers and Judge Byers went over the lists of possessions taken at the Hotel Latham, indicating the ones at stake.

Government lawyers readily disclaimed interest in what they called "purely personal" items—the thirty-three white handkerchiefs, the pairs of white socks, the paintings, the foot powder, and all the rest; but they did want to hold on to the following articles, which were read into the record:

The first of several unfathomable messages, this one typed:

" 'Balmora,' Avenida Oberon. 3 p.m. Display left of entrance. I. 'Is this an interesting picture? L. 'Yes. Do you wish to see it, Mr. Brandt?' L. smokes a pipe and has a red book in left hand."

Still another: "Mr. Vladinec, P.O. Box 348. M-w, K-9. USSR Sign 'Arthur.' W. Merkulow, Poste Restante, M-a, USSR (Russia). Sign 'Jack.' "

A third printed message was put into the record, with no statement of where it had been found: "As you told, will wait in London 2-3 day while your message arrives. P."

Several keys, one accompanied by a tag which identified it as a safe-deposit box key.

Several strips of graph paper, one with a series of digits in groups of fives, another with six lines written in what was identified only as "a foreign language."

A bill from the Camera Craft Company for one hundred twenty dollars and change; an International Certificate of Vaccination made out to Martin Collins; a Hallicrafters Model S-38-D radio.

Two roles of green insulated wire; a wiretap apparatus.

And the "personal" records: Emil Goldfus's bankbook from the East River Savings Bank; hotel bills from the Daytona Plaza in Florida and the Hotel Latham in New York; bills from Fifth Avenue Laundry, Wright Arch Preserver, and Peyton, Ltd., a men's clothing store, all

made out to Martin Collins. A birth certificate in the
name of Emil Robert Goldfus; another for Collins.

The government wanted to add to this list of possessions that they laid claim to whatever Colonel Abel had
abandoned in the wastebasket of his hotel room. Kevin
Maroney, a special attorney of the Department of Justice
who would handle much of the courtroom work, said so.

"Now, is there any way," Judge Byers asked, "we can
tell what those items are?"

Maroney explained that the "items" he was talking
about had been taken by the FBI "after the Immigration
people had left the hotel room." He was careful to put it
that way, and he would get a list from them very quickly.

There was a short scuffle over the wastebasket items.
Did Abel not relinquish ownership by throwing the things
away? No, said the defense, he claimed he owned them.
Maroney was quick to get into the hearing a specifica-
tion of what was in the scrap basket—"particularly," he
said, "a pencil, a wooden pencil which was a container,
and which contained some frames of microfilm." Byers
stepped in and asked Fraiman to draw up another affidavit in which the colonel specifically claimed ownership
of what was in the wastebasket. "All right," said the
judge, exasperated and anxious to get on with business,
"are we ready for the hearing?"

They were. The government produced its first witness,
Robert E. Schoenenberger, supervisory investigator for the
INS, who recited his role in the arrest: a man following
orders. Quickly Donovan made clear what he was after.
As Schoenenberger was describing leaving Washington on
the evening of June 20 and being met by Edward Farley
of the New York INS branch, Donovan asked if there
was any conversation between them about the imminent
arrest of Colonel Abel. Schoenenberger said yes and then
Donovan wanted to know what was said, to which Maroney objected. Judge Byers asked what bearing that had
on the motion and Donovan, answering, reiterated the
point in question—one which he had made in all the papers filed before the court, one which he would make
throughout the hearing.

"We believe, sir," he said, "that by the manner in
which I am approaching this we will show that at all times
the Federal Bureau of Investigation was actually directing
the movements of the Immigration Service."

Byers would not allow the question of what was said between the two INS men, and Donovan had trouble getting Schoenenberger to describe the "arrangement" between the FBI and INS. Schoenenberger had not been privy to that arrangement; but he had gone from Washington to New York with the papers for the arrest and he had supervised the INS agents at the Hotel Latham and had been in the room when Colonel Abel was taken into custody. On those points, Donovan began to question him.

Schoenenberger described leaving FBI headquarters at six-thirty in the morning, arriving at the Hotel Latham in a car belonging to the FBI accompanied by two special agents of the FBI, and driving around the block for a while.

"Was it not by prearrangement that you were simply cruising around while these other events were taking place?" Donovan asked him; it sounded sinister.

"Yes."

"What was the arrangement?"

"Special Agents Gamber and Blasco were designated by the FBI to interview the suspect shortly after seven A.M. I designated Farley and Boyle to stand by, and at the end of the interview by the FBI, they were told to serve the order to show cause and the warrant of arrest. . . ."

Schoenenberger described himself as being in the hotel room "for the purpose of supervising the arrest of Abel and the examination of his personal effects in an effort to locate documentary evidence of alienage."

"And did you find," Donovan asked, "any such documentary evidence of his status as an alien?" The question touched the most important point in the hearing: Was the INS search of that room really (in legal terms, "in good faith") to find evidence that the man was an illegal alien, or were they actually, *sub rosa*, looking for evidence of espionage? But Donovan could not get it in.

"I think he should ask what was found in the hotel room," Maroney objected.

Judge Byers thought so, too. "The witness doesn't need to give his opinion as to the value of the papers in the evidentiary sense. Ask him what he found."

"Your Honor," Donovan pleaded, "this is extremely important."

"All right, don't ask him what he found. I am telling you what I would like to have you do. Of course, you can disregard my instructions; I realize that."

Donovan, still trying, turned back to Schoenenberger and asked him if what he "did find in that room confirmed . . . the information the FBI had given you?"

The question was excluded by the judge; Donovan was reminded that "the witness does not need to characterize the probative value of the documents."

"Yes, your Honor, but he did make that statement."

"I know you like to argue," Judge Byers said, "we all like to argue. Will you please just move along?"

Donovan tried once more and was cut off again. "I am not going to listen to the witness's opinion as to what those documents show," Byers said. "Now, take that from me."

Donovan took it. Maroney cross-examined Schoenenberger and asked, "During that hour did you observe any FBI agents making a search of any of the effects of the defendant?"

"I did not."

Byers asked his own question. "Were there any FBI agents in the room during that hour?"

"No, your Honor, with the exception of Gamber and Blasco, who were just——"

"You said they were in the doorway, as you were entering."

"That is correct."

"During the hour that elapsed was there any FBI agent in the room?" Byers again, annoyed at the way counsel on both sides were handling the questioning.

Maroney moved on to put in the record some testimony about the things found in the wastebasket. Byers interrupted to ask, "Did you see him put anything else in the wastebasket than pencils?"

"I believe he discarded some Kleenex. I believe he discarded a package of contraceptives in the wastebasket."

No one objected. The government had no further questions.

Arnold Fraiman went back to the days of preparation in Washington just before Schoenenberger came to supervise Abel's arrest. He asked what the evidence was that Schoenenberger had reviewed in order to determine that there was cause to issue an Immigration warrant. Maroney objected. Schoenenberger, he said, had already tes-

tified that he made "an independent review from the
Immigration standpoint."

"We are entitled to know what the information was
that the FBI supplied Immigration, your Honor," Fraiman said.

"I question that," answered Byers. "What is it you want
to establish about that?"

"I want to establish, your Honor, what the evidence
was upon which he reached this conclusion."

"Why? Why are you entitled to know that?"

"It is our contention that the object of this search and
seizure was to obtain materials relating to espionage. . . .
It is our contention that as part of the proof to show that
it is material, to show what information it was that the
FBI turned over to this Immigration officer——"

Byers interrupted and Fraiman did not get to finish.
Immediately after Schoenenberger was excused, Edward
J. Farley of the New York office of INS took the stand,
and Fraiman questioned him about what he knew of the
suspect on the night before the arrest. Farley said that he
knew only what was in the report that the INS men from
Washington, Schoenenberger and Lennox Kanzler, had
brought with them. Fraiman jumped right in.

"What type of report was this?"

"It——"

"Was it an Immigration report?"

"It was a report furnished to the Immigration Service."

"At this time," Fraiman says, "the defendant asks that
the government produce that report for our inspection."

"The government opposes the motion," Maroney said,
"and thinks that it is immaterial to this hearing."

"I think, your Honor," Fraiman said, "it goes to the
very heart of this hearing, which is to determine what the
object was by the Department of Justice conducting this
search. I think that report, based upon what Mr. Farley
has testified to, would indicate what the information was
that the men had which was the basis for this entire investigation."

Byers sustained the objection and said, "I am going to
ask you to take me into your confidence to this extent—is
it your theory that the FBI, having reason to believe that
a given individual has broken the law, may approach the
solution of the problem by investigating what you might

consider a minor offense, there being a major offense in the background? Is that your theory?"

"No, your Honor."

"What is it?"

Fraiman explained that "in arresting this man in the manner in which they did, that is having information that he was a Soviet espionage agent, but not having sufficient information to obtain a warrant charging him with that, but having additional information that he was an alien illegally in the United States——"

"And, therefore, subject to arrest?"

"Subject to arrest, your Honor."

"They were not at liberty to arrest him?"

"No, your Honor. They were perfectly proper in arresting him. We don't contend that at all. As a matter of fact, we contend it was their duty to arrest this man as they did. I think it . . . showed admirable thinking on the part of the FBI and the Immigration Service. We don't find any fault with that. Our contention is that although they were permitted to arrest this man, and in fact had a duty to arrest this man in a manner in which they did, they did *not* have a right to search his premises for the material which related to espionage."

"What we are seeking," Donovan added, "to bring home through this hearing is that, as your Honor has pointed out, the man was suspected of two crimes: illegal entry and espionage. . . . The ordinary legal process that would be followed in pursuit [of] a person suspected of either one of those two crimes was not followed in this case and what we hope to . . . show [is] that the dominant motivation of the Department of Justice . . . was to keep this entire proceeding as secret as possible."

Donovan explained that the civil warrant served on Abel at his arrest required no return before a United States commissioner or judge and that the measure was "extraordinary," done to "serve the dominant *counterespionage* objective of the Department of Justice." That objective, Donovan argued, included having the FBI spend a half hour with the man and then bring in the Immigration officers with their civil warrant of arrest. Donovan summarized: "These Immigration officers were simply used as pawns." As a professional intelligence officer himself, James Donovan was the perfect man to point out, as he did, that persuading a top Soviet agent "to come over to our side" was "far more in the national interest" than giving him the maximum sentence for illegally entering the United States. But, Donovan argued, "having gone down that road, the road of counterespionage in which it is [taken for granted] that you keep it as secret as possible, and having taken that gamble for weeks down in Texas and lost, then you cannot come back up the other road to follow as though you had issued a criminal warrant." Donovan concluded by referring to a Supreme Court decision that established the precedent of "good faith" in questions like this one; Donovan argued that the arrest was not made in good faith and "that the search and seizure was illegal."

Judge Byers was less ornery. "Thank you for explaining your views to me," he said, but made it very clear that, "I should be very reluctant to have any court assume the function to tell the FBI how to perform their functions. I think it is the job of the FBI to bring to light information concerning violations of the law and I don't think it is part of the court's duty to tell them how they should function."

On that note, the court recessed for lunch and returned at two o'clock when Farley went on the stand again describing arrangements that had been made in New York between the FBI and the Immigration Service.

"Agents would enter the hotel room," he said, "and they would talk to [Abel] in an effort to have him cooperate with them; we would be present as Immigration officers with the warrant of arrest to take him into custody."

No one, he said, had elaborated on what the word "cooperate" meant. He described waiting in a room down the hall while several FBI men went in to talk with the colonel, then coming into the room and "standing by," as he said, while his partner, Boyle, served the show cause order and the warrant. Farley identified the man they had arrested. The record indicated that "the witness had identified Rudolph Abel as the man whom he knew as Martin Collins."

They went around the same story again, Farley testifying nearly as Schoenenberger had. He went so far as to say that two FBI agents were standing in the hallway while the arrest and search were made. Asked whether he had been instructed to make a search for evidence of espionage, he said no. Then the same stumbling block loomed: the contents of the FBI memorandum to Immigration based upon which the decision to arrest Abel was made.

Donovan began to talk about the report and Byers stopped him short.

"I have told you that that report is not going to be produced so far as I am concerned."

Maroney suddenly offered, for the government, to submit the FBI memorandum to Judge Byers. Byers agreed to examine the document but, he insisted, "I am not willing to have any time elapse which will delay our proceedings."

The rest of the afternoon was taken by the testimony of Lennox Kanzler, who worked directly under Schoenenberger and could testify to little that had not already been said in court, only that he and Schoenenberger and Mario Noto had gone in Washington to the offices of the FBI and conferred there before taking off for New York.

Byers continued in his usual mood saying, when a motion was made to strike some of Kanzler's testimony as irrelevant, that, "If I should strike all the irrelevant matters that have been produced at this hearing today, there would be very little left, my friend."

Byers kept insisting that they were "wasting time," usually that the defense was; he became so irritable that at one point he asked Fraiman to "go on with something else; if you have something else in mind."

Paul Blasco, special agent of the FBI assigned to the New York office, took the stand. Blasco spoke like a true policeman. He talked of "interviewing the occupant of the hotel room," "instructions being issued," and he said often "that is correct, yes, that is correct"; he described events as taking place at 7:04, and when Donovan asked, "Now the three of you remained in that room for the next twenty-five minutes, is that correct?" Blasco corrected him. "Approximately twenty-three minutes."

Blasco was reciting what happened during the FBI interview with Abel when Byers interrupted.

"Mr. Witness, I think this is liable to be quite a recital."

Court was adjourned. The next day, Blasco said that his partner had presented Abel with "Colonel, we have received information concerning your involvement in espionage." Then the questioning got sticky.

"Before interrogating Mr. Collins," Donovan asked, "did you warn him of his right not to answer your questions?"

"He was given no such warning."

"Did you warn him that anything he said might be used against him as evidence in a criminal proceeding?"

"We did not give him any such instruction inasmuch as we were interviewing him to solicit his cooperation."

"Did you tell him that he was entitled to consult a lawyer?"

"He was not told that he had a right to consult a lawyer."

The questions were asked over a continuing string of objections by Maroney, interspersed with Judge Byers's insistence that he be allowed to ask the questions although they were "purely argumentative." Donovan kept trying to ask whether or not the FBI had standing instructions to give those warnings and Blasco finally got the distinction he was making as this— "When an individual is to be arrested by an agent of the Federal Bureau of Investigation, all agents are instructed . . ." And so on. But in this case, the arrest was being made by an Immigration officer.

Blasco said that he had been in the room after the INS officers were called in and that from his position ("I stood in the room with my back to the bathroom door") he could see the search of the room being made but did not take part in it.

Mario Noto was called. On his testimony the case hinged, for Noto had been the link between INS, where he was deputy assistant commissioner for Special Investigations, and the FBI. He told of receiving a report on Colonel Abel from the FBI's liaison man Papich; he said that Papich told him the FBI was interested in the man because of his espionage activities but that he, Noto, did not ask about it. He told, too, of preparations for Abel's arrest. Noto insisted that his interest was purely from an Immigration standpoint.

"On matters of this type it is just a routine operation to coordinate . . . with the FBI."

Had Noto told Schoenenberger to confer with the FBI when he got to New York?

"I did not . . . but I told him that in the interest of coordination, in view of Mr. Abel's background, that when he arrived in New York after his conversations with the district director that I would appreciate it if he would get in touch with the New York office of the FBI."

Had there been discussion in Washington about the FBI interviewing Abel before Immigration agents arrested him?

Noto did not recall that. He also did not recall "being aware" that the FBI was going to talk to Abel at all.

Two things, Noto told the court, could have been done with Colonel Abel based on the information that the INS and FBI had about him: deportation proceedings or criminal prosecution. "Election of deportation proceedings," he insisted, "does not foreclose the bringing of subsequent criminal prosecution."

Noto was excused, unfinished business was put out of the way, and Judge Byers said that he had read the report that the FBI had turned over to the Immigration authorities.

"I find nothing in it," he said, "that could be interpreted as a suggestion that [Rudolph Abel] should be made the subject of inquiry by the Immigration authorities for the purpose of having him arrested as a cover for an investigation by the FBI or in the hope that the arrest . . . would afford information to the FBI in connection with the alleged character and activity of the defendant."

It was clear what Judge Byers's decision would be. On October 11, the motion to suppress evidence was denied. The case went to trial.

Taking of testimony began on Monday, October 14, in the federal court of the Eastern District of New York on Fulton Street, just across from the Ovington Studios. The accused appeared, dressed in a dark blue suit, hair cut, composed. You looked at him. Who was he? You had been told that Rudolph Abel was a pseudonym. You did not even know his name. And the face you had been seeing in the press and on the television news reports, a face tense and hard, often photographed through the bars of his prison cell, that was not his real face. It was his *persona,* the mask through which he looked at the world.

Ask his friends in Brooklyn. They do not recognize that face at all. They grasp the reality of the man rather well; the person whom they knew as Emil Goldfus for nearly four years is genuine. They point to his gentleness, his generosity, his spirit. Those things cannot be fake. A man does not come back again and again to an unfinished canvas, trying each time to shape it more in the image of the world he sees, if he is faking. A man cannot hide his identity from the people who see him constantly and open themselves to him. It is impossible, you see, to deny that although he is being called Colonel Rudolph Ivanovich Abel he is, in reality, that arch, sympathetic fellow, seedy, pleasant Emil Goldfus.

Ask the government of the United States of America, his accuser. Its lawyers know Rudolph Abel's identity. They know that everything he has done was staged and calculated. They know that he only pretended to be Emil Goldfus and that his life in Brooklyn Heights was an elaborate masquerade. It counts for nothing; it testifies to his adroitness. Goldfus was a role; Abel played it because it gave him good cover. The real man is a professional soldier and a spy. He is the enemy. Do not trust him. Those young men taken in by his deception were innocents. Fortunately, the government is not innocent. Abel's disguise has been penetrated and he is about to be unmasked.

EIGHT

TOMPKINS sat at the prosecution table folded into a chair.
You heard the street traffic through the windows and the
rustle and coughing of intermission time. Tompkins had
made his opening speech to the jury. You prepared to
listen to Donovan, who began, "May it please the Court,
ladies and gentlemen of the jury. This is a case in which
you, the jury . . . are to decide whether or not the defendant has been proven guilty beyond a reasonable
doubt of a crime for which he could be sentenced to
death. . . . It is important to remember with respect to the
three counts in this indictment that it is only under count
number one, that is the conspiracy to transmit information
to Russia, that the defendant could be sentenced to
death. . . ."

Tompkins had spoken confidently of his case to the
jury, to the press, to his colleagues. And yet he had some
doubts himself. Not about the evidence or the guilt of Rudolph Abel; those were unclouded in his mind. As Donovan spoke, Tompkins dwelt on his witness, Reino Hayhanen. He turned over the pretrial days when Hayhanen
and his wife Hannah were firmly ensconced in a
government-rented suite at the St. George Hotel, a Brooklyn landmark on Clark Street, a short walk from the
courthouse. The suite was headquarters for the staff now
sitting at Tompkins's table in the courtroom, and there
Hayhanen had been kept amused by the government's
lawyers, who talked and ate and played chess with him.
They had been with him since his defection and had come
to know him, if not well then simply better than anyone
else did. Tompkins was on good footing with the defector
because he had been honest and had not let Hayhanen
get away with too much; it established some ground of respect.

"This case is not only extraordinary," Donovan was

saying, "it is unique. For the first time in American history a man is being threatened with death as a sentence on the charge that he acted as a spy for a foreign nation with which we are legally at peace."

Hayhanen had been in "tremendous emotional turmoil," as the government lawyers put it. But after he accepted the decision to defect and testify, after he faced it, he seemed to be more in control. He had been talking about establishing himself in this country after it was all over, about making an independent life for himself. Up to the night before his appearance in court, he seemed to be holding his own, but then, in the government suite at the hotel, he had broken down again and refused to testify. Tompkins and James Featherstone had calmed him, reassured him, convinced him. Monday morning, Tompkins was still listening to Donovan. . . .

"The defendant is a man named Abel. It is most important that you keep that fact uppermost in your mind throughout the days ahead. This is not a case against communism. It is not a case against Soviet Russia. Our grievances against Russia have been voiced and are being voiced every day in the United Nations and in various other forums. But the sole issues in this case, on which you are going to render the verdict, deal with whether or not this man Abel has been proved guilty beyond a reasonable doubt of the specific crimes with which he is now charged."

Donovan described Hayhanen, and you understood immediately that part of the defense strategy would focus on discrediting Hayhanen's character.

"The prosecution has just told you that among the principal witnesses against the defendant will be a man whose name is Hayhanen, who claims that he helped the defendant to spy against the United States.

"This means that within a very short while this man will take the stand and testify before you. Observe his demeanor very carefully."

Tompkins knew that if Hayhanen were to break on the stand it would come right at the beginning of his testimony, right when he would be asked to identify Colonel Abel in the courtroom. Anyone who had been watching Hayhanen since May would have pin-pointed that confrontation as the source of greatest strain; the intuition had been confirmed by two psychiatrists. Anticipating the moment, Tompkins turned back to hear Donovan's attack:

". . . Bear in mind that if what the government says is true, it means that this man has been here for some years living among us, spying on behalf of Soviet Russia. . . . It means . . . that he entered the United States on false papers . . . that he has lived here every day only by lying about his true identity, about his background, about every fact of his everyday life . . . he was trained abroad in what his 'cover' should be here, meaning that he was trained in the art of deception. He was trained to lie. In short, assuming that what the government says is true, this man is literally a professional liar.

". . . Bear in mind that the man's sole hope of clemency presumably is not only that he implicate as many as he can in his crimes, but that he make as important as possible the information which he says he has to give our government . . . consider what motivation the witness has to tell the truth; and what justification or motivation he would have to do again what he has been doing for some years, and that is lying. . . ."

Donovan ended his address with, "I know this jury will do its conscientious duty and render a just verdict, in the tradition of a fair American trial," and sat down.

Tompkins called the government's first witness and Reino Hayhanen came in through the rear door and walked to the front of the courtroom.

He took the oath, sat in the witness chair, and Tompkins began:

"Will you speak up, so that your voice is heard all the way back here to the last juryman, please? Now, what was your last permanent address in the United States?"

"Peekskill, New York State."

"You are a citizen of Russia, is that correct?"

"Yes, I am."

"And from 1939 roughly until 1957 you were employed by the Soviet Union?"

Arnold Fraiman stood and objected to "Mr. Tompkins leading the witness."

"Who is going to conduct the trial for the defense, please?" Judge Byers asked.

"I believe, your Honor," Donovan said, "that Mr. Fraiman's objection was that Mr. Tompkins was leading the witness."

"Now, what is your objection?"

"I make the same objection."

"I don't think it is harmful leading thus far."

Hayhanen agreed that he had been employed by the Soviet Union.

"Now," Tompkins said, "would you please describe your employment, briefly?"

"Do I have to tell before espionage and counterespionage work or just that one——"

"No. I am getting at what agency in the government of the USSR were you employed by?"

Hayhanen began reciting his history.

"The last time I was employed with the KGB. It means espionage work."

"Is that *KGB?*" Byers asked.

"Yes, that is Committee of State Security," Hayhanen answered.

"But, your Honor, up to 1948 I was working in *N*KGB. It means counterespionage work in Russia."

"*N*KGB?"

"NKGB, your Honor."

"Now," Tompkins began, "would your original employment with the NBGD——"

"No. NKG-*B*."

"Did it subsequently change its name?"

"It was NGVD; then when NKVD was divided to NKVD and NKGB, I was still working in NKGB section."

Tompkins dropped the alphabet. He established that Hayhanen had entered the United States in October 1952 with a passport issued in Finland. The passport was marked Government Exhibit Number One and introduced into evidence. Judge Byers asked to have a look at it. "I suppose," Byers said, "at some time you are going to ask the witness if in 1952 his name was Maki?"

"We will connect it up, your Honor; these are just general questions and we will go into more detail later on."

Hayhanen had been on the stand for nearly ten minutes. You could feel the waiting. Tompkins pressed toward the moment when Hayhanen would identify Abel, anxious to get it over with, and dreading it. He led Hayhanen to say that his arrival in the United States was in connection with his "employment" and that he was "sent to this country to be resident assistant in espionage work."

"Now, do you know the name of the resident officer?"

"I know him just by the nickname Mark."

"Do you know him by any other name?"

"No, I don't. I didn't know him by other name. I know him just for security reasons by his nickname."

"Now, do you see him in the courtroom here?"

"Yes, I do."

"Would you please point him out?"

"Yes. He is sitting there at the end of that table."

Hayhanen pointed his finger toward the table at which Fraiman, Donovan, and Abel were sitting. The foreman of the jury had been watching that table and thinking how alone they looked sitting there. Tompkins, having asked the question, turned away and looked, not at Hayhanen, nor at Abel, but at the two psychiatrists, sitting in the courtroom. Hayhanen pointed.

Tompkins turned his head back. "The end of the table?"

"That is right."

"Will the defendant stand up, please?"

Abel stood. There was absolute silence.

"Is that the gentleman?"

"Yes."

"I would like the record to note that the witness has identified the resident officer Mark, Rudolph I. Abel."

Byers spoke. "Is there any question that the witness identified the defendant?"

"No, your Honor," Donovan said, from the table. Abel sat down.

How long? Thirty seconds? The confrontation, enacted, was done, and Hayhanen had survived it. He didn't crack, Tompkins thought; we are in the clear.

Hayhanen and Abel had not seen each other since the spring, when Hayhanen was being urged to take his trip "home." Whatever Abel must have felt about him then—the disdain, the annoyance—he kept it controlled. But the last vestige of his illusions about Reino Hayhanen were being stripped in the courtroom; he had told Donovan that he "bided his time . . . hoping [Hayhanen] would work out or that his gross inadequacy was part of a more devious Soviet design meant to lead Hayhanen to the FBI in an assigned role of a triple agent." "Abel's faith," Donovan explained, "in the Soviet and its intelligence service would not permit him to believe the KGB had sent him so dangerous an incompetent."

There, in the courtroom, with Hayhanen's finger pointing from the witness stand, the nightmarish *j'accuse* being realized, Abel had to believe it. But his control was impeccable. No sense of betrayal showed on his face, no hatred, not even the rancor he must have felt as Hayhanen went on with his story. At each grotesque distortion Hayhanen wreaked on the English language, at each incomprehensible answer, Abel must have thought back on his admonitions to his then-assistant: "I told him to spend more time with native-born Americans, because I wanted him to speak English that wouldn't attract attention. I repeatedly emphasized this because he spoke with such a heavy accent."

On Hayhanen's side of the confrontation, enormous relief. The resentment against Abel, the lifetime resentment of superiors who made him feel inferior, of a father who had abandoned him, of unreachable figures that had haunted his thirty-five years—against them all, Hayhanen had his revenge. What had kept him from testifying at first—oh, yes, the fear of reprisals against his family, as he had said, but also the deeper fear—the retaliation he feared from Mark, the vengeance he continually felt Mark would have on him, although Mark was safely in the custody of the government, although Mark was safely behind bars. Still, that fear that had kept him from testifying and that had made him buckle only the night before—it was all, for the moment, exorcised. He had pointed his finger, he had waited, and nothing had happened.

All the caught breaths were released; Tompkins launched into the direct examination and Hayhanen answered quite easily, in spite of the enormous difficulty he was having with the English language.

For a moment Mark had been real; Rudolph Abel had assumed flesh and blood as he stood to be accused. But the moment passed and, as the trial went on, grew dim. Tompkins asked the questions necessary to establish the conspiracy he was out to prove.

"Now, do you know what his occupation is?"

"He told me that he worked as a photographer, that he had somewhere a photo studio."

"Do you know whether he is an employee of the Russian government?"

"Yes, he was—or he was up to this time."

"And what agency of the government, if you know, was he employed by?"

"He was employed by the KGB."

"Did he have any rank?"

"Yes, he had the rank of colonel."

"Throughout the rest of the trial," Tompkins said later, "I was aware of Hayhanen's tendency to great strain, and I had to be on the alert for it. He needed to be eased into things lest he blow up before the line of testimony made its point." First, then, Tompkins eased Hayhanen into his biography. Hayhanen said that he was born May 14, 1920, in a village called Kaskisarri, about twenty-five miles from Leningrad, that he attended school in Russia through the level of teacher's college and taught school for three months until he was drafted, in 1939, into the NKVD which, he explained, was "like secret police." He worked first as an interpreter, helping Russian troops to interrogate prisoners of war, just after the end of the Finnish-Russian war. Tompkins asked about his training.

"I got just short course of training. It was about ten days course. We got several lectures during that nine- or ten-day period. How to question war prisoners, how to try to find that maybe there is somebody who is a spy to send as a war prisoner and then also we got short training as for future NKVD officials or workers, how to work on counterespionage work, how to find anti-Soviet people, or some espionage agents from some other countries on Russian territory."

Were it not for the language, the story would have seemed remarkably straight and well rehearsed. From the morning's proceedings, if you tried hard, you could piece together the story: at the end of the war, Hayhanen continued in the same kind of job in Karelia. In 1948 "that assignment was completed and I was called to Moscow." He had become a member of the Communist Party and risen to the rank of first lieutenant. In Moscow, he said, "my bosses explained to me that now they need me instead of counterespionage work on espionage work." He named his bosses, one of whom was Colonel Korotkov, "the assistant boss of PGU," which Hayhanen translated for the court as "first division" of the KGB.

"Now," Tompkins asked, "I don't want the conversations of any of those who participated, but as a result of

your visit was your assignment changed from counterespionage to espionage?"

"That is right."

"Now, after your visit in Moscow, where did you go?
Did you return home?"

"I returned to Karelia, and I prepared everything for
moving from Karelia to Estonia."

In Estonia, Hayhanen was trained for espionage work.
Tompkins asked what kind of training.

"I received training on photography, then on driving
car and how to make some repairs in cars, to show I can
work as a car mechanic, auto mechanic. . . . In photography, I got training as all photographers were getting, I
was getting training on how to copy some documents or
how to make some copies from some photos, and then I
got some training of using Minox cameras."

"Now, did you receive any other training in anything
else while you were in Estonia?"

"I got training in to talk English, to write English."

"Now, how often did you take English lessons?"

"English lessons I was getting about once or twice a
week."

In Estonia, Hayhanen was told about his future. The
witness started to tell how a Major Abramov had come to
see him, but Donovan objected. Tompkins explained that
Major Abramov was a "coactor who has been in this
conspiracy from the original conversation and the meeting back in 1948 when the witness first went to Moscow."

"Does it appear in the record," Judge Byers asked,
"that Abramov is one of the unnamed coconspirators?"

Tompkins said no. Donovan insisted that he had "never
heard of him before and . . . there has been no proof on
the conspiracy in the case to date."

"We are not going to prove the conspiracy in the first
hour with this witness, as your Honor well knows," Tompkins said.

Donovan repeated that the testimony was not binding
and Tompkins withdrew the question. The plot continued, minus Major Abramov.

In Estonia, Hayhanen was informed that he would be
assigned to the United States of America. He began to
build his "legend." He explained, obtusely, "A legend is
that for which somebody who has to live another life by
another name, that has to show himself for another per-

son as he is." Hayhanen became Eugene Maki. Tompkins was explaining the connection with the passport, Government Exhibit Number One, how Hayhanen built the Maki legend from 1949 until he applied for an American passport in that name three years later. "When my Moscow bosses," Hayhanen said, "they have been certain that my background is well built, that it is now to apply for United States passport."

In August 1952 Hayhanen was, as he put it, "called to Moscow." He described his travel route—"by train from Porkkala territory to Leningrad and from Leningrad to Moscow."

"And how did you cross the border?" Tompkins asked.

"I crossed the border the same way like I came from Finland, in the trunk of the car."

No one in the courtroom seemed surprised. All through the day, Hayhanen would recite the tricks of his trade— the way meetings were arranged, hiding out in a car trunk, establishing drops and going out to check them, codes, code names—all the bizarre paraphernalia of his "employment"—and it was just what you were expecting.

At the meeting in Moscow, Hayhanen said, he met Mikhail Svirin, who was assigned to Soviet "official work," which meant that he was connected with the embassy or the Soviet Legation to the United Nations. Hayhanen was told that he would contact Svirin in the United States. He also met a man called Pavlov who gave him instructions.

"Those instructions contained," Hayhanen said, "that as Mark's—a resident assistant I will get some illegal agents, and I have to get some espionage information from those agents." The agents, he said, were to come to him from "Soviet official people," which he defined as "Soviet officials who are coming to the United States or to some other country by Soviet passports."

Methodically, Tompkins was drawing out the government's picture of the conspiracy. He had established, in Hayhanen's first public hour, that Reino Hayhanen, alias Vik, was part of that conspiracy; that Rudolph Abel, alias Mark, was also, and that Vitali Pavlov and Mikhail Svirin, safely in Moscow, helped to direct it. As though he were drawing an organization chart of a large corporation, Tompkins had put in the record not only a list of "members," but the salary scale (Hayhanen testified that he was paid five thousand dollars for cover work, a salary of four hundred dollars a month, a hundred dollars for trip expenses, and another salary in Russian currency which was paid to his relatives) and then he came to the "goals" of that organization.

He asked Hayhanen to tell what Pavlov had told him at the Moscow meeting.

"Pavlov explained me that on espionage work we are all the time in war, that—but if real war will be for everyone or between several countries, that I don't have to move—to forget about espionage work. Even if they don't have connections with me, so still I have to do my espionage work in the country where I was assigned. And he explained that after war our country or our officials will ask from everyone what he did to win this war."

"During this conversation," Tompkins asked, "or during the receipt of these oral instructions from Pavlov, did he give you any directions as to the type of information?"

"Yes, he did. He told that it depends then what kind of illegal agents I will have, so it depends then what kind of information they can give, where they work, or whom they has as friends and such and such things. He told that I have to consider with their help in every different occasion or with every different agent."

The answer was not good enough, not quite what the government needed. Tompkins persevered.

"Now, let me ask you this directly: What type of information were you seeking?"

"Espionage information."

"Would you describe that, what you mean by espionage information?"

"By espionage information I mean all information what you can look to get from newspapers or official way, by asking from, I suppose, legally from some office, and I mean by espionage information that kind of information what you have to get illegal way. That is, it is secret information for——"

Byers stepped in. "Concerning what? What kind of information?"

"Concerning national security or——"

"What do you mean by that?"

"In this case, United States of America."

"What do you mean by national security?"

Hayhanen, bewildered, seemed not to know for the moment what answer they were looking for; like a child

questioned by his teacher, eager to please and be re-
warded, he floundered around and came up with, "I mean
it—that some military information or atomic secrets."

It satisfied Tompkins and Judge Byers stopped asking
questions, but Donovan said he was "not clear with respect to the witness's testimony. . . . As I understood him,
your Honor, he was answering your questions as to what
he meant but I did not understand him to testify that this
was part of his instructions." Tompkins and the judge
thought he had said it was part of his instructions. To
make sure, Tompkins repeated:

"Now, as I understand, your testimony was that your
instructions were to get secret information; is that correct?"

"That's right."

"Those were the oral instructions you were given by
Pavlov?"

"Yes."

"By secret information, as I understand it, you mean
atomic energy or defense information, isn't that correct?"

"That's right."

And there it rested. The answer conformed to the statutes that made espionage a capital offense. It had taken
some irritating time and tried some tempers to get it from
him, but Hayhanen had, finally, found the right answer.
Right from the government's point of view and sufficient
in the eyes of the court. Sufficient, too, to Donovan and
his assistants. And insufficient, puzzling, and empty to
anyone else. The grand jury charged that the information
being collected or transmitted by this conspiracy was "information relating to the national defense of the United
States of America, and particularly information relating
to arms, equipment, and disposition of the United States
Armed Forces, and information relating to the atomic energy program of the United States," but beyond that did
not, nor was required to, specify.

The existence of a conspiracy, its members, and its object—all this had been established before the lunch break
on Monday. For the rest of the day, and on until Thursday, when he stepped down from the witness stand,
Hayhanen described the operation, especially its communications system: hollow containers, coded messages,
holes in brick walls, lampposts, and park benches.

In Moscow, Hayhanen was given the location of sev-

eral drops to be used once he arrived in New York. He
defined, for the court: "By a drop I mean secret place
which you or several people just know, where you can
hide some container that—suppose if I will hide container
in that drop and will let know to another person that I
have there information, and another person will pick up
that container and will get it."

He listed the drops. Each one had a number and
Tompkins led his witness through eleven drops and four
signal areas. Each time, Tompkins showed the witness a
photograph of the area he had described, asked him if he
recognized and could identify it. "Yes," Hayhanen would
say, "that is . . ." and he would give the drop number and
tell the court where it was.

Before midday Monday, Tompkins got through three
drops. Drop Number One, soon to be known as "original
Drop Number One," was a hole in a stairwell on Jerome
Avenue in the Bronx. Hayhanen left a message in that
drop just once, and received just one from his "Russian
officials." After that, it proved inconvenient. "Original
Drop Number Two," as the government called it, provided a moment of mild humor in the courtroom. Tompkins showed Hayhanen a photograph of a bridge and the
witness pointed out a white spot on the photograph.
"Where is this white spot, that's for—that's the hole where
there was that drop."

"What bridge are you talking about?" Judge Byers dutifully asked. "I think there is more than one bridge in
Central Park."

"This bridge is close to that water reservoir. It is—if
you enter that Central Park, it is around One Hundred
Tenth Street, I think—One Hundred Fourth Street or One
Hundred Sixth Street, I think. That big water reservoir
what is. I cannot tell you more exactly. Otherwise I have
to show it over there where it is. I know how to go but I
cannot remember exactly the street number from what
you have to go."

Byers offered, "I think it is located near the reservoir."

Tompkins tried to move on: "The witness testified that
the drop was where this white spot is showing on the photograph, so we have the precise location of it."

Not for Donovan, they didn't.

"Your Honor," he said, "I would just like to point out

that as far as my memory serves me, the reservoir is nowhere near One Hundred Tenth Street."

"Well, I don't think it is near One Hundred Tenth
Street, but I think it is just generally on the west side of
the park, and I think——"

Hayhanen cut in. "Maybe it is Ninety-Fourth, Ninety-
Sixth."

"And the witness corrected it to One Hundred Fourth,"
Byers said.

Donovan didn't "think it is anywhere near One Hundred Fourth Street."

Hayhanen, plaintive, said, "I cannot remember exactly
the street," and it went on like that for a while, with Byers trying to settle the matter by asking Donovan to agree
that it was simply a bridge spanning a bridle path and let
it go at that. But Donovan said he "would wish that the
witness would locate it more accurately. . . . The man has
had the bridge moving from One Hundred Tenth Street
down to various other places."

"Wait a minute," said Tompkins. "Wait a minute. I
didn't understand that. What did the witness say?"

"Never mind what the witness said," Judge Byers answered. "This is a physical fact. There is only one bridge
to which that photograph refers. Now, if you gentlemen
can agree as to which bridge that is, well and good. If you
can't, we will get somebody who can tell us precisely
where it is. That is all there is to this."

It was not. Donovan kept it going: "Your Honor, I
again say that so far as claiming that there is such a
bridge, or having someone testify there is such a bridge,
there is no question in my mind that there is such a
bridge."

It is a tribute to Hayhanen's influence over the scene
that he could reduce two straight-speaking attorneys and
an articulate judge to this. Hayhanen was contagious. At
long last, Tompkins pulled the group out of the quicksand
by interjecting that Hayhanen had never testified that he
used the place, only that it was assigned to him. Byers
asked the witness, "Did you ever see this drop?"

"Yes, I saw it."

Byers pressed on. "Did you ever use it?"

"No, I never used it, but I can——"

"But," Byers cut him off, trying to keep control, "You
did *see* it?"

"No. I saw it and I was there, but I never used it, and by the map of New York City I can show almost the exact spot where that bridge is located."

The map seemed to settle it. Tompkins tried to move on to the next drop. He introduced two photographs. Hayhanen marked one and stated that the drop was located under a lamppost and that the area shown in the photograph was Fort Tryon Park.

"Your Honor," Donovan asked, judiciously, "do I understand that this man was instructed in Moscow to use this drop beneath this electric pole?"

"He was given the location, as I understand it," Tompkins said.

"And from a map of New York City, is that correct?" Hayhanen answered for himself, "No."

"I submit," Donovan said, "I have yet to see a map of New York City where you could identify, in Moscow, a drop under this one pole——"

"Oh, please," said Byers.

"—in Fort Tryon Park." Donovan objected to the admission of the photographs on the grounds that "while it is understandable that anywhere in the world you could properly describe these two locations, I respectfully submit that I wouldn't know how to send anyone to that place; and I say that to say that the witness was instructed to find this pole in Fort Tryon Park is simply incredible."

It was. But Tompkins led his witness to an explanation.

"On that lamppost," Hayhanen said, "there is a certain number, too. By that number I found it."

"The number on the lamp pole?"

"Yes."

Tompkins turned to Judge Byers. "I again offer it."

Hayhanen repeated, "By that number I found it."

"I again offer this," Tompkins said.

There was no objection, and the court recessed for lunch. The afternoon session ran until four o'clock and reflected the morning's session, except there was more of it.

Three more drops: in a flight of stairs in Prospect Park, Brooklyn; on the West Side of Manhattan, at Riverside Drive and 89th Street, near the Soldiers and Sailors Monument; at a bus stop on Seventh Avenue, at the tip of Manhattan, near the Macombs Avenue Bridge. Testifying about each of them, Hayhanen stumbled and fell, tripping over his words, managed to tell the courtroom that the Riverside Drive drop and the Seventh Avenue bus station drop were for magnetic containers, which he defined as "a magnetic container is that kind of a piece of metal that sticks to another metal, and holds onto." At Riverside Drive he stuck the metal onto part of a long fence; at the bus stop it went behind a pole. He told the courtroom that Mark had gone with him to that last drop, standing guard to make sure no one saw what was going on, or, as Hayhanen put it, "He was walking around that nobody can notice that I put that magnetic."

Tompkins picked up all the photographs and took them to the jury box, where he handed them first to the foreman, John Dublynn. "I am just going to let the jury look at these exhibits, your Honor," he said, and the room was still as the photographs went from hand to hand.

"Now, to get back to the drops that were given to you in Moscow, in addition to those drops, Mr. Hayhanen, were you given in Moscow the location of a signal area?"

"Yes," Hayhanen said. He was given a signal area at 86th Street and Central Park West. At first the area was at the entrance to the Eighth Avenue subway station, but it was later shifted to the other side of the street, near Central Park. Hayhanen answered the prosecutor's request for an explanation of "signal area" with, "By signal area I mean the place where I leave some kind of signal that in certain place I left a message, that it is hidden in Drop Number One or in Drop Number Two or in Drop Number Three or Four. And by those stakes on that fence, if I put that signal on second one it means that I have magnetic message or magnetic container with message in Drop Number Two. That is what I mean by signal area."

Tompkins tried to help. "To clarify that," he said, "by this signal area, this is a signal area which you advise somebody else what you are doing, is that correct? In other words, it is how you signaled somebody?"

Byers asked for himself, "What did you do in order to make a signal?" Tompkins did not understand the question and Byers repeated it; then Tompkins asked Hayhanen, who answered, "I made signals usually with colored chalk, mostly with blue chalk."

"How did you use the chalk?"

"I was using chalk that if there——"

Byers, impatient, said, "What did you do with it, my friend?"

"I marked on that fence horizontally line. It meant that I have message for Soviet officials. And when I put vertical line it meant that I got a message from them."

That was as coherent as the explanation would get. The jury was left to interpret for themselves how this signal business really worked. Tompkins went on to introduce three more signal areas: one at New Utrecht Avenue near 46th Street in Brooklyn; a second at the Market Street exit of the Pennsylvania Railroad Station in Newark, New Jersey; a third at McCarren Park in Brooklyn. Those three were used by Hayhanen's "Russian officials" to signal that they had left messages for him at one of the drops.

Throughout the testimony, Donovan objected. The witness had not said from whom he received instructions to use the drops or signal areas, when the instructions were given, or what use he made of them. He had said nothing about the messages left in those metal containers. Judge Byers overruled each objection and told Donovan not to tell the government how to develop its testimony. He assured both Donovan and the courtroom that Tompkins would tie in this testimony to the conspiracy and to Rudolph Abel.

Hayhanen began the saga of his activities in the United States. He told of arriving in New York City and, for once, he could give the court a specific date: "It was twentieth of October 1952 when I arrived in New York City." He went on then with a list of his addresses: the first night in a midtown hotel, then a furnished room, the apartments in Brooklyn, Peekskill, Newark, Peekskill again. He told the court how he had signaled his safe arrival. You could feel the lips smacking in the audience for it was, again, straight from a thriller:

"First of all, I lived about one week—I was walking around and checking that nobody was following me, and I was checking it very carefully. Then when I noticed that nobody followed me I went to Central Park close to Tavern-on-the-Green and I put white thumbtacks to that sign, and it meant that nobody is following me and I arrived all right in this country, there is no danger for me."

Then, Hayhanen said, he sent a message through one

of the drops—he wasn't sure which one—saying that he arrived safely, that "there is everything going okay with me," and asking for money. That was, he said, at the end of November or the beginning of December, and his request was answered close to Christmas time, when he received three thousand dollars through the Fort Tryon Park drop.

John Dublynn, jury foreman, had as much imagination as anyone and considerable common sense. He kept thinking how bizarre Hayhanen's story was, how extreme the system he was describing seemed. But apparently the roundabout cloak-and-dagger stuff was really the way these spies worked. Not for a moment did the juror disbelieve Hayhanen; still, it seemed an awful waste of time. And at so-and-so-many-dollars per hour, Dublynn put it to himself, what an expensive waste. In any other operation, the unions would not stand for it.

Hayhanen was describing his rendezvous with Mikhail Nikolaevich Svirin, whom he first had met in Moscow in 1952. On the twenty-first of each month, he would ride to the Prospect Park station on the BMT subway line, walk to the Lincoln Road exit and stand there. Those were visual meetings—no contact was made; Hayhanen had only to stand on the corner and be observed. Describing the procedure, Hayhanen let himself in for a little more courtroom humor at his own expense.

"What did you wear," Tompkins asked, "at these visual meetings?"

"I had to wear a blue tie with red strips, and I had to smoke a pipe."

"Blue tie with what?" asked the judge.

"Stripes or strips, how it is."

Tompkins helped him out. "Stripes."

"Stripes?" asked the judge.

"Yes," said Hayhanen, "with red stripes."

Tompkins began asking his next question, but Judge Byers wanted to clear up one more detail. "You say you also smoked a pipe?"

"Yes, but I do not smoke myself, but I had to smoke that time."

Tompkins struggled on. By late afternoon he had managed to elicit from Hayhanen the story of two meetings with Svirin. At the first, Hayhanen received a package with photographed letters from his relatives in Russia and

a message that he described as, "to my best recollection
that message said that I got May first greetings and that
my family is all right and they hoped me success." At the
second meeting Svirin told him that there would be no
more visual meetings and that he would soon receive a
message, through the drops, about new arrangements.

Tompkins put in evidence a photograph of Svirin from
a United Nations booklet that identified him as first secretary of the Soviet delegation there and then a new character appeared in the story.

"Mr. Hayhanen, do you know an individual by the
name of Asko?"

"Yes, I know."

Asko was a code name. Hayhanen did not know him
by any other, but he had met Asko several times. The
man was a Finnish sailor who brought, Hayhanen said,
"some pencils or pens or some coins in which I got some
messages from my relatives or some messages from my
bosses."

Hayhanen began to delineate the system he had used
with Asko—the drops, the meetings, the signal areas. It
looked like the beginning of a new chapter. Judge Byers
decided to wait for the next morning to hear the exploits
of Lieutenant Colonel Reino Hayhanen and his courier,
Asko.

Court was adjourned. The jury left, overwhelmed and
bewildered by what they had heard. The details of the
testimony were difficult to keep in order. Simply understanding Hayhanen's words required hard concentration.
The jurors were weary.

On Tuesday, Hayhanen told of meetings with Asko
and the prosecution put in evidence photographs of two
drops: under a lamppost in Riverside Park near 74th
Street and under a lamppost in Riverside Park near 80th
Street. Then Hayhanen went over his relationship with
Mark: their first meeting in 1954 at the Flushing movie
theater and his visits to the vicinity of 252 Fulton Street,
Brooklyn, the Ovington Studios, where he had picked up
photographic supplies from Mark and, once, had gone upstairs to the storeroom where Mark gave him a shortwave
radio.

Of Mark's operations, Hayhanen could tell little. He
did know of some drops that Mark had used, and he
identified them for the court. Two were for magnetic con-

tainers; Hayhanen said they were near 96th Street and
the Henry Hudson Parkway, off the West Side Drive.
Another was for thumbtacks; on Riverside Drive near
104th Street, Mark would leave a tack under the middle
slat of one of the park benches and the tack somehow,
the witness did not explain how, contained a message.
Then there was a "walking drop" on Central Park West
in the Upper 70's; on each street corner between 74th
and 79th streets there was a place for a magnetic container; Mark would leave his message, usually under a
mailbox, and signal the ubiquitous "Soviet officials" on
which corner the message waited. "If he had a message
on the corner of Seventy-Seventh Street," Hayhanen explained, "so he used the number seven, that he has there
a message." The Symphony Theatre served two functions:
there was a drop under a carpet in the balcony and
Mark often met "Soviet officials" there. There were two
more drops, one at the fence around the Museum of Natural History and another at a 95th Street subway station,
but Hayhanen could not remember much about those,
and Tompkins did not bother with them. Donovan objected to each photograph of a drop site as irrelevant to
the charge. Byers consistently overruled him. The government put fifteen such photographs into evidence.

Then the prosecutor eased his witness into recounting
his activities with Mark, and the activities were alike in
that they led nowhere. Hayhanen trudged through his
story of all the frustrating attempts he had made, alone
or with Mark, to accomplish something: once they had
set out to locate a United States army sergeant named
Roy Rhodes, whose code name (or nickname as Hayhanen said in court) was Quebec. They went first to Red
Bank, New Jersey, where they thought Rhodes's family
lived, found no one, contacted Moscow for more information, were told his family was in Colorado. Mark had sent
Hayhanen out there, armed with the telephone number
of Rhodes's parents that Mark himself had sleuthed out
of a Colorado telephone directory in the New York Public
Library. Hayhanen had gone, telephoned the family, received a mailing address for Rhodes in Tucson, Arizona,
and returned to New York. Nothing more was done until,
Hayhanen said, Mark told him he would look Quebec up
on his way to Moscow. On his return, sadly, Mark reported that he had not located Rhodes.

There were several other expeditions to locate people:
one a Swedish ship engineer named Olaf Carlson who
lived in a suburb of Boston, Massachusetts. Hayhanen
told the court that the "main thing was just to look at the
man, is he the same, because I got instructions only to locate him, but not talk with him as an agent." With Mark,
Hayhanen said, he went to Arlington to locate an agent;
but they could not do so and that was duly reported to
Moscow. There was a trip to New Hyde Park, Queens,
where Hayhanen watched the home of an unnamed man,
did not see the man emerge from the house, and duly reported that to Mark. There was another trip à deux, this
one to Hopewell Junction, New York, where the pair in-
quired about buying land, which was, Hayhanen said, to
be used for an "illegal radio station." The land turned
out to be too expensive and nothing came of that trip either.

And then came the grand moment of that day. Hayhanen said that he drove around New York State, New
Jersey, and Pennsylvania with Mark, mostly taking photographs. Tompkins led him easily.

"Well, on one of these trips did you have occasion to
go to Bear Mountain Park?"

"Yes, we did."

"All right; were you accompanied by the defendant?"

"Yes."

"And how did you go?"

"We went by the car."

"And what was the purpose of your trip to Bear Mountain Park?"

Donovan objected. Judge Byers asked it more properly.

"Did you have any conversation about or with Mark
concerning the trip to Bear Mountain?"

"Yes."

"What did he say?"

"He said that we have to find couple of places to hide
some money."

"How much money?" Tompkins asked.

"Five thousand dollars."

"Now, will you tell us what else he said?"

"And he said that five thousand dollars we have to give
to Agent Stone's wife."

Tompkins trod gently. "Agent Stone's wife?"

"Yes."

"Was Stone a code name?"

"Yes, code name." The word was awkward on Hay-hanen's lips. He was accustomed to calling it "nickname." But this part of the testimony had been painfully committed to memory.

"Will you tell us," Tompkins said gingerly, "the name of Stone's wife?"

"His wife is Helen Sobell."

And there it was. The linked-up spy ring, in all its grandeur. Through Helen Sobell, who had never been convicted of anything, to her husband, Morton Sobell, then in prison for having conspired to give atomic and military secrets—that phrase, again—to a foreign power; and through Morton Sobell to his coconspirators, Julius and Ethel Rosenberg. The newspapers, of course, made headlines of this testimony: Abel linked to Rosenbergs and variations on the theme. Was he? Whether Abel was linked to the Rosenbergs in fact is impossible to know. Government lawyers said they knew he was, but they said so in private. "I think," Tompkins said, "there was a really hard connection between Abel and the Rosenbergs." Arnold Fraiman, who was on the other side, thought so too. Fraiman was not at all surprised when the name Sobell rang out in the courtroom, for he had understood throughout the trial that there was indeed a connection and that the five thousand dollars Hayhanen said was meant for Helen Sobell was intended for the defense of the Rosenbergs. But Fraiman's assumption is peculiar; the Rosenbergs had been tried in 1950 and executed in 1953. Hayhanen told the court that this had taken place in the spring of 1955. Perhaps Fraiman meant that he assumed the money would be used for the continuing appeals of Morton Sobell, then imprisoned. Still, it was no more than an assumption.

The sources of that assumption are easy to point to. They lie, first, in the conspiratorial mentality and the propagandistic belief that the intelligence services of the Soviet operate efficiently. The Rosenbergs were spies for the Russians, this reasoning goes, and Rudolph Abel, Master Spy for the same master, operating in the country at the same time, must have been connected with them. The speculation was, at the time of Abel's trial, that his job was chief intelligence officer for the entire United States and, as such, the Rosenbergs would have been under his command, at least for a time. For these assumptions, there is no real evidence and thus no way to refute them. They are no more than a frame of mind. They were never introduced into the trial; they formed no part of the accusations against him; they simply clouded the atmosphere.

There is another route by which Abel gets connected with the Rosenbergs; this one seemingly more tangible. Again, the connection was made outside the courtroom, in conversation, in the press, in the public mind. It involved Morris Cohen and his wife, Lona. "Abel definitely knew Lona Cohen," said Tompkins. And he did. There were several ways of making that connection, none of them ever made public. There was no testimony about the connection, but there was a single piece of evidence. In Colonel Abel's room at the Hotel Latham, a series of twenty-dollar bills was found in an envelope, along with photographs of a man and a woman. The FBI identified the couple as Mr. and Mrs. Morris Cohen, who had lived in New York and been active Communists until the middle of 1950, when they disappeared from the country and left no trace. When Abel's trial was in progress, in 1957, the Cohens were still missing. Four years later, they were arrested in London, where they had been living under false names as Peter John Kroger and Helen Joyce Kroger. Along with a man calling himself Gordon Lonsdale, who turned out to be a Russian national in the Soviet intelligence service, they were tried and convicted as members of a spy ring stealing naval secrets in Britain.

At the time, the connection made between Abel and the Rosenbergs went through the Cohens. Abel knew the Cohens, the Cohens knew and worked with the Rosenbergs—that is the chain. But the last link is questionable. No one has ever proved that the Cohens were involved in espionage with the Rosenbergs at all. They did mysteriously disappear from their New York apartment just after the Rosenbergs were arrested in June 1950 and it *was* suspicious timing. There have been stories that Abel paid the rent for the Cohens' apartment, which are unsubstantiated. Two journalists (Walter and Miriam Schneir), who investigated the Rosenberg case, tried to find evidence that the convicted spy couple and the Cohens worked together, but they could not.

* * *

In Brooklyn Heights, in the middle of an autumn Tuesday, the prosecution's star witness had just told the court that he had buried five thousand dollars meant for Helen Sobell. Ripples went through the room and Abel reacted, according to assistant defense counsel Tom Debevoise who was sitting next to him, as though the whole thing were a fabrication. Tompkins pursued the line of questioning.

"His wife is Helen Sobell," Hayhanen had said.

"S-O-B-E-L-L?" In case no one got it.

"That is right," the witness answered.

"Now, what were you to do with the money in Bear Mountain Park?"

"Mark told that we have to locate Stone's wife and ask her to come to Bear Mountain Park where we can talk with her and give her that money."

"Did you actually bury the money in Bear Mountain Park?"

"Yes, we did."

"All right. Did you at any time in the future bring Helen Sobell to Bear Mountain Park?"

"No, we did not."

Like all the other escapades, this one had come to nothing. Mark had said, according to Hayhanen, that he had tried several times to locate Helen Sobell, but could not because "close to her apartment on street corner near there was almost all the time a policeman."

Tompkins asked whether or not Mark had been told how to identify Helen Sobell. Hayhanen answered, "Mark told me that he got a letter from the man who recruited Stone as an agent, just that when Helen Sobell would read that letter she will know then that that is right man who will give that money."

Throughout the testimony, Donovan tried to get Judge Byers to insist on the witness saying when all this had happened. The best Hayhanen could do, however, was "springtime in 1955." Just after the trip to bury the money and a drive past the house where Helen Sobell lived, Hayhanen said, Mark had to leave for a trip to Moscow (Donovan objected to the trip to Moscow being used for identification, insisting that no such trip had been proven) and he left Hayhanen with instructions to turn the buried money over to Helen Sobell himself.

"Did you follow Mark's instructions and give Mrs. Sobell the five thousand dollars?" Tompkins asked.

"Did I follow—No, I did not."

"Did you report what you had done in connection with Mrs. Sobell?"

"Yes, I did."

"And how did you report your action?"

"I reported that I located Helen Sobell and I gave money and told her to spend them carefully."

The moment was priceless. In the flattest tone imaginable, Hayhanen was telling the court that he had lied to Mark and kept the money for himself. No one in the room reacted to the testimony, although the press picked it up for the day's stories. Tompkins proceeded mechanically and had Hayhanen tell that he had sent his report through a drop and received, again through a drop, an answer instructing him to "locate Helen Sobell once more and talk with her once more and decide is it possible to use her as an agent."

"Was it your impression from that message that Helen Sobell had been an agent prior to that time?"

"When Mark explained to me that money should be given to Stone's wife, he explained that usually in Soviet espionage practice they recruit husband and wife together as agents."

"So is your understanding from Mark that both husband and wife had been agents for the Soviet Union?"

"Yes."

Hayhanen said that when Mark returned from Moscow he related instructions to give Helen Sobell five thousand dollars more, and told Hayhanen to "locate her once more," a phrase which took on additional auras of absurdity each time it was repeated. Tompkins asked if Hayhanen did have a meeting with Helen Sobell. No. Did he have any communication with her? No. And that was the end of it.

Thus the idea of a Great Spy Ring, involving several people already convicted of what amounted to treason and extending to the man then there on trial, was firmly planted in the minds of everyone present, including the jury. Among the members of that jury ("all from Catholic-dominated southern Brooklyn," Tom Debevoise observed, "a very conservative atmosphere") a preconditioned set of responses was awakened. The foreman, for example, believed the testimony entirely, even though not one piece of evidence had been introduced to corroborate it (and in a trial where every other statement was supported by a photograph or document and the government was equipped with an imposing number of those to introduce, this piece of testimony seems remarkably bare). He understood this to be "the most important spy case ever; higher than the Rosenbergs, top drawer."

The only point in the testimony at which his reason balked was the burial of the money in Bear Mountain Park. He thought that was a goof. "The best place to bury money," he said, "is in the Flatbush Savings Bank."

NINE

AT the end of each day's testimony, Rudolph Abel was returned to the West Street jail. In the evening he was permitted to confer with his lawyers. Those conferences, along with the notes he took in the courtroom, did not help his case much, but they did keep him occupied and give him a sense of being actively engaged in his destiny.

Debevoise asked Abel frankly about the conspiracy's alleged attempt to get military or atomic information. Were there any overt acts, he wanted to know, that the prosecution might introduce? Did Abel remember anything that might be construed that way? Abel thought a while.

"Well," he said, "one day I was driving with Hayhanen across the George Washington Bridge. One of us, either I or he, said, 'This is the first place to drop the bomb.' Maybe they'll use that."

On Tuesday afternoon Hayhanen told the court about Abel's attempts to get him to go home for a "vacation." Several false birth certificates were put into evidence—machinations for Hayhanen's leaving the country. There was more drop testimony and the introduction of messages from Hayhanen to Abel about the "vacation."

Hayhanen told the story of his defection without any emotion. Step one, arrived in Paris. Step two, made some telephone calls and contacted a "Russian official" from whom he received his itinerary: from Paris to West Germany, from West Berlin to East, and home. Step three, signaled to the Russian that he would be leaving the next day; went to the movies and to his hotel room. Step four, on Saturday morning, May 4, 1957, went to the American Embassy. On this point there was some peculiar testimony:

"Now," Tompkins asked, "did you communicate with the embassy before you went there?"

"Yes, sir."

"What did you do?"

"When I came to embassy?"

"When you communicated with them, did you call them on the telephone?"

"No, I did not."

"You went into the embassy?"

"Yes."

Whatever Hayhanen did mean by having communicated with the embassy before he went there remained mysterious. Perhaps he did not understand the question, for there were many put to him those four days that he did not. Or perhaps he had communicated with someone attached to the embassy before he actually went to the building. If so, that someone would have to have been an American intelligence officer. Tompkins obviously did not want to touch that base.

Once inside the embassy, Hayhanen said, he gave the officials he was talking to one of his hollowed-out coins and gave it, in his own words, "as proof." Tompkins had the coin marked Government Exhibit Number Twenty-three. Then he led Hayhanen through the weeks after his defection, his permission to the FBI to search his house in Peekskill, a listing of the things the Bureau had found there that connected the witness with Mark and the conspiracy. There were Government Exhibits Numbers Twenty-four through Twenty-nine: a shortwave radio, earphones, a lens and copper plate used for making microdots, a box of spectroscopic film, several mimeographed pages stapled together and headed "Color Photography," and a typewritten pamphlet entitled "Vacuum Board for Making Matrices." All of them, Hayhanen said, had been given to him by Mark.

Tompkins interrupted this part of the testimony to ask Hayhanen if he would demonstrate to the courtroom how the hollowed-out coin worked. Caught up in the trial, the prosecutor had forgotten to bring with him the steel needle he planned to use for this vignette. Tompkins dispatched someone to get it and when it was in his hand he handed it to Hayhanen, who pried the coin open easily. Then Tompkins returned to the identification of the tools of the trade passed from Mark to Hayhanen and found in the Peekskill house, which went on until that day's session closed.

Wednesday was dull. Tompkins began by tying up a few loose ends of the previous day's testimony. He came back to Helen Sobell and the five thousand dollars that Hayhanen was told to give to Mrs. Sobell at Bear Mountain, asking just one question about that.

"Will you tell us what you did with it [the money]?"

"I kept it myself."

He had to bring that out first, Tompkins said, lest Donovan "kill us in cross-examination."

"Now," said Tompkins, "yesterday afternoon you also testified that you had told the defendant you were being trailed by FBI agents. Is that correct?"

Hayhanen had described one of the messages he had sent to Mark when they were negotiating about Hayhanen's "vacation" to Moscow. He had repeated the message and Tompkins had produced it: the Immigration and Naturalization Service had found the message after they had taken Abel from the Hotel Latham. It was handprinted on a page from Hayhanen's memo book, on the back of a page dated Tuesday 27-Wednesday 28, and it said, "I bought a ticket to next ship Queen Elisab. for next Thursday—1.31. Today I could not come because 3 men are tailing me."

"Yes," Hayhanen answered Tompkins's question, "I told him so."

"Now, was that true or not?"

"No, it is not."

The rest of the testimony that day was technical. People shuffled in and out of the courtroom. Everyone was bored. By the end of the day, Hayhanen had identified and described several hollow containers used for hiding messages, among them a hollow bolt and old screw; a Trav-Electric converter which converts six volts to one hundred ten volts and works by being plugged into a car cigarette lighter. Hayhanen gave a garbled explanation of how one prepares microdots and said that Mark often sent microdots stapled into the spines of magazines to Paris.

Then Kevin Maroney took over and questioned Hayhanen about his code, which took up the rest of the session. As Hayhanen was explaining the way his code operated and Maroney was introducing charts that illustrated the testimony, nearly everyone fell asleep. Several cryptographers in the room tried to follow the testimony, fruitlessly, for, they said, it made no sense.

Byers, too, balked at the cipher testimony. "Don't come back with stuff like this again," he told Tompkins, "or I'll throw the case out."

The day concluded with Hayhanen answering Maroney's question of whether the defendant had a code similar to his by saying, "Mark told me that he had the code but he was using—he was ciphering and deciphering different way; that he was using special small books with numbers what makes ciphering easier by this method."

You would have to wait some time to find out what *that* meant, but, in fact, Hayhanen was referring to one-time cipher pads that Mark had been using. The government would introduce a cipher pad into evidence before the trial was over.

The next day, Thursday, was Donovan's. As he rose to cross-examine the witness, there was a stir of renewed interest among the wearied spectators. For the most part, it was a hostile atmosphere into which Donovan moved. You feel at every major trial that the people in the courtroom have taken sides, either as a body or among themselves. At the trial of Alger Hiss, you felt the room responded in divided ways: for Hiss, for Chambers. At Alice Crimmins's trial, the room was uniformly against her. At Abel's trial, it was harder to tell. Had Colonel Abel taken the stand, you would have sensed the reaction strongly: for him or against him. But he did not. So you had to be for or against an idea. You had to hope A Spy would get off; or hope he would be punished. Donovan had taken pains in his opening address to remind the jury and spectators that a man called Abel and not Soviet Russia was on trial; it was difficult to expect the audience to remember that.

So when he rose to cross-examine, the atmosphere was hostile. There was little feeling for Donovan. The government wanted to see him go through the motions; but not to make too much trouble.

The only aspect of the case that Donovan dealt with in his cross-examination, the only point at which he could find an opening was, as he had indicated it would be when he first addressed the court, Hayhanen's character.

"Mr. Hayhanen, did you testify before the grand jury with respect to this case?"

"Yes, I did."

Hayhanen was extremely tense and Tompkins felt as he had on the first day, when his witness was asked to point out the man he had known as Mark.

"Mr. Hayhanen, to your knowledge have you ever been indicted in the United States?"

There was considerable scuffling about whether Donovan would be allowed to ask that question and, if so, in what form. Byers told him how to do it: "If your question is—have you been indicted with respect to any matters concerning which you have testified in this trial, I will allow the question."

Hayhanen said that he did not understand the word "indicted."

"Have you ever been formally charged with any crime with respect to these matters? . . ."

"For my best knowledge, no."

Donovan then brought out a long statement that Hayhanen had made to the FBI soon after his defection. Again, there was a squabble. Donovan asked the witness to identify the original statement, which had been written in Russian, and a translation of it, which Donovan gave him. Byers wanted to know who had made the translation; Donovan would not tell him; it had been translated, the night before, by Abel himself; Hayhanen insisted there were inaccuracies in it; Tompkins objected to its being admitted at all; Donovan complained that he had only received the Russian statement at four o'clock the day before and that he had done his best to have it translated; Tompkins said Donovan got it at noon; they jibed at each other, and finally Tompkins offered the government's own translation of the document and it was accepted. Donovan put one page of the translation in evidence. To it, he added two more exhibits for the defense—Hayhanen's passport application file containing the documents by which he got his first American passport in the name of Eugene Nikolai Maki in 1951 and a renewal in 1956, and the lease signed by Eugene and Hannah Maki when they rented their storefront on Bergen Street in Newark.

Donovan had the witness explain to the court that when he married Hannah in 1951, he had a wife and son in Russia. Hayhanen was bewildered by the fuss Donovan was making. Donovan tried to ask whether it was legal in Russia to have two wives at once, but Tompkins objected to the question and Byers sustained the objection. Hayhanen continued to look puzzled. Of all the things he had to hide about himself, this was the least troubling. He tried to explain. When Donovan asked if he had written on his passport application that his legal spouse was Hannah Maki, Hayhanen said, rather helplessly, "It was part of my legend because—that is why I wrote—answered this way questions."

"Now," Donovan pressed on, "with respect to your testimony that in 1953 you were joined here by a woman, who is the woman who joined you?"

Tompkins, Byers, and Donovan argued over the tone of the question and Byers instructed Donovan that the "correct question is: Who joined you in the United States in 1953?"

Donovan did not like it that way; it took the bite out, but he asked it. By that time, Hayhanen, comprehending what was going on, got angry.

"My wife," he answered emphatically, "by church marriage."

"What is her name?" Donovan asked.

"Hannah Maki."

"And is this the Mrs. Maki who signed the lease with you on the Bergen Street premises?"

"Yes, she is."

From his torpor, Hayhanen had risen to a point at which he was nearly spitting those answers and, afterward, he bitterly complained to the government's lawyers about Donovan's questions. It was, Tompkins said, the only time he blew up. Hayhanen could endure, had endured, exposure as thief, liar, drunkard, and coward. But the slur on his marriage, perhaps even the implied smudge on Hannah—these enraged him. Clearly, thief-liar-drunkard-and-coward were epithets Reino Hayhanen might have hurled at himself; they described his own vision of himself. But this man, peasant from the provinces that he was, raged at Donovan's moral smugness about his wife.

Donovan, backing away from the witness's ire, having made that point, went on to expose Hayhanen's ineptitude: how he had kept the storefront on Bergen Street covered with Glass Wax and never opened the photography shop he had been assigned as cover work. Donovan brought in all the dirt he had managed to muster about this man. He got Hayhanen to agree that one night an ambulance had been called to his home and Hayhanen, with a deep knife wound in his leg, had been taken to a hospital.

Donovan asked if it was not "a fact" that the ambulance was called because there was "blood all over the premises."

"Yes," Hayhanen said. "Not all over, but in couple rooms."

"Yes," countered Donovan, "and isn't it a fact that, I ask you, Wife Number Two had stabbed you in a drunken brawl? Isn't that true?"

"No, it is not. I can answer more if you like about that whole situation."

Donovan did not like. "If you deny that she stabbed you, there is not anything more I can do at this time."

"She didn't not," Hayhanen insisted. "She did not."

Donovan tried something else. He asked if Hayhanen had been beating his wife and Hayhanen said no. He asked if "one day you entered a bakery store on Bergen Street with your wife, bought a loaf of bread, and threw it on the floor and ordered the woman to pick it up?"

Tompkins could not see what the materiality of throwing a loaf of bread on the floor was in an espionage case.

This was the stuff a courtroom audience loves. Unfortunately, Donovan did not get much of it into the record, for he had surprisingly little sensational material to offer and once Hayhanen had denied something, there was no choice but to move on. He tried to pin down the alcoholism, but it was difficult.

"Now, returning to the subject of drink, Mr. Hayhanen, do you still drink?"

"Yes."

"How much did you drink yesterday?"

"The whole day?"

"The whole day and the evening."

"About four drinks as they serve in bars."

Many in that courtroom had done the same, if not more. So Donovan had failed to pin the label "alcoholic" on him and the government had taken good care that he could not.

At the end of his cross-examination, Donovan read a portion of the statement Hayhanen had made to the FBI just after his defection:

I resided and worked in Finland from July 1949 to October of 1952. There I received my American passport and arrived to New York on October of 1952. I did not receive any espionage or secret information from anyone during my stay abroad, neither in Finland nor in the United States of America.

With that, on what he hoped to be a triumphant note, Donovan said, "No further questions, your Honor" and sat down.

It was puzzling, perhaps damning; surely in need of explanation. But Tompkins did not get his witness to explain. He merely asked, on redirect examination, "Mr. Hayhanen, what were you sent to the United States for?" And the witness answered, "I was sent to the United States as Mark's assistant for espionage work."

It need not take an expert to make sense of Hayhanen's statement. Most important, what Donovan read was an English translation of words Hayhanen had written in Russian. The translation was accurate but it could not possibly capture the distinctions between the Russian and English words for espionage. Hayhanen did not really understand the English word. He thought of himself as a spy, a man who is interested in every kind of information he can get, even what may be innocuous. In Hayhanen's mind unclassified information was as important as secret information. When he said that he had not engaged in espionage activity, by which he meant that he had received no espionage information, he meant that no secret information had been turned over to him by anyone. And indeed it had not. Nor had the United States government claimed that it had.

Donovan's flourish at the end of his cross-examination was meant to cast doubt on whether or not Reino Hayhanen had been sent here by the KGB. It cast no such doubt. It simply told us that whatever his assigned purpose, the bumbling spy had not succeeded in obtaining any secret information. Hayhanen had been telling that all along.

Kevin Maroney took over for the government. The most dramatic part of the trial was over. Maroney put into the court record some data about Mikhail Nikolaevich Svirin which traced his comings and goings and indicated that Svirin had arrived in New York with a Soviet diplomatic passport in August 1952, left in April 1954, returned again in September 1954. On the documents that the government introduced there was no record of another departure, but Svirin had indeed left the country again. The dates of his comings and goings coincided with Hayhanen's testimony. Svirin had been in New York when Hayhanen said he met him and in Moscow at the time Hayhanen said he was given his instructions about his work in the United States.

Much of Hayhanen's testimony was corroborated by the parade of witnesses that afternoon. Four agents of the FBI told how they had dug in the basement of Hayhanen's house in Peekskill. As each agent gave his testimony, the government put in evidence a box of hollow bolts, a diagram of the Peekskill house drawn by Hayhanen to help the agents find the treasures buried in his basement, the false birth certificate wrapped in a bread wrapper and buried in the basement, and a message inside a bolt, again in that bread wrapper. This was the famous Quebec message and it was read in court:

Quebec. Roy A. Rhodes. Born 1917 in Oilton, Oklahoma, U.S. Senior Sergeant of the War Ministry, former employee of the U.S. Military Attaché Staff in our country. He was a chief of the garage of the Embassy.

He was recruited to our service in January, 1952, in our country which he left in June, 1953. Recruited on the basis of compromising materials but he is tied up to us with his receipts and information he had given in his own handwriting.

He had been trained in code work at the Ministry before he went to work at the Embassy but as a code worker he was not used by the Embassy.

After he left our country he was to be sent to the School of Communications of the Army, C. I. Service which is at the City of San Luis, California. He was to be trained there as a mechanic of the coding machines.

He fully agreed to continue to cooperate with us in the states or any other country. It was agreed that he was to have written to our Embassy here special letters but we had received none during the last years.

It has been recently learned that Quebec is living in Red Bank, N.J. where he owns three garages. The garage job

is being done by his wife. His own occupation at present
is not known.

His father, Mr. W. A. Rhodes, resides in the U.S. His
brother is also in the States where he works as an engineer at an Atomic Plant in a Camp in Georgia, together
with his brother-in-law and his father.

Earlier that day, Arlene Brown, the sister of Roy
Rhodes, had testified that a man with a heavy foreign accent had telephoned her in Colorado and asked after
Rhodes. Sister and message together convinced you that
Hayhanen had, as he said, actually taken that fruitless
trip. And then the spotlight shifted. Hayhanen and his
empty bolts and frustrating missions was no longer the
focus of attention. The prosecution read aloud the rental
records for the Ovington building, which showed that
Emil Goldfus had leased studio 505 at 252 Fulton Street
from January 1, 1954 through August 1957 and taken
storage space in room 509 from June 1955 through July
1957. A rental agent came on the stand and testified that
he was acquainted with the defendant and had rented an
apartment to him; the real estate man identified a signed
lease and told the court that the man who signed it, Emil
R. Goldfus, was the defendant. The public knew him as
Colonel Abel.

These were the first pieces offered at his trial that related directly to the man known as Abel. You sat forward
a little, listening, and you looked at the slim, birdlike man
about whom the witness spoke. He seemed immersed in
the proceedings and every once in a while he was scribbling on the yellow legal pad placed squarely in front of
him. You felt that he would not take the stand at his trial;
whatever you learned about him would come from what
others said. So you listened. When the real estate man left
the stand, court was adjourned for the day and Judge Byers said there would be no session on the next, so it was a
long weekend's pondering before the trial resumed on
Monday morning and the first witness to be called was an
artist, Burton Silverman.

The Silvermans, on their honeymoon trip, had reached
Rome at the beginning of October and had there the classic American tourist experience: they were robbed. Their
first night in the Eternal City, close by the shadow of the

Forum, their car had a flat tire, and as they got out, grumbled, and began to repair it, a man slipped from the dark, reached for Helen's purse on the front seat, and disappeared on the back of a motor scooter. They went to the police and muddled their way through explaining and listing the contents of the purse: money and Helen's passport. The next day she went to the American Embassy to report the loss and apply for a new passport.

In the middle of the week the couple sat disconsolately in their *penzione*. A visitor was announced. He identified himself as a representative of the embassy. Our embassy. He was eagerly asked to sit down, and had he found the thieves?

What thieves? No, he was sorry; he did not know anything about that. He is here on another matter: "Do you remember the Abel case?"

The man said Silverman might be needed in connection with the trial.

"But why? The FBI said there was nothing for us to do."

"I can't say. I've just been assigned to relay this information to you."

"Well, all right. But when?"

"I don't know any more about it."

The man, about to leave, hesitated. "You know, I had a hell of a time finding you. I've been at it for almost three weeks."

"How come?" Helen asked. "Where were you looking?"

"Everywhere. Nice. Florence. Venice. About four days here in Rome."

"Did you check the register at American Express in Florence and Nice? We signed in everywhere in case there were friends looking for us. And, here in Rome, we put a huge star next to our names in the book and wrote a note for a couple we're going to meet later this week. Furthermore," Helen warmed up, "we've been to the embassy twice, the Central Police station four times because my passport was stolen."

"Well, I don't know anything about that. All I can say is it was very difficult to track you down."

"I hope you don't have to find people who are running away," Burt said, as he opened the door.

That was the middle of the week. By Friday night there

had been no further word from the embassy and Burt was in bed, sleepless, when the telephone rang in the hall. It was two A.M. The owner of the *penzione* shuffled to Silverman's door.

"Signor Seelverrman?"

On the telephone, a strained voice said Silverman was booked on a Sunday flight to New York to appear at the trial of Colonel Rudolph Abel.

"Goddammit, it's two in the morning. Who the hell are you? OGPU? You mean this idiot message couldn't wait another six hours?"

He hung up, angry. Silverman thought of escaping Rome right away. But on Sunday, Silverman boarded the plane for New York.

Monday morning, October 21, a full week after the trial of Colonel Abel had begun, Silverman walked into the Brooklyn courthouse. Nothing that morning matched his mood; it was a good Indian summer day, shiny. The brown gloom of the United States Attorney's office did nothing to calm him. Behind the desk, James Featherstone rose, grinned a ruddy grin, and extended his hand. Silverman grimaced.

"What the hell is going on here? I mean, why am I here?"

Featherstone was cheery. "Why, about the typewriter, of course."

"What do you mean 'of course'? No one told me anything about this. What the hell am I supposed to say?"

And still Silverman was not convinced that there was no "cooked up" plan to implicate him or his friends in the career of Colonel Abel.

"What am I supposed to say?"

"You just have to identify the typewriter."

"But I can't. Not positively. That machine is like ten thousand others. Besides, I never looked at it carefully."

Featherstone was blank. Then he remembered. "Didn't you sign it over to the FBI?"

"Yeah, but I don't have the receipt with me."

"Why not?"

"Hell! I've been trying to tell you that until I stepped into this office, I didn't have the slightest idea what testimony I was required to give."

Featherstone paused. "Well," he said, "no matter. We'll get it from the Bureau. How was your trip, by the way?"

Silverman was irate and silent.

"Where to, now?" he asked, as Featherstone led him out into the corridor.

"You're due to go on the stand in a few minutes."

Oh, no, Silverman thought. This guy must be kidding. Kafka Through the Looking Glass. By Silverman's time clock it was late in the evening, and he had not adjusted to Brooklyn or his friend's trial or to being in that very· courthouse. And now Featherstone was telling him,˙with aplomb, that he was about to go on the stand.

"Uh, suppose my plane had been late? Or I stopped off to have breakfast? Or got sick? What then?"

Featherstone was unbothered. Instead of answering, he waved his hand toward a set of double doors and told the young man to go in.

Silverman stood with his back against the large brown doors until he heard his name called. The courtroom was drab, musty, and far from the grandeur the occasion demanded. A small-town courthouse, or the New York traffic court, or a stage design. The space was barnlike, stifling. The windows tall and grimy, the worn rows of bench pews—in his eye flashed an old image of the synagogue in Boro Park, of the scattered figures come in the morning to pray. And everywhere, in the real room and in the images of his mind, a strange bluish mist, hanging.

Suddenly, Silverman was aware of a court official marching beside him. Together they reached the witness stand and the official melted away.

"Do you promise to tell the truth, the whole truth and nothing but the truth. . . . Raise your right hand and swear."

He sat in the chair and saw Emil. Across the space between the witness stand and the defense table, the two looked at each other, locked in. On Emil's face, a faint smile that wiped out gravity and worry. Silverman felt himself smiling in return, just a faint flicker, an exchange of rueful knowledge, regret, and good-bye. It lasted no more than ten seconds; summed up everything with nearly nothing. It was no more than a human sign; and then they looked away. Rudolph Abel did not look up again during the testimony and Burt Silverman did not see him again.

Kevin Maroney began by having his witness identify the man he knew as Emil Goldfus.

"Do you see him in the courtroom?"

"Yes."

"Would you indicate where you see him?"

"Sitting at the table over there," the witness said. The trial transcript notes that he "indicated" where the defendant sat; Silverman indicated without looking.

Maroney got the important facts out—that Silverman had known Emil Goldfus since early 1954 and knew him to have a studio near his own. Then, the only question this witness had been called to answer: "I show you what has been marked as Government Exhibit Number Fifty-two for identification, and ask you if you can identify that?"

Silverman did.

Maroney showed him Government Exhibit Number Fifty-two-A, the receipt given to Burt Silverman by the FBI when he turned the typewriter over to them.

". . . and I ask you if that is your signature, sir?"

"Yes."

Fraiman came forward to ask if the particular Remington portable was different from any other and the witness said no. Fraiman asked how the witness knew, then, that it was Emil Goldfus's typewriter and the witness answered that the serial number on the back of the typewriter corresponded to the serial number on the receipt given him by the FBI. He answered grudgingly, for the defense counsel's questions confirmed his own earlier reluctance about identifying the typewriter. Judge Byers interrupted:

"Why don't you gentlemen agree in the record on what the serial number of the typewriter is? It appears on it, doesn't it?"

"Yes," said Maroney.

"Then open it, look at it, read it, and agree to it."

They did. Fraiman agreed, Maroney agreed, the skirmish was over. If it seemed for a moment that this might become a forgery-by-typewriter case, too, the moment was lost and the ordinary questioning began again. Just a few things by Fraiman on cross-examination, to establish what acquaintanceship Silverman had with the colonel. Yes, he had visited him on a number of occasions; yes, the defendant had known his family; yes, he was on friendly terms with the defendant; yes, he knew other people who knew the defendant; and oh, yes, he had talked about the defendant with other people.

"And what was the defendant's reputation in the community for honesty and integrity?"

Maroney objected. Byers said he would allow it and asked the witness if he had ever discussed the defendant's reputation for truth-telling.

"Yes. It was beyond reproach."

"Beyond reproach?"

"Yes."

"Did you ever hear anything bad about the defendant in any way, sir?"

"No."

Fraiman said he had no further questions and Judge Byers slipped in edgewise with what he thought put the testimony in perspective. "And these discussions," he said, "had to do with a man by the name of Goldfus. Is that it?"

Silverman acquiesced, and it was over. The court excused the witness and the witness went out, past the defense on his way from the room, not looking at anyone, and quickly down the stairs out into the world where it was still morning.

What had just happened made no sense. To Silverman, reality had been Emil Goldfus. The hard-nosed spy in the press and the man in the courtroom were an illusion. Some were ready to believe the story they read daily in the newspapers and the testimony they heard in court; others were not. The artists at the Ovington building read with different eyes from the general public or the defense lawyers or the attorney general's office. They could do nothing else. If Goldfus's activities at the studio were so sinister, they had asked themselves and each other, why did they always have access to his place? Why did he leave a key behind when he left the city? Why were they allowed into the studio; why, in fact, encouraged? What if they had come across some of its secrets?

As he walked away from the courthouse Silverman realized that there was more than metaphysics at stake in those questions; there was honor and trust. Beyond the shock of the first days of Goldfus's "exposure," one troublesome question muddled the minds of those young men. Betrayal. Why, they wondered, had Colonel Abel chosen to enter their circle and become their friend? Had he done it in his role of Master Spy, it would mean that they had all been somehow used, or that he intended to exploit them. Had he done it innocently, simply as a man, if any of that were possible?

The "authorities" were saying that the spy had chosen to rent the studio and be interested in art because it was a perfect cover. Around artists, or "Bohemians," as they were being called, one could come and go quite easily. No questions; a great deal of privacy and acceptance of what might be, to others, eccentric behavior. It did not fit. If Colonel Abel wanted to surround himself with unconventional people who would not pry, he would surely have invented some other activity that did not demand overt results. No, the spy's studio and his painting were genuine parts of the man.

The largest question Silverman and his friends had been asking had the greatest number of possible answers. Take a Russian spy whose primary job is to keep himself from being discovered. Does he immerse himself in a group of people who might attract attention because of their political activity? It was possible, very possible, in the 1950s, that someone would be investigated by the FBI. One or two had been members of the Communist Party; many others had "radical" political ideas. There was no way of determining the reality of that situation: to what extent was the government interested in keeping an eye on or making trouble for these people? They did not know. In an age when statesmen voluntarily went before congressional committees to insist that they had been 4-H Club members in their teens and that their records showed consistent true-blue Americanism and stringent anticommunism, who could be sure that unpopular political beliefs, even without unpopular political activity, might not bring trouble? The press knew nothing about these people who had been Abel's friends and thus the question never came up before the public. In their own minds, however, it was persistent.

One answer was that the "group" was potentially dangerous to Abel. They were people he ought to have stayed away from, had he conducted his affairs according to the book. That he did not, attests to his genuine feeling for them, for the reality of their friendship with him. In spite of the fact that those friends expanded the possibility of attention and thereby detection, this answer goes: Abel stayed on at the Ovington building because he had a human need to do so. This way, the spy is seen as a bureau-

crat who breaks the rules of the game because he is a
man. It is comforting to think so. But others had different
answers. Perhaps the "unorthodox" politics of the young
men in Brooklyn Heights provided the best camouflage.
Protective coloring, it is called. Perhaps the rules of the
game are sophisticated. And, then, a third answer: perhaps it did not matter at all, either way. Perhaps they did
not put Abel in any special danger and perhaps they were
not calculated to be protective coloration. It was possible
that they did not enter into the picture at all.

Silverman had expected Abel's trial to answer those
questions. When he left the courtroom, he knew that it
had not. Throughout the weeks of the trial, he and his
friends held to their expectation that some light would fall
on Abel's relationship to them, but it weakened as days
went by. They referred to the man on trial as Emil-Abel,
slipping back and forth, waiting for the moment when
reality would fall quietly into focus.

There was no focus either, in Silverman's mind, about
what his testimony might have meant; of where it fit into
the pieces of the government's case. Still, he felt relieved:
he had not, in fact, betrayed his friend. He had not, he
was sure, done damage. His testimony might have been
given by anyone. That was the center of Silverman's anger and his relief—he had been, in the courtroom, anonymous. His face in public and the words he spoke touched
not at all his relationship with Emil Goldfus. Touched
nothing and were empty, then. Having played his part,
the witness had been dismissed.

TEN

MONDAY afternoon, Master Sergeant Roy A. Rhodes took the stand. He answered Tompkins's questions with military precision, recalling the exact dates on which he had gone from one post to another in his army career and adding "sir" to every response. It took a few minutes to get the roster of places Rhodes had been with the army into the record—one of them, curiously, was Fort Monmouth, New Jersey (a major Signal Corps installation where the Rosenbergs were alleged to have maintained a spy ring), and when the army heard about that one they had been considerably upset—but the focus of the government's interest in Rhodes was his work in Moscow. In that city, Rhodes testified, he was motor sergeant for the embassy garage. He had arrived in Moscow alone, but just before Christmas, in 1951, his wife was granted a visa to join him. Tompkins questioned the witness about that day.

"And what did you do after lunch?"

"Well, during lunch—I had a few drinks—that is what you want me to bring out?"

"Well," Tompkins said innocently, "whatever happened."

"I think he is going to leave this to your judgment," Judge Byers said. We were obviously on delicate ground.

"All right, sir," said the sergeant, and told his story.

"Well, during lunch—I went down to the Marines. There had been a few drinks. In fact, several drinks, before I got around to going back to the garage. On arriving back to the garage, the two Russian nationals, mechanics that worked for me there in the garage, I believe, as I can recall it, that I decided that they should have a drink with me, and so one drink led to another, and apparently it went on all afternoon. At three-thirty or four o'clock in the afternoon, I suppose, something like that, the youngest mechanic's girl friend had his car that day, and she came up to the garage to pick him up, and there was still some of the vodka left that we had been drinking that afternoon, so I said, 'Why don't you bring your girl in for a drink?' And when she came in there was a girl with her, and I had never seen the girl before.

"So we had a few more drinks from whatever was left of the vodka, as I can recall it, and I don't know who suggested it, that maybe we should have dinner that night, but possibly I did. I just can't recall exactly how it got started, but we left the garage in his car with the two girls, and I know we made a trip to, I guess it was his apartment. I never was inside of it. I don't know what was on the inside of this building.

"But anyway he was gone fifteen or twenty minutes. He cleaned up and changed his clothes, and came back to the car, and the four of us went to one of the hotels in Moscow, and the party just rolled on through the night, and I know that I was dancing, drinking, and eating with these people, and I have no recollection of leaving the hotel in any way, shape, or form. I don't know exactly—possibly I passed out there and they had to carry me out.

"I know I woke up the next morning in bed with this girl in what I had taken to be her room."

Donovan hesitated a second to see if Rhodes had finished his story and it seemed he had, so the defense lawyer moved that "all this recital be stricken from the record on the ground that it is not binding on this defendant."

"Not at the present time," the judge said. "I don't know how much of this is material. I have no way of telling at the moment."

So the story continued. Rhodes said that he had seen the girl again "as best I can recall it would be anywhere from five to seven weeks after this party . . . there was this phone call to the mechanic, originally, I mean he answered the phone there in the garage because most of the time it was some Russian who called on the phone, and he spoke a good deal of English, so he normally answered the phone. . . . He told me it was this girl. She wanted to talk to me."

He went to meet her and as Rhodes and the girl were walking along the street she telling him "that she has trouble," they were, as Rhodes put it, "accosted" by two Russians, one of whom said he was the girl's brother and the other who told Rhodes to call him "Bob Day." The foursome went to a room which Rhodes thought was the room he had found himself in after the drunken party. Only the men entered the room; the girl kept walking down the hall and Rhodes never saw her again.

The rest was predictable. Rhodes, trapped, went on seeing the man he called Bob Day and eventually met other Russians, some civilians and some in military uniforms. Rhodes gave them information and they paid him for it—the first payment, he remembered, was five hundred dollars—and for each payment he signed a receipt.

Tompkins asked if the information Rhodes gave to the Russians was truthful or untruthful.

"Some of both," he said.

Everyone in the courtroom understood that it would violate national security to have Rhodes elaborate on what information he had given. Instead, Tompkins simply listed some categories.

"Did you furnish these people with information as to your place of birth?"

"Did you furnish them with information with relation to your duties in the embassy?"

"Did you furnish them with information that you had been trained in code work?"

"Yes, sir," Rhodes said.

"Yes, sir."

"Yes, sir."

". . . information relative to the habits of military personnel assigned to the embassy?"

". . . relative to the habits of state department personnel?"

"Yes, sir."

In Moscow, the arrangement between Rhodes and the Russians was terminated by a change of duty assignment that sent the sergeant to San Luis Obispo, California, U.S.A. Before he left, he was given three systems for communicating with the Russian Embassy in the United States, for no one was about to let Rhodes off easily. He described the systems to the court and as he did so his words stirred the memory:

". . . I was to furnish, from *The New York Times,* any article I picked out that was critical in relation to the Russian economy, the Russian Embassy, whatever you have, as long as it was critical of Russia. Three of these articles from any paper were to be lettered with a big question mark in red crayola or pencil, and sent to the Russian Embassy in Washington, D.C. These were to be dispatched on any given day of the week, but the same day for three weeks running. . . . On the fourth week, on the same day, I was to be in front of a theater in Mexico City, in Old Mexico, for a contact with whoever they designated to meet me. . . . I was to be carrying or smoking a pipe that they furnished me."

As crimes are said to bear the imprint of the personality that committed them, thus enabling criminal psychologists to track down the man behind them, so, it seems, do espionage operations. You hear, in Rhodes's description of his communications system, echoes of things past. You hear the sense behind the mysterious messages found in Colonel Abel's hotel room. "In Mex: Signal 'T' on pole opposite #191 Chihnaahva (Chihvahaa) St. (Fonolia Roma), using side of pole towards roadway. Sat or Sun, Tues, Thur. Met on Mon, Wed, Fri at 3 p.m. movie 'Balmora.'" and "'Balmora,' Avenida Oberon. 3 p.m. Display left of entrance. I. 'Is this an interesting picture?' L. 'Yes. Do you wish to see it, Mr. Brandt?' L. smokes pipe and has red book in left hand." You hear Reino Hayhanen going to meet Abel for the first time at the Keith's movie house in Flushing, with his pipe and book and his passwords, and Hayhanen, again, in Paris, just before his defection, smoking that same pipe and signaling a watching Russian official that he was leaving for Moscow the next day.

The personality of this operation is clearly stereotyped, melodramatic, trapped in its own ritual language and gestures. It is not a creative mind that lies behind Abel's operations. And Abel knew that—"I know you are the right man," he had said at his first meeting with Hayhanen, waving aside the passwords. Listening to Rhodes, Abel must have been as bored with the tedium of the system as the audience was intrigued.

When Roy Rhodes finished telling the court of the elaborate system devised for keeping him in touch with the Russian Embassy, he told them, too, that he had never used it. Once Rhodes left the surveillance of his Moscow "contacts," he obviously tried to forget the whole mess. Whoever wrote the Quebec message that had been found

in the basement of Hayhanen's house was not willing to
let it go.*

Tompkins took Rhodes over the ground covered in the
message.

"No, sir," Rhodes said. "I never lived in Red Bank."

"Is your wife employed?"

"She is, yes, sir."

"Is she in the garage business?"

"No, sir."

His brother, Rhodes said, had never worked in Georgia
and never in an atomic energy plant. Tompkins asked if,
after returning to this country, Rhodes had tried to communicate with anyone or with the Russian Embassy and
Rhodes said no. There were no further questions. Tompkins did not need to ask where the Russians could have
gotten that peculiar information about Rhodes's brother
working in an atomic plant, for he knew that it had come

---

* Quebec. Roy A Rhodes. Born 1917 in Oilton, Oklahoma,
U.S. Senior Sergeant of the War Ministry, former employee of
the U.S. Military Attaché in our country. He was a chief of
the garage of the Embassy.

He was recruited to our service in January, 1952, in our
country which he left in June, 1953. Recruited on the basis of
compromising materials but he is tied up to us with his receipts
and information he had given in his own handwriting.

He had been trained in code work at the Ministry before he
went to work at the Embassy but as a code worker he was not
used by the Embassy.

After he left our country he was sent to the School of
Communications of the Army, C.I. Service which is at the
City of San Luis, California. He was to be trained there as a
mechanic of the coding machine.

He fully agreed to continue to cooperate with us in the
states or any other country. It was agreed that he was to have
written to our Embassy here special letters but we had received none during the last year.

It has been recently learned that Quebec is living in Red
Bank, N.J. where he owns three garages. The garage job is
being done by his wife. His own occupation at present is not
known.

His father, Mr. W. A. Rhodes, resides in the U.S. His
brother is also in the States where he works as an engineer at
an Atomic Plant in a Camp in Georgia, together with his
brother-in-law and his father.

from Rhodes himself and was a mere thread in the cloth
of lies he had told them. As for the other discrepancies,
the Russian network had simply made mistakes.

Rhodes was excused and did not appear for cross-
examination by Donovan until the following afternoon. In
the interim, Donovan moved again that Rhodes's testimony be stricken and asked "that the jury be instructed to
disregard it as incompetent and immaterial and not binding on this defendant." The opinion of the judge was
clear: "I don't think this is offered as binding on the defendant," he said in answer to Donovan. "I think this is
offered as evidence tending to show that a conspiracy existed, and that one of the purposes of the conspiracy was
to avail the conspirators of the services of this witness."

"Your Honor," Donovan said, "ninety-nine percent of
this man's testimony this afternoon is with respect to a
conspiracy, if it existed, totally unrelated to that charged
in this indictment. There is no testimony, your Honor,
that this man ever knew the defendant, and no testimony
that this man ever knew Hayhanen. There is no testimony
that he ever knew anyone named as a coconspirator in
this indictment."

"In this kind of conspiracy, Mr. Donovan, it wouldn't
be any surprise to you that several of the conspirators do
not know several of the other conspirators. This is not the
kind of a little two percent conspiracy entered into to
burn down a building. This is a pretty widespread conspiracy," said the judge.

In the end, Byers denied the motion and allowed
Rhodes's testimony to remain in the record. He told the
jury that the witness had been discredited to some extent,
for he had made conflicting statements to the FBI and the
army about his activities in Moscow. Those statements
had not been brought out in court because, as the judge
put it, "it would not have been in the interests of national
security." Then Roy Rhodes took the stand again.

"May it please the court," said Donovan, "would the
defendant rise?"

Rudolph Abel stood.

"Sergeant Rhodes, have you ever seen this man before?"

"No, sir."

"Do you recognize him as anyone you have ever
known under any name?"

"No, sir."

"Do you know a man named Rudolph Abel? . . . Emil Goldfus? . . . Martin Collins? . . . Reino Hayhanen? . . . Eugene Maki? . . . Mikhail Svirin? . . . Vitali G. Pavlov? . . . Alexander M. Kortov . . ."

Rhodes knew none of them.

Donovan draped over his shoulders the mantle of moral outrage, the shock all "decent" people must feel at the spectacle of Roy Rhodes. The witness was meek. Donovan asked if Rhodes had made any report on his treasonable activities to his superior officer. Rhodes said no. Donovan asked if, long after his wife and child had arrived in Moscow, the errant Rhodes was not at another party and that time found himself in bed with a girl. Rhodes said he was on the bed, not in it. Donovan asked if Rhodes frequently drank intoxicating liquors.

"I did, yes, sir."

"What liquor?"

"Whiskey, vodka, almost anything you want to name."

Was it not true, Donovan asked, that for the last two months of his stay in Moscow, Rhodes was drunk every day?

"I believe that is right, yes, sir."

Donovan tried to pin down some large sums of money Rhodes had been sending home from Moscow, but the sergeant denied or did not remember most of it. In the jury box, foreman Dublynn was listening intently and the next exchange stuck in his mind. It got to him. It led him to call Rhodes the prosecution's most effective witness.

"Did you ever hear of a man named Benedict Arnold?" Donovan asked.

"Yes, sir."

"How does he stay in your mind as a figure in American history?"

"Not so good."

"Why?"

"I . . ."

"Isn't it because he betrayed his country?"

"I think so."

"Do you know enough history to know that even Benedict Arnold didn't do it for money?"

"I know it."

"Sergeant, Benedict Arnold may have been the greatest traitor in American military history, but it was only until today."

"Is that a question?" said Judge Byers.

The cross-examination was over. On redirect Tompkins asked Rhodes if he was in arrest of quarters and Rhodes said yes, explaining that meant that he could not leave the post. The witness was excused.

By this time, well into the second week of the trial, you relaxed a little as you watched. The figures on center stage were familiar; you were used to Tompkins's lankiness and the Legion of Merit badge that appeared on the lapel of James Donovan's suit every day. Abel sat scribbling his notes and the women on the jury wore different dresses each day but looked exactly the same. You had a sense of the end drawing near.

All the rest of Tuesday afternoon, after Rhodes stepped down, and part of Wednesday morning, special agents of the FBI told the court how they had staked out the studio at Fulton Street and observed the man there on two separate occasions. Meticulously, they described the man leaving the building, walking east nine paces, west five, taking the bus, walking north, and all the rest of their police blotter account of a routine experience. The agents who had been at the Hotel Latham the morning of the arrest described what had happened there and Robert Schoenenberger gave his dry account of the actual arrest. Then the special agent who had searched the hotel room after Colonel Abel "vacated" it told what he had found there: "Magazines and sundry articles on the dresser and a wastebasket which was full nearly to the brim." Anthony Palermo, who was conducting the direct examination, showed the witness two government exhibits and they were identified as objects seized from the wastepaper basket: a pencil and what the witness called "a block of wood in a casing that appears to be sandpaper." This same agent told the court that he had, on August 17, gone with a legal search warrant to room 509 of the Ovington building and "observed" there an extraordinary list of items: "photographic equipment, such as a camera, film, enlarger, various chemicals and trays, a densitometer, rubber tanks . . . approximately one hundred electronic tubes of various sizes, a transformer, a converter . . . hollow screws and flashlight batteries and other items which were used as containers, also maps for Boston, Los Angeles, Chicago, New York City, and New Jersey."

The witness identified objects he had seized in his search: "a canister containing film marked 'one roll, Eastman spectroscopic film, type 649GH,' two sheets of paper containing five-digit groups of numbers, ten columns of numbers to the page . . . found in a Kodak photographic book . . . a piece of electronic equipment marked 'A Trav-Electric converter' . . . two screws."

The defense objected to the admission of all those exhibits on the grounds that they were taken on a search warrant issued as a result of Abel's arrest. That went into the record and would be considered by the Court of Appeals. Judge Byers allowed the evidence to be entered, but reserved the right to have it stricken if the argument made by the defense later proved meritorious. The FBI man continued identifying objects he had taken from Abel's studio:

". . . a flashlight battery . . . a hollow piece of brass tubing approximately one inch and a half long [that] unscrews at one end, a smaller brass cylinder, tie clasps, a cuff link."

The defense objected and Judge Byers made the same ruling he had before. The witness showed the courtroom that all of those objects were hollow inside, and was excused.

The last witness returned the trial solidly to the real world. If much that had unraveled before the court for the week and a half past was fantastic in every sense, the testimony of FBI Special Agent Frederick Webb, a laboratory expert, stuck perilously close to what was real. These were just the facts, then, and the audience, trapped in its own passion for detail, listened.

And watched. Webb had photographic enlargements to show the court and he moved professorially to prove his point: that the birth certificate made out to Martin Collins, which had been found in his room at the Hotel Latham, was forged. Webb had some blowups of Dorothy Adams's handwriting and he showed how that handwriting differed from the signature, "Dorothy Adams" on the Collins birth certificate. "I reached the conclusion," he said, "that Dorothy Adams did not prepare the signature on the birth certificate."

From the birth certificates, Webb moved on to tie

clasps. With the full authority of those fellows from the FBI laboratory one sees constantly solving the most perplexing crimes on television and in films but without that Sherlock Holmes sense of joy at having "got it," Special Agent Webb revealed for all to see the secret of the tie clasps. Two of them had slightly raised ornaments on the front of the clasp which held secret compartments. Webb said that the cavities were "large enough for microdot messages or microfilm messages in which film backing has been removed so the film can be folded or rolled." A third tie clasp had an inlaid wood ornament on its face which, Webb said, "comes apart and inside the wood is a cavity big enough for microfilm, microdot, or even messages on thin paper." All of those objects, along with a hollow screw container for messages, a battery for the same purpose, and a hollowed-out cuff link had been found in storeroom 509 at the Ovington building. David Levine had said that he did own them. You felt yourself caught by the incontrovertible existence of those things.

There were more. Two of the objects Abel had thrown into the wastebasket at the Latham, already put into evidence, were shown to Webb and it was his job to interpret them. Of the first, he told the court, "This was found to be a block of wood with sandpaper wrapped around it. The block of wood comes apart and inside the block of wood, rolled in this paper, sealed with adhesive cellulose tape, is a small booklet which was found to consist of about two hundred fifty pages and on each page a series of numbers appears. In one section, the numbers were in red printing and the numbers were in five-digit groups. The other section were black numbers printed, but the numbers are also in five-digit groups."

"Mr. Webb," asked Kevin Maroney, "do you know what that little book is?"

"I would recognize this as a cipher pad which would be described as a one-time cipher pad."

The second object Webb had examined at the FBI laboratory was what looked to be an ordinary wooden pencil. It was not. The eraser end came out and inside was another one of those cavities. "The eraser end," Webb said, "had on it a little wooden plug which fitted into that hollowed-out cavity and made it appear as an ordinary stub end of the pencil."

Unlike the tie clasps and the cuff link and the battery, the cavity in this container was not empty. When it was opened by the FBI, out tumbled eighteen microfilms. Photographic prints had been made of the films and the government put three print frames into evidence after Webb identified them as being enlargements of the films found in the hollow pencil.

Then the court recessed for lunch and it was one of the few times during this trial that resembled the suspense you expect of a spy trial. Throughout the recess, you wondered what was on those films, dreading that it turn out to be another cryptic message, like those about Balmora and telephone poles and Mexico. You returned and were relieved, for the contents of this set of films were wonderfully clear. In some ways, too clear.

Kevin Maroney read Government Exhibit Number Ninety-eight into the record. It had been written in Russian and translated into English. "It contains a heading," Maroney said, " 'January-December, 1957,' and under that, 'Data of the Center,' and then there is a schedule . . . for each of the twelve months, January through December, with two major headings, 'Basic Sessions' and 'Alternate Reserve Sessions.' And then there are seven columns: 'Days of Work,' 'Time of Beginning of Transmission GMT,' 'Frequency Kilocycles,' 'Signal (Call Signs)' and then under the 'Alternate Reserve Sessions,' similar columns."

Maroney read an example of what the schedule said and then passed the exhibit among the jury members while he went on to the next, which was a letter that began, "Dear Dad."

He tried to read just the opening paragraph, saying that it was a letter written in English, but Arnold Fraiman "wondered . . . if we could request the government to read the remainder of the letter to the jury?"

"Why don't you do it to save time," Judge Byers suggested, "because the other side can, if you don't." There glimmered the idea that the contents of this exhibit would be somehow useful to the defense. Maroney read the entire letter:

Dear Dad:
   It's almost three months since you went away. Although it's not so much as compared with eternity, still

it is a long time and the more so as there is a great quantity of news to tell you.

First of all, I am going to marry. Please don't be astounded. I am much surprised myself, and still it is a fact to be taken for granted.

My future husband seems to be a good guy. He is thirty-four and a radio engineer. Mother likes him very much. We met at the birthday of our friend who lives in our bungalow. On February 25 we shall celebrate our wedding. I hope you will like him when you come back; I think you will have much to talk about.

News number two: We are to get a new flat of two rooms. It is not what we're supposed to get but it is a flat for ourselves and it is much better than what we have now.

News number three: I have found a job—engineer referrant in aviation, so now I shall be somewhat closer to you. The job seems to be a decent one. They promised to pay well, and my future boss seems to be an intellectual and a polite guy. I did some odd jobs there and received a pretty sum of money.

My future husband and I are both deeply interested in photography, especially color photography. He has an Olympia car and we both enjoy meddling with it.

We received both your letters and the key from the suitcase but the latter is still wandering somewhere.

Our aunt, the one we took home with us, still lives here.

Our childhood friend writes regularly and sends you his and his family's best regards and wishes. All our friends wish you health and happiness and a happy and quick way home.

Well, this is all I have to say.

> Yours,
> Evelyn
> February 20, 1956

Witness Webb returned to demonstrate the gadgets he had described. He pointed to photographic enlargements, hung for the jury to see, of two hollow screws ("this shank portion here had been hollowed out, the top part of it threaded to fit the threaded cap, which comes out, leaving inside the cavity within the shank of the screw itself. . . . This cavity . . . is something over an inch deep"); and two tie clasps with similar cavities. Maroney had no further questions and the gadgets were passed among the members of the jury, who turned them over and over with considerable interest. Judge Byers asked for cross-examination.

"Your Honor," Arnold Fraiman said, "at this time the defendant would like to offer in evidence as a defense exhibit, Government Exhibit Number Ninety-nine for identification," which was the rest of the microfilms found in the hollow pencil.

Maroney objected; the microfilms, all of them letters, were "personal letters which have nothing whatever to do with the issues charged here in the indictment."

"Yes," said the judge, "but they were part of a government exhibit and doesn't that entitle the defense to offer them for what they are worth?"

Maroney did not press.

Fraiman and Debevoise read the letters. There were eight of them: four written in English and signed "Evelyn," the other four in Russian, signed "Elya." Evelyn appeared to be Abel's daughter. She wrote about her job, about trying to compose poetry, and about her forthcoming marriage. Her husband, she said, did not compare at all with her father, whom she missed deeply. Elya, Evelyn's mother, Abel's wife, sent catalogues of domestic details: her health, their new dog, the plum trees, a television set, a new apartment. She, too, wrote sadly of the wait until her husband's return. Some of the letters were dated—February, April, June, August; one gives a year —1956. Both wife and daughter wrote about presents they had received from Abel, a visit they had with him, and their anxiety about his coming home again.

Some said there were tears in Rudolph Abel's eyes as the letters were read in the courtroom. Some doubted their authenticity and thought of them as coded communications, not from family, but the Center. At the trial, though, no one objected to their admission into the record. Since the trial, the letters have not been decoded and they remain stubbornly on record, ambiguous.*

The last exhibit, Number One Hundred for the government, came from the Department of Defense. At the re-

* The letters are printed in their entirety in Appendix A.

quest of the Justice Department, they had monitored at the times and frequencies shown on Abel's radio schedule and picked up five-digit messages. Donovan objected to the admission of that monitoring on the grounds that it "flowed from a document obtained at the Hotel Latham," which had already been objected to as being seized illegally. Judge Byers overruled the objection. Donovan then objected on the grounds that "there is no showing that this related to the defendant" and that a different set of call letters were used in the broadcast that the Defense Department picked up. Tompkins answered the objections and it quickly became a muddle. Not even *The New York Times* man covering the trial understood the argument over the admissibility of those radio schedules. One man did, though. Tompkins was arguing that the schedules ought to be admitted into evidence and Rudolph Abel rose from the defense table and whispered to Donovan what it all meant. The jurors laughed, Abel sat down, and Judge Byers admitted the exhibit. Shortly before four in the afternoon, the prosecution rested its case.

The next to the last day, Thursday, was given over to summations for each side. Donovan began with, "This trial has been an experience I know for me, and I feel sure for you as well. Like all experiences they are meaningful when we can look at them with the benefit of hindsight." With hindsight, then, Donovan went back over the trial, reminding the jury that they were to use common sense in deciding whether the defendant was guilty or not guilty. As he surveyed the charges in the indictment, Donovan asked the jury, "What evidence of national defense information or atomic information has been put before you in this case? When you and I commenced this case, certainly we expected evidence that this man is shown to have stolen great military secrets, secrets of atomic energy and so on."

Judge Byers interrupted to lecture Donovan and the charge was conspiracy to get that information. "The charge doesn't involve a substantive offense. When you undertake to tell the jury what the law is, be accurate in your statement, please."

Donovan left the law and moved on to character, setting up Abel as "a devoted husband, loving father . . . outstanding type of family man . . . a very brave patriotic man serving his country on an extraordinarily hazardous

military mission and who lived among us in peace during
the years"—setting that against "a bum, a renegade, a
liar, a thief," Hayhanen. Donovan retraced what had
come out in court of Hayhanen's unsavory character and
added a few touches like: "When the case began, I
thought [he defected because] he was simply afraid to go
back to Russia. By the time he finished his testimony, I
think he was more afraid to go back to his wife," and
"furthermore, he used all of those fantastic methods of
communicating with someone. At times he said he used
those drops and hollowed-out bolts and so on to communicate with the defendant. One minute after he testified to
that, he was telling you he met him every week and they
used to go for drives for an hour. If he met him every
week and went for drives by the hour, what would be the
object of communicating with him through this melodramatic, boyish device?"

Then he set Abel up against Rhodes: "dissolute, a
drunkard, betraying his own country." Donovan said that
Rhodes's activities in Moscow did not relate to the defendant in any way, nor did mention of Mrs. Sobell whom the
government "pulled in by the ears." He warned the jury
against what "you have heard condemned for the last
some years . . . guilt by association," and reminded them
that "you are not serving your country and you are not
fighting communism to convict a man on insufficient evidence. . . . Ladies and gentlemen," he said at the end, "if
you will resolve this case on that higher level so that you
can leave it with a clear conscience, I have no question
but that certainly on counts one and two in this indictment, you must bring in a verdict of not guilty," and sat
down.

By afternoon, the courtroom was stifling hot. Inside,
you could feel the impatience. A lawyer's summation, by
its nature, goes over the ground covered during all the
days of testimony and unless the lawyer can give to his
final speech some arresting rhetoric, some brilliant twist
of logic or urgent passion, it is bound to be boring business. There were no Perry Masons in this trial, the jury
foreman said.

Tompkins talked about the death penalty, which had
sounded ominously through Donovan's speech. He reminded the jury that "prior to your being sworn, each
and every one of you said that you could decide the case

on evidence without consideration of penalty." He asked
that the jury leave the matter entirely to the judge. Again,
the jury listened to an explanation of the conspiracy
charge:

"If we agree, two persons agree, to assassinate the President and one of them procured a gun, that would be all
that you needed to complete the crime and it need not be
completed to be a crime. In other words, we don't have to
stand idly by and permit an individual to commit espionage, to get our secrets. We are not powerless in that
case. We may intervene. We may prevent the consumma-
tion of the crime."

Point by point, Tompkins countered Donovan's arguments. First, the attacks on Hayhanen. Tompkins took on
Donovan's assertion that Hayhanen was a bungler and
claimed he had "the same training as the defendant, but
less time." Tompkins reminded the jury of Abel's "family
living very well in Moscow with . . . a summer home and
servants." To Donovan's assertion that Hayhanen had
been vague about the "faceless" Soviet officials he had
taken orders from, Tompkins repeated the testimony
about meeting Mikhail Svirin in Moscow and later in a
a Brooklyn subway station. To counter the name-calling
("bum," "renegade," "liar," "thief," Donovan had said),
Tompkins described Hayhanen as a "trained, skilled espionage agent." And about Rhodes's testimony that he
did not know either Abel or Hayhanen, Tompkins twisted
it to his own side: Rhodes did not know them, he said,
but "Abel knew about Roy Rhodes and so did Hayhanen." The names Rhodes had been called were true,
Tompkins said. "If he wasn't a weakling who sold out his
country and was susceptible to use by this conspiracy by
the Soviet government, this conspiracy would not have
sought him out. Abel wasn't seeking decent citizens. He
was seeking the Roy Rhodeses because the decent citizens can be of no help to a Soviet conspiracy. . . ."

Had Burt Silverman been in the courtroom he would
have blanched at Tompkins's next remarks. The prosecutor was illustrating how Hayhanen's testimony had been
corroborated. Hayhanen had said that a drop in Prospect
Park had been sealed up and an FBI agent had testified
to going to the drop, unsealing it, finding a bolt inside; another FBI man had identified the message inside the bolt
as having been typed on a certain typewriter.

"And that brings me to one of the most important items of proof in the case," Tompkins said, and pointed to the Remington portable sitting on the table, "this typewriter. Who placed a typewriter definitely in Abel's possession? Who was the person who testified that it was Abel's typewriter? I do not even think the defense would complain about this. Of all people, one of the defendant's character witnesses. He testified that he got this typewriter—he gave you the serial number—from Abel and he turned it over to the FBI."

As additional corroboration, Tompkins held up the pamphlets titled "Vacuum Board for Making Matrices" and "How to Make Microdots," both found in Hayhanen's Peekskill house and both typed on that typewriter. It was, Tompkins said, "overwhelming proof."

Toward the end, Tompkins waxed sentimental about the FBI. The agents "did a magnificent job in a very difficult case"; theirs was the "painstaking work of a great organization"; they were "thirteen plain American citizens with no interest except that justice be done."

His pace increased. He went over the list of exhibits, the tools of the trade that had been brought into court. "Now these items," he said, "have been referred to as toys, as were the [hollow] coins. Toys. I don't believe anybody would call these toys for amusement. They are not toys for amusement. Ladies and gentlemen, they are tools for destruction, destruction of our country; that is the purpose of this conspiracy. These toys, tools for destruction, believe me . . ." and so emphatic was Tompkins on this point that he pounded the table as he spoke. He felt a pain in his back, stabbing, but he continued his address smoothly, ignoring it.

He insisted that Abel was "professional, a highly trained espionage agent . . . a master spy, a real pro." "Just remember this," he said, "this was the man's chosen career. He knows the rules of this game and so do his family, so does his mature daughter. He is entitled to no sympathy.

"I simply say this: this is a serious case. This is a serious offense. This is an offense directed at our very existence and through us at the free world and civilization itself, particularly in light of the times. And I say this, and I don't believe I have ever said anything more heartily or more seriously: I am convinced that the government has proven its case not only beyond a reasonable doubt as required, but beyond all possible doubt."

Tompkins walked back to the table at which the government's lawyers sat and lowered himself gingerly into his chair, thinking that the pain in his back must be a college injury acting up. He put his hand behind his back as the courtroom sat silent in the aftermath of his speech and there felt what had happened: nothing more than a snapped suspender. He smiled to himself.

On Friday morning, the last day of the second week of the trial, Judge Byers addressed the jury and explained once again the difference between a conspiracy to commit a substantive crime and the substantive crime itself. By that time, the jury must have understood so well that they could mouth the explanation themselves. Byers read the entire indictment out and when that was done urged the members of the jury to consider that the defendant must be proven guilty beyond a reasonable doubt to overcome the presumption of innocence they were supposed to have about him. "The emphasis," he said, "is upon your reasoning faculties and that necessarily excludes your emotions. You know that two of our favorite emotions are sympathy and prejudice. You may not rely upon either of those or any other emotion and call the result the creation of a reasonable doubt. The emotions, as you know, and this is true of every one of us, sometimes fly in the face of our reasoning processes, and that is why it seems necessary to warn you."

The judge asked the jury to put aside what might happen if an American were being tried under similar circumstances in the Soviet Union because they could not possibly speculate what might happen and because it was irrelevant to their function. "We are not interested in the standards which prevail in any other part of the world," he said. "We are responsible only for the way in which we discharge our duties as American citizens."

The charge of the court took up the entire morning and it was a quarter past twelve when the alternate jurors were dismissed, the United States marshals who attended the jury were sworn and those nine men and three women left the courtroom to deliberate. In the room, in the corridors, among members of the press, over luncheon tables, the talk was of the death penalty. That is, among the uninitiated there was such talk. Among the lawyers for the government, none was heard at all. In spite of the insistent reminders by Donovan and journalists—you found in each day's story of the trial the tag line that "if convicted, Colonel Abel could be sentenced to death" —in spite of all that, the government at no time wanted the death sentence. "The trial judge," Tompkins said, "knew this and was very clear about it." Which explains why Tompkins could tell the jury that Colonel Abel was entitled to no mercy but that they should not think about the sentence, leaving that to the judge.

In the jury room there was no real dissension, none of that film makers lead us to expect, no holdout convinced Abel was innocent to manipulate the other jury members to his point of view. Although one member did vote "not guilty" on the first ballot, he was soon to change his mind.

For the luncheon break, the jury was taken to Joe's Restaurant on Fulton Street, across from the courthouse. In that restaurant, only a year before, Rudolph Abel had eaten meals with Burt Silverman and there, framed by mirrors, tile floors, and high, ornate ceilings, Abel had been sketched by the young painter. Later, Silverman had made a painting of his friend sitting alone at a table in Joe's.

Back in the jury room, the foreman sent a request for three trial exhibits: Hayhanen's statement to the FBI in which he said that he never commited espionage, the Quebec message, and the message found in the hollow nickel. Four o'clock passed and the jury had not come out. There was talk that it might be deadlocked. Then, at ten minutes to five, the call went out that a verdict had been reached. Twelve people filed solemnly into the courtroom and took their seats in the jury box. The clerk of the court stood.

John T. Dublynn, jury foreman, stood also. Dublynn, a short, muscular man who could have been a lumberjack but worked instead at a sewage disposal plant in Brooklyn, was to deliver the verdict. He set his square-jawed face forward and fixed his eyes on the clerk.

"Members of the jury, have you agreed upon a verdict?"

"We have."

Dublynn knew that death was the maximum penalty for the crimes of which Colonel Abel was accused. He had thought about it hard, trying not to let it affect his decision. He tried to be fair about the evidence presented in court. He had opinions: Roy Rhodes turned his stomach, stuck in his mind. "I wouldn't hesitate to have dinner with Abel," he said, "but I wouldn't share a stick of gum with Rhodes."

"In the case of the United States of America against Rudolph Abel, how do you find the defendant, guilty or not guilty on count one?"

Dublynn stared straight ahead, deep into the eyes of the clerk. His hands stiffened. He could not meet Rudolph Abel's eyes.

"Guilty."

"How do you find the defendant, Abel, guilty or not guilty on count two?"

"Guilty."

"How do you find the defendant, guilty or not guilty on count three?"

"Guilty."

Dublynn was sure that Abel would be executed.

ELEVEN

ABEL went back to West Street to wait for sentencing. His lawyers brought books to keep him occupied: lots of technical material, books on mechanics and electronics, one about cube tables. He was, they said, well up in the thousands doing cube tables in his head as he lay in his cell trying to get to sleep. And, like many highly trained minds, he read detective novels for quick relaxation. Of which there was little between the delivery of the verdict and the date set for sentencing.

He wrote a letter to *The New York Times* asking for a subscription. One morning, a letter arrived at 75 West Street from the *Times* subscription department addressed to R. I. Abel. That very day his photograph was on the front page of the paper; the printed form letter that arrived in the mail simply told Dear Sir that it did not have a delivery route covering his address on West Street; they would, the letter said, surely be installing one in the near future. Unfortunately, Dear Sir would, for the time being, have to continue buying his copy of the *Times* at his newsstand when he goes out for his morning coffee.

Talk among the lawyers in the case was that if anyone could execute Abel, Judge Byers could. But, they reminded one another, the government did not want the death penalty. Before the sentencing, Donovan prepared a list of arguments against the death penalty: that no evidence had been produced to show that Abel "actually gathered or transmitted any information pertaining to the national defense"; that the death penalty is usually justified as a deterrent to subsequent crimes but in this case "it is absurd to believe that the execution of this man would deter the Russian military"; that the government ought to consider the effects on our own citizens abroad of executing a man for a peacetime conspiracy to commit espionage (Donovan, of course, not so naïve to believe that only *they* had spies; Donovan, who had been a member of the OSS); that although Abel had not yet "cooper-ated," that was still possible; and that "it is possible that in the foreseeable future an American of equivalent rank will be captured by Soviet Russia or an ally and at such time an exchange of prisoners through diplomatic chan-nels could be considered to be in the best national interest of the United States."

On November 15, in the same courtroom in Brooklyn, Donovan read out his arguments. Tompkins made a speech in which he repeated that Colonel Abel was no novice; said that although a substantial sentence would not deter the Soviets from continuing their "espionage operations directed at this country and at the free world," still it would "serve notice upon the men in the Soviet Union, in the Kremlin, and those who carry out their as-signments, that the commission of espionage in the United States is a hazardous undertaking." He urged considera-tion of "the present dangers which this country faces from the country whose leaders tell us they will bury us." And while "no shooting war exists with the Soviets, we are en-gaged in a Cold War with that country, the outcome of which could well decide who would be victorious in a hot war." He urged upon the court "a substantial and very strong sentence."

Judge Byers prefaced his sentencing by saying that he lacked insight into the "man known as Abel" and thus could deal with him only as "one who chose his career with the knowledge of its hazards and the price that he would have to pay." The only question involved in setting the price was serving the best interests of the United States. Therefore, on count one of the indictment, conspir-ing to transmit defense and atomic secrets, Byers imposed a fine of five thousand dollars and imprisonment for thirty years. The clerk of the court informed the judge that the law provided for no fine for that offense, so the judge re-scinded it. On count two, conspiring to obtain defense and atomic secrets, he was sentenced to ten years' imprison-ment and a fine of two thousand dollars, a penalty which the law did provide. On count three, failing to register with the United States government as a foreign agent, the sentence was five years' imprisonment and a one-thousand-dollar fine.

Colonel Abel returned to West Street and remained there well into the next year. While he sat in his cell doing cube tables in his head and making a remarkable peace with his prison mates (everyone said criminals are notoriously anti-Communist; everyone expected the cold shoulder given political prisoners by inmates to be turned on Abel, too, but it was not), Donovan began the process of appealing the conviction and Reino Hayhanen disappeared for a while and Roy Rhodes was sent back to his duty station in Fort Meyers, Virginia.

In February of the next year, at Fort Lesley J. McNair, Washington, D.C., Roy Rhodes was tried by an army court-martial for conspiring to violate the espionage laws of the United States. The maximum penalty for the charges against Rhodes was life imprisonment, dishonorable discharge, and loss of all pay and allowances. The army court heard, as star witness for the prosecution, Reino Hayhanen, who told again about the Quebec message he had received and the attempts made to locate the man described in the message, Sergeant Rhodes. Hayhanen had survived the four months since Abel's trial without noticeable change. He was still heavy; his hair and mustache were still dyed black, his command of the English language had not improved. Still, he was as useful as before. Rhodes was convicted on February 21, given a dishonorable discharge, and sentenced to five years at hard labor.

When Hayhanen left the army hearing in Washington, he walked off into the dismal oblivion reserved for turncoats and stoolies. He lived protected by the government; he was provided with food, shelter, and whatever he wanted; yet he could not live at all, even had he wanted to. Hayhanen's sanctuary was suffocating, dismal, and lonely; very much like the life he had lived before his defection. He and Hannah were constantly secluded, constantly watched. After Abel's trial, in preparation for Rhodes's, Hayhanen was "kept" somewhere in the South. Then he was moved to New England, shut away in the countryside with Hannah and someone to watch over him. He was drinking heavily.

In Washington, William F. Tompkins got a telephone call and left almost immediately. He traveled north, to a small New England town near the Vermont border and trudged through deep snow to the house in which Hayhanen, sprawled on a bed, had been in a stupor for several days.

"Gene!" Tompkins shook him.

"Gene!"

He could not be roused.

True to the best melodramatic script, Tompkins rushed for a doctor and had to face keeping Hayhanen's identity and whereabouts secret while getting him well. He found a local country doctor and told him there was a man sick, but that Tompkins would only identify himself and no more questions. The doctor agreed. Tompkins showed his Justice Department identification; he was still chief of Internal Security. Not only a real enactment of second-rate crime thrillers, but with the roles reversed: the government's man this time keeping to back roads and allowing no questions. The bewildered country doctor, when he saw Hayhanen, had him taken straight to the local hospital. There he stayed a few anxious days, drying out. When he was well enough to leave, back to his house in the bleak countryside, Hayhanen was told that his liver was in very bad shape and that if he came back in the same state again, they would not be able to help him.

From the federal detention headquarters, prisoner Abel sent a letter in April 1958 to the Honorable Matthew T. Abruzzo, judge of the United States District Court. It was a curious letter, very much like the one he had written from Texas to his friend David Levine, mixing formality and informality, sounding old-fashioned and formal, yet colored throughout by a weary cynicism. The business of the letter was to ask that ten thousand dollars be approved by the court to be taken from his funds and given to Donovan to pay for his defense. "This application is being made at this time because I am about to elect to serve my sentence, pending my appeal; further communication may be difficult, in view of the uncertainties of life. . . ."

Two weeks later, Donovan, Fraiman, and Debevoise argued the case before the United States Court of Appeals, Second Circuit. Seven lawyers for the government, most of them from the Department of Justice in Washington, argued again the reality of the search and seizure made by the Immigration and Naturalization Service Agents at the Hotel Latham at the time of Abel's arrest.

The month of April brought a parting in the band of men who had coalesced around Colonel Abel the year before. The uncertainties of life, as he had put it, took over.

William F. Tompkins left the Department of Justice that month. He still felt himself the best friend Reino Hayhanen (Gene, as he called him) ever had; his connection with Hayhanen remained and kept cropping up in Tompkins's life the next few years. Like everyone who had worked with the star witness during the trial, Tompkins retained his conviction that Hayhanen was smarter than most people thought. Abel, he was convinced, was brilliant, absolutely professional and, Tompkins said, "I always thought he was more than a colonel." Each of the principal players had been fascinating in his own way and Tompkins was thinking as he left the case that if he could, he would like to write about them.

On the other side, Arnold Fraiman had left the defense. The reality of Abel that Fraiman took with him was totally different from Tompkins's and his memory of that reality, too. "He never impressed me as having any special character," Fraiman said. "I mean, I was impressed by his talents as a linguist, an electrical expert, a cartographer, a cryptographer, a mathematician, but he left no impression on me, personally. I found him rather humorless." Illustrating Abel's lack of humor, Fraiman remembers that letter he got from *The New York Times* telling him that there was no delivery route in his area. "His response was serious, completely humorless, even plaintive. He said, 'Well, what should I do? Should I write another letter? I mean, *I* can't go out for coffee in the morning.'"

More pieces of the puzzle. Fraiman said he did not get to know Abel well, that Donovan and Tom Debevoise knew him better. Debevoise remembers the *Times* letter and that Abel fully appreciated its humor. Fraiman says no. But Fraiman corrects himself, he has to admit now that in 1958 he was more rigid, more black-and-white in his perceptions than he is today. To him, Abel was a bad guy. You could not like one of the bad guys.

Some did like the bad guy. Burt Silverman, for one, clung to his memories and tried to incorporate the reality of Rudolph Abel who had stood trial for his activities as an espionage agent and been convicted and sentenced to jail. All along, through nearly an entire year following the conviction, the traces of Emil Goldfus endured in the mind of his friend and the reality of that exposure-trial-and-conviction was bent and bruised to fit the memory, but it never did. Then Donovan called Burt Silverman and told him that Abel had gone to prison in Atlanta and arrangements were being made to ship his personal effects to his wife in East Germany. Silverman still had the guitar. Would he, Donovan asked, bring it down to the office? Incidentally, Donovan also had a personal request from his client.

In his office at 15 William Street, Donovan sat behind his huge, shiny-top desk with a view out the window of the bridge to Brooklyn and a reminder of what part of life Silverman had shared with the convicted spy. They were cordial, Donovan correct and lawyerlike, Silverman nervous. Donovan's connections with naval intelligence and the official aura that surrounded him kept the young painter reserved, sitting in a chair by the side of that very large desk. Between them, a bare hint of friendliness, a brief encounter on common ground: between them, they shared Rudolph Abel.

Donovan presented the personal request from his client immediately. "He has asked me to tell you that he would like to correspond with you."

Silverman went blank.

"It would be about general things, you know, like what is going on in the art world. Of course, everything relating to his present circumstances would be out of bounds. . . ."

Impossible, Silverman thought. Writing about art seems so unimportant. Impossible. All the time, I'd want to say something personal. About what happened. About who he really was.

Silverman said he wanted some time to think it over before giving his answer. Donovan was content with that.

Donovan set a time for turning over the guitar.

"It's being cared for in the best way possible," Silverman said, "by being played. Will you tell that to Emil?"

He started to go and stopped at the door to ask if Abel had seen an article that he had written about his friend the spy for *Esquire* magazine.

"Yes," Donovan said. "We both found it very fair, very fair indeed.

"You know," Donovan said, as though he had just remembered, "Abel talks about you and your friends all the time. He really thinks very highly of you and your work."

The Court of Appeals considered the case of Rudolph

Ivanovich Abel, also known as Mark and also known as Martin Collins and Emil R. Goldfus, Appellant, until July. On the eleventh of that month the court affirmed Abel's conviction. Judge Waterman, who wrote the opinion of the court, agreed with the pretrial findings of Judge Byers:

". . . Judge Byers, who heard the motion to suppress, rejected the appellant's contention that federal agents had violated the Fourth Amendment. He held that INS agents making an arrest pursuant to an administrative warrant may, as an incident of that arrest, conduct a search of the hotel room in which the arrest is made, and he found that the search of Abel's room was made in good faith for the purpose of discovering weapons and evidence of alienage and not for the purpose of uncovering evidence of Abel's espionage activities. . . . We agree with this conclusion of law and decline to reverse this finding of fact."

The court denied several other contentions made by Appellant Abel: "It is true that there is no evidence indicating that Abel or his coconspirators ever succeeded in gathering or in transmitting any unlawful information. There is not the slightest hint in the record that these espionage agents met with any success." However, the court reiterated that a conspiracy need not be successful to be criminal and that the existence of a conspiracy had been proven in court. The court agreed, too, that Roy Rhodes's testimony should not be stricken from the record because "it tended to prove the truth of Hayhanen's testimony, not because it tended to confirm some of the details of the latter, but because the circumstances which Rhodes related made it more likely that Rhodes was, as Hayhanen had testified, being sought by foreign agents." The opinion of the court ended with high praise for Donovan, Fraiman, and Debevoise for "having represented the appellant with rare ability and in the highest tradition of their profession."

In the federal prison at Atlanta, Fred T. Wilkinson was waiting for his new prisoner. Wilkinson was having a busy year; some of his prisoners, he said, included the "biggest names; the whole gamut from underworld bosses to overworld political activists." He had been warden of Atlanta since 1956. This Russian spy was a sensitive case, Wilkinson said: "He was highly publicized and therefore more ripe for attacks in prison by patriots, punks, and young roustabouts who wanted to make a reputation."

It never happened. When he arrived in Atlanta, Abel was put in a cell with men whom the warden felt were safe: "intellectually and emotionally removed from current affairs; conservative people who couldn't care less what he was." Twenty-four hours a day, in a population of over three thousand men, the warden worried about his new prisoner's security. But nothing happened. After a few weeks, Abel was moved to another cell with, as Wilkinson put it, "more diverse companions."

In New York, Silverman had been thinking about Abel's request and decided that he had to say no. The problem had hung heavy for a long time. Back and forth his mind had gone: yes, he wanted to be in touch with Emil; but no, how could he? It was not just a man jailed for some petty crime, but, they said, the top Soviet agent ever caught in this country; and it was still in some ways Joe McCarthy's America and there were still dossiers being compiled; then Burt would be engulfed by the image of his friend, lonely and vulnerable, gripped by the machines of a mighty, impersonal government; yes, the urge to open an avenue of contact that would be comforting to the older man was strong but he was afraid. Burt had gone to ask the advice of a civil liberties lawyer and been told what he already knew: that Abel was a big fish and the FBI was waiting for any links with anyone that might show up; writing to him would mean opening oneself to probable harassment. No, in the end he could not and he wrote a note to Donovan telling him so, shouldering at the same time the guilt he felt at abandoning his friend.

Throughout the summer of 1958, with Abel already in Atlanta, Donovan and Tom Debevoise had waited for the decision of the Court of Appeals. It had come down in July, the conviction affirmed, and the two lawyers had immediately gone on, without missing a beat, to file a petition for certiorari to the Supreme Court. In that document, counsel for the petitioner sets forth the legal issues that he hopes fall within the jurisdiction of the Court and on which he asks to be heard. In his petition, Donovan listed six:

First, the procedure at the Hotel Latham. If an alien is suspected and officially accused of espionage, taken into custody for deportation pursuant to an administrative warrant issued by the Immigration Service, but has not been arrested for the commission of a crime, are the Fourth and Fifth amendments of the Constitution violated by a search and the seizure of evidence without a search warrant? The Supreme Court had never decided this question and Donovan asked whether an administrative warrant for deportation allowed federal police to "conduct an unlimited search of a suspect's home and all his effects." The question was of fundamental importance "with respect to the protection afforded by the Fourth and Fifth amendments to all who are aliens or who are believed by federal authorities to be aliens."

Second, the use of evidence gathered at the time of the arrest in a later prosecution for a different crime. The Immigration warrant charged that Abel was subject to deportation because he was an alien illegally in the United States. Donovan allowed that certain items might be properly seized under that warrant; namely, as the law provided: "instrumentalists by which the crime charged in the warrant was committed, fruits of the crime, weapons or property which it is criminal to possess." Under those provisions, the birth certificates for Emil Goldfus and Martin Collins along with the certificate of vaccination for Collins were properly seized. But everything else taken from the hotel room and later used as evidence was not.

The third question was whether a conviction for conspiracy to gather and transmit defense information can be upheld when there is no evidence of conspiracy to gather or transmit classified information or anything not accessible to the general public. At Abel's trial, the petition read, "there was no evidence of even an attempt to steal information not generally available to the public." The lower courts that had upheld the conviction had based their decision on the recital by Hayhanen that he was seeking "national security information . . . military information or atomic secrets"; but, the petition argued, Hayhanen had also said that the information he would get depended upon what agents he had once he arrived and "it was never shown that he ever acquired any agents in this country."

Next, the testimony of Rhodes. The Court was asked to hear whether a conspiracy conviction can be upheld when the trial court admitted testimony about "heinous crimes" that were neither related to the alleged conspiracy nor to the defendant.

The last questions charged deprivation of a fair trial
and due process. One point dealt with the charge of conspiracy to commit sabotage which was in the indictment
but about which no testimony had been given in court.
The rest were errors which Donovan said had been committed in the conduct of the trial having the cumulative
effect of shifting the burden of proof to the defendant and
depriving him of a fair trial. Reading page after page of
those errors, in spite of the seriousness of Donovan's al-
legations, a peculiar tone emerges: it sounds a little like a
lovers' quarrel, long after the affair, over who said what
to whom, but you said, but you said. Donovan insisted
that the chief witness, Hayhanen, had been led by the
prosecutor and quoted the "highly prejudicial leading
questions" at length from the transcript. He cited Tompkins's explanation that it was necessary to ask questions
the way he did because the witness was not "as conver-
sant in the English language as the rest of us." On appeal,
Donovan could answer, as he could not have in the courtroom, "Whether Hayhanen, a confessed Russian intelligence agent trained in the English language could understand or not, the prosecutor placed an impossible burden
on the defendant if he was not to appear to the jury to be
obstructing the trial by objecting to every question." Then,
the questions were answered vaguely; Hayhanen could
rarely fix a date or place for many of the events he testified to. The justices must have had a moment of amusement as they read Donovan's example of that vagueness—
"It was fall," Hayhanen had said in response to when
something had happened, "because it was raining, and I
believe it was fall. It was raining that night, and I believe
it was fall, 1953. Or maybe it was in—could be even
spring 1954, because in springtime it is raining, too."

Donovan objected to the witness being asked why he
did something and to the admission of testimony about
events that took place after Hayhanen said he had left
the conspiracy. "The government knew that Hayhanen
had left the conspiracy, but said nothing and continued
the line of questioning," he charged. And that photographs were offered in evidence that were not accurate;
irrelevant testimony that was not binding on the defendant was allowed; the prosecutor put facts in evidence himself; immaterial and irrelevant exhibits were introduced;
the judge tried to cast suspicion on the microfilmed letters

read in court. In sum, then, Donovan contended that the general climate of the trial had deprived his client of the protection guaranteed by the Constitution.

In October of that year, the Supreme Court answered granting a hearing with respect to questions one and two, the questions dealing specifically with the search-and-seizure. Since the Court is accountable to no one but the Court, no explanation is required for its choice of what it agrees to hear. Conceivably, there was no merit in the other points of the petition and the lower courts had ruled on those to the satisfaction of the highest one. The specific grievances that Donovan had about the conduct of the trial were set aside. With Debevoise, he began to prepare his case for argument.

More waiting. More writing briefs and filing them and hearing the answer from the government's lawyers and filing again a counterargument. As the disembodied voices of government and appellant spoke back and forth to one another, the subject of all that argument was making do in Atlanta.

Wilkinson, the prison warden, had seen many men come and go, into the drab life of Atlanta and out again; he had a keen intuition about what happened to men in prison and Rudolph Ivanovich Abel, from the start, was unique. Ordinary men cannot withstand the loss of identity that is required to endure in prison; they submerge, get lost, cease to be, at least for a while, as they must if they are to be controllable. But Abel managed to be a model prisoner and, in spite of being tagged 80016-A, in spite of being told when he could eat, sleep, or walk around, in spite of having every letter he wrote or received screened by an official, he maintained himself. It could have been no other way: he was a military man with the rank of colonel, surely trained in methods of survival in case of capture, mental survival as well as physical; the life he had led before being sentenced to prison equipped him to endure there. Abel had, in his life and work, taken on as many masks as he needed. He had worn them well, became the masks and still remained himself. He had made the masks work for him, juggled the identities required of him, and not lost his talent for living inside himself when he got to Atlanta. The man who had been Milton, Emil Goldfus, Mark, and Martin Collins adjusted immediately to a new role: he packed himself up for a while and did what he could to retain the core of his self while he waited for the curtain to come down on this act.

He endured because he was indestructible. He stayed alive because he had a mind that could be nothing but lively. Many prisoners maintain ties to the world outside by taking part in their own "cases"; the jailhouse-lawyer stories about all of them are infinite. Abel was no exception. He followed the course of his appeals closely, corresponded often with Donovan about his case, offered suggestions, and, characteristically, maintained a balanced view of his prospects. He thought that his case was legally very strong but that, given the nature of the times and the structure of politics in the world, he doubted the outcome would be in his favor. He was a realistic man.

Abel stayed close to the legal machinations as they ground and ground, but he kept in touch with the world, too, which he knew was larger than himself. When he talked about that world, which he did often with Donovan or with Warden Wilkinson, he stuck to his feelings about how things had changed in his own country since Stalin's death and leveled consistent criticism at the major flaw in American society which, he said, was the plight of the poor and the dispossessed. Life in Atlanta confirmed those ideas for him. He looked, he studied the other prisoners, and told Wilkinson that they were largely victims of social disease and dislocation. He had a lot of information and genuine feeling for the pain of black people, especially in the South. In spite of all the masks he had worn and the parts he had played, Abel was consistent in those social attitudes. Emil Goldfus had talked much the same way to his friends in Brooklyn Heights; Emil Goldfus had filled sketchbooks with lonely old men on park benches and bums in the doorways of the Bowery. It was not Party line that Rudolph Abel was spouting, and the warden recognized that. "Well, you know," Wilkinson said, "though he was an antagonist to our system, he was not an antagonist to the welfare of people. He was very human."

Human he was, and a loner. Quiet, introspective, self-disciplined. He could fit amazingly well into the heterogeneous prison population, but few warmed up to him. There were two exceptions, two men with whom Abel did spend time, men he enjoyed talking to or playing chess with or strolling around the prison yard with: Kurt Ponger and Morton Sobell. Ponger, an Austrian, was a naturalized American citizen who had been sentenced in 1953 to five to fifteen years in Atlanta for conspiracy to commit espionage; Ponger had pleaded guilty to one count of the charges against him, that he had been involved in a conspiracy to transmit information about the national defense of the United States to agents of Soviet Russia. Morton Sobell was familiar in most American households as the codefendant in the espionage trial that sent Julius and Ethel Rosenberg to the electric chair. That case had hounded Abel for some years by the time the two men met in prison—there had been a great deal of talk before Abel's trial of his involvement in the Rosenbergs' spying, with no evidence to support it, and talk, even on the part of lawyers at his trial, of how the money Abel had given his assistant, Hayhanen, was meant for the legal defense of the Rosenbergs and then Abel, the still point in the tempest, had sat in court listening to Hayhanen testify that the two had tried to recruit Mrs. Sobell. Face to face the first time, Abel and Sobell must have flinched a little. Still, the two men became friends and though that might raise an eyebrow somewhere, the warden thought it had no special significance—by which he meant no political significance. In the populace of that prison, which included Joseph Valachi, Vito Genovese, and some other big- and small-time Cosa Nostra members, Morton Sobell and Kurt Ponger, educated, intelligent, in many ways refined, were simply Abel's type.

In the yard at Atlanta, just by the side of the *boccie* court where the Italians were amusing themselves, Sobell and Abel played chess. Between moves, they talked a little. Sobell thought of his companion as an aloof character; you could talk with Abel at length and come away with an impression of the man, but with a gaping hole somewhere behind it, a nagging sense of not really knowing whom you were talking to. Abel was well liked by the other prisoners, Sobell said, and looked up to. In fact, he impressed Morton Sobell, too, especially where their interests intersected. Abel played with mathematics the way some people play sports or watch television. Diophantine equations was his hobby. He was an expert linguist, Sobell thought, and spoke English without accent. When it came to electrical engineering, Sobell's expertise, he thought the colonel rather "old school," as others in his earlier life in Brooklyn had thought of him in other categories: personally, in his painting, and knowledge of photography.

From October 1958 to February 1959, while the Eisenhower epoch extended itself and Khrushchev was clearly boss of the Soviet Union and Fidel Castro made his revolution successful in Cuba, Rudolph Abel was being given vocational training in the Atlanta prison, working in the commercial art section of the printing shop, and supervising the design, printing, and distribution of seven thousand cards that said "Merry Christmas and Happy New Year," and his lawyers were at work on his appeal to the Supreme Court.

The government had filed its papers with the Court; there was nothing new to be said. The government repeated, first that Abel's arrest had been legal; that a search may be made incident to a lawful arrest for a crime with or without a warrant, "the crucial thing is the lawfulness of the arrest rather than the nature of the offense." Second, the government briefs pointed out that the argument that the arrest lacked "good faith" relies on the inference that the Immigration and Naturalization Service made the arrest for the sole benefit of the FBI (an argument that had been dealt with in the motion to suppress the evidence and denied by Judge Byers at the hearing that was held before Abel's trial); that inference was, according to the government, contradicted by direct evidence.

Only seven items found in the hotel room had been introduced into evidence at the trial; the papers submitted by the government listed the items and the legality of their being introduced: (1) birth certificates for Emil Goldfus and Martin Collins, a vaccination certificate in Collins's name, a bankbook in Goldfus's name; these were "properly seized" because they were "instrumentalities and means by which he maintained his illegal status in the country"; (2) a coded message taken from Abel's sleeve when he tried to conceal it as he was being taken into custody; this was "properly seized to prevent destruction of evidence"; (3) a hollowed-out pencil with microfilm inside and a cipher pad, "properly seized" because they had been abandoned by the prisoner.

The government defended the testimony of Roy
Rhodes at the trial because it corroborated Hayhanen's,
"by establishing his own existence and providing positive,
direct evidence of the motive for locating him—his usefulness in Soviet espionage as manifested by his past cooperation." That testimony "established an additional link
between petitioner (Abel) and the Soviet espionage system, but also tended to support a strong inference that
Hayhanen was a trustworthy witness and the remainder
of his story was true."

In conclusion, the lawyers for the United States said,
"It is clear from the entire record that the exclusion of all
the allegedly tainted evidence would not have substan-
tially harmed the government's case."

Against those arguments, Donovan went to work. On
February 24 and 25, 1959, he presented his case.

Rudolph Abel paced the yard of the prison with great
long strides, not like a man meditating, but rapidly, restlessly, squeezing maximum exercise from the small activity he was allowed. He looked ill, they said at Atlanta,
but very determined. A month after Donovan appeared
before the Supreme Court, the decision was handed
down, and it was an unusual one: the Court ordered re-
argument and asked each side to appear on October 12.
Both Abel and Donovan were surprised by the order,
knew it to be out of the ordinary, and expected that it
boded well for their case.

The disembodied voices on each side, petitioner and
government, continued their conversation on paper, in
briefs filed back and forth, arguments made and met and
remade. Through the spring, through the summer, when
the hearing was postponed from October until November
to accommodate another case in which Solicitor General
Rankin was involved, through the early fall, the voices
continued, strophe and antistrophe, endless.

In one of his briefs Donovan quoted a passage from
Masters of Deceit, written by FBI Director J. Edgar Hoover and published in 1958. The first words in that book
explain Hoover's reasons for writing it:

Every citizen has a duty to learn more about the menace that threatens his future, his home, his children, the

peace of the world—and that is why I have written this book.

If you will take the time to inform yourself, you will find that communism holds no mysteries. Its leaders have blueprinted their objectives. The time is far too late not to recognize this "ism" for what it is: a threat to humanity and to each of us.

and the last, his formula for combat:

. . . the truly revolutionary force of history is not material power but the spirit of religion. The world today needs a true revolution of the fruitful spirit, not the futile sword. Hypocrisy, dishonesty, hatred, all these must be destroyed and man must rule by love, charity and mercy . . . With God's help, America will remain a land where people still know how to be free and brave.

In between those paragraphs, J. Edgar Hoover tells the American public, as it says on the jacket of the first paperback edition, "what the communist bosses are doing now to bring America to its knees." And part of that story is Rudolph Abel. Hoover tells it this way:

More and more Soviets are concentrating on building illegal networks and planting "sleeper" agents. Such was the case of Colonel Rudolph Ivanovich Abel, of Soviet intelligence, who was arrested by the Immigration and Naturalization Service in June, 1957, *at the request of the FBI* after we had identified him as a concealed agent. [Emphasis added]

Donovan had quoted Hoover's words—"at the request of the FBI"—against the government. That assertion, he said, supported his point that the arrest had not been made in good faith, that the FBI had been directing the movements of the Immigration agents all along, and that the administrative warrant on which Abel had been arrested was a "subterfuge."

The government countered:

. . . Assuming that this was so, the issue is not whether the petitioner was arrested at the request of the FBI, but whether the arrest was a bona fide step in effecting his deportation.

The Immigration Service had deliberately decided to institute deportation proceedings rather than criminal charges, the government papers argued, and the "subsequent decision to proceed under the espionage statutes was made possible only after the belated decision of the previously reluctant witness [Hayhanen] to testify." At the time of the arrest, however, Hayhanen was still refusing to testify and, said the government, "the FBI could hardly sit back and permit petitioner to continue his activities. If he could not be prosecuted and imprisoned, at least he could be stopped by deportation."

The briefs for the government and the subsequent argument heard before the Supreme Court once again took the case far beyond the "instant" one, as they called it, far beyond mere Rudolph Ivanovich Abel pacing around in Atlanta, and into consideration of constitutional guarantees as they apply to aliens. Deportation proceedings are considered civil matters, not criminal. The courts have "consistently refused to engraft upon them constitutional protections limited to criminal cases." Among the protections not applicable in civil cases are: the right to trial by jury, privilege against self-incrimination, defense of former jeopardy and all the provisions of the Eighth Amendment which guarantee the right to reasonable bail and prohibit cruel and unusual punishments. The government's briefs on this point cited reams of cases in which the Court had held those protections "not applicable." The Court had also, government lawyers said, "upheld the power of Congress to enact legislation declaring as grounds for deportation the past misconduct of aliens, despite prohibitions in Article I, section 9 of the Constitution against the passage of *ex post facto* legislation." All this history was set down dispassionately in the government's papers; it was not the job of the lawyers who wrote those papers to have opinions about the precedents, simply to lay them as the foundation for the next step in the argument: that the Fourth Amendment ("the right of the people to be secure in their person, houses, papers, and effects, against unreasonable searches and seizures, shall not be violated, and no warrants shall issue, but upon probable cause, supported by oath or affirmation, and particularly describing the place to be searched and the persons or things to be seized") was also inapplicable.

In support of their contention that the Fourth Amendment was by precedent inapplicable to the "instant case" and that the Court should not decide to make it applicable, the government quoted a recent Court decision:

The history of the constitutional protection against official invasion of the citizen's home makes explicit the human concerns which it was meant to respect. In years prior to the Revolution leading voices in England and the Colonies protested against the ransacking by Crown officers of the homes of citizens in search of evidence of crime or of illegally imported goods. The vivid memory by the newly independent Americans of these abuses produced the Fourth Amendment as a safeguard against such arbitrary official action by officers of the new Union.

By this the government was insisting that the battle for fundamental liberty, which resulted in the drafting of the Fourth Amendment, was "the issue of the right to be secure from searches for evidence to be used in *criminal prosecutions.*" Not civil proceedings. The Court had, in the past, held that houses could be inspected without a warrant for the purpose of "ascertaining compliance with local health and safety regulations"; or that an officer of the law could enter a premises to seize "goods or chattels" in compliance with "an attachment, a sequestration, or an execution," again without a warrant; a warrant is not required for the search of a business premises and the seizure of goods to be used in a proceeding to revoke a manufacturer's license; nor to collect delinquent taxes; nor to seize adulterated and mislabeled food and drugs. When the Immigration agents arrived at the Hotel Latham that hot June morning three years before, they had been about to institute a civil proceeding against an illegal alien. The government insisted on that; the proceeding was civil and therefore exempt from every constitutional guarantee that exists. The agents were free to do whatever they liked with that alien. The presence of FBI agents at the same hotel, at the same time, in the same room, was irrelevant: "The FBI had no operative jurisdiction with respect to illegal residence in the United States."

There it rested, strophe and antistrophe, performed out loud once again before the nine eminent justices of the Supreme Court in the fall of 1959 and decided by them quite some time later. On March 28, 1960, the decision was issued: the Supreme Court upheld the conviction of Rudolph Ivanovich Abel, also known as Mark, and also known as Martin Collins and Emil R. Goldfus, Petitioner. But, and this is what surprised everyone, it upheld that conviction five to four. Felix Frankfurter wrote the opinion of the majority of the court, representing Justices Clark, Harlan, Whittaker, and Stewart. The dissenting opinions, one written by Justice Douglas and one by Justice Black and Chief Justice Warren.*

Beyond the Supreme Court, there is no place to go. A convicted prisoner, if he has held out to himself the hope that the appeal of his case will work, if he has managed to go from morning to night day after day with eventual freedom always in mind, resigns when the legal process is exhausted. Not so Abel. He had, all along, been cynical about the success of his own case before the Court. Hearing the decision on the prison radio, Abel was buoyed by the closeness of the opinion. He thought, and later told Donovan, that the case might be brought before the Supreme Court once again. But he was not counting on it. Neither was he resigned to Atlanta. Abel, in the eyes of everyone who had known him those two and a half prison years, was becoming extremely irritable and impatient. He had had trouble with his correspondence privileges, which had been severely curtailed. He was, according to Morton Sobell who saw him nearly every day, "thin and ailing." He continued to play chess or bridge; he made prints and painted (Sobell remembers a painting of Orchard Street on New York's Lower East Side, a painting full of pushcart vendors, which was hung in the prison library), and he carried with him, from morning to night day after day, a current of tension; waiting, flexed, as though something were about to happen.

* Excerpts from these opinions appear in Appendix B.

TWELVE

SOMETHING about round numbers makes you think they signal new beginnings or the death of old things. History arrives in centuries. Our time is packaged in decades—the forties, the fifties, the sixties. We know it is a lie, but we impose the lie to shape our thinking about time. Fortunately for the lie, the round-numbered year 1960 did mark a beginning and an end. In May, the Cold War was radically altered. The end of one thing and the beginning of another arrived for Colonel Rudolph Abel.

Early in the morning on May 1, a Russian missile connected and brought tumbling from the sky over Sverdlovsk, more than twelve hundred miles inside the Soviet Union, a weird black apparition that turned out to be an American plane. This Black Lady of the skies, long, with a high tail and wide wings, a one-man cockpit and a single turbojet engine, came to rest on the ground in surprisingly good condition. So good that the Russians determined right away that its sole function was aerial photography. Spying from the sky. Also in surprisingly good condition was the pilot, Francis Gary Powers. He was taken very much alive.

At home, no one knew anything about it for four days. When Khrushchev told us, a mad scramble began in Washington: caught with their pants down, all kinds of people lied, made excuses, and blushed coral. It was a weather plane that had been sent over Turkey and strayed east. It was not, said Khrushchev. Unveiled plane and pilot. More blushing. Oh, we said, maybe it *was* a plane on an aerial photography mission; but certainly no one in Washington had authorized it. A Summit Conference, scheduled for May 15 in Paris, hung in the balance. Finally, on May 11, after days of Abbott and Costello routines in the capital (No, you said it. No, he said it. You said he said), President Eisenhower held a news conference. He told the country that U-2 spy planes had been flying for some time and that those flights over the Soviet Union were not only acknowledged, but defended, by our government. They were necessary to our own defense. We must—and do—and will—have spies of our own.

Good guys and bad guys, remember? One of Colonel Abel's defense lawyers had said that for him the world was divided into good guys and bad guys. The lawyer was a good guy, spy Abel a bad one. On the whole, the rest of the country felt the same way. Ignorant people had been saying all along: Look, the Russians, bad guys, have spies which they sneakily send into our homeland while we, good guys, are horrified. We would never do such a thing. Those ignorant people were most of us. And here we were faced with a statement by our own apple-pie President who said we did indeed have spies. And that we needed them. In the press conference at which he said that, our President also talked about the convicted Soviet spy Abel. Here, he said, is an example of how the bad guys operate. Here is why we must do it, too.

Abel was introduced into Eisenhower's May 11 news conference (and all over that day's press), not only as a tit-for-tat smack at the Russians and not only to propagandize the public about how necessary and "all right" espionage is, but also to bring out into the open a speculation long in the minds of everyone who had to do with Abel's case: a spy trade.

From the day of his capture, Abel had considered a trade and rejected the idea because the Russians, he said, had no one of equal value. For three years there had been no one. In May 1960, perhaps there was. So Abel came out of mothballs, where he was growing anxious anyway, and into the public eye again. Editors dug into the morgues of the newspapers and reprinted the details of Abel's "case," in case it had been forgotten. The FBI chimed in, calling the case "the classic example of Soviet espionage operations in the United States." Out came the photographs again.

James Donovan had applied to the Supreme Court for a rehearing of the decision that upheld Abel's conviction. He had asked that the case be heard again because "the full impact of this decision upon the rights of alien residents has not been, but should be, fully presented to the Court." Donovan said that his request came "on behalf of

the Immigration and Naturalization laws, whose personal
liberties have been severely and unjustly curtailed by this
Court's decision . . . [which] grants to administrative officials possessing no search warrant greater power over a
suspect's person and property than is permitted to law enforcement officers who obtain judicially authorized . . .
warrants. . . . The way has been opened for every type of
police subterfuge."

On May 17, with the colonel's picture still on front
pages, the Supreme Court announced that it would not
rehear his case. It seemed, for the space of a few days,
that James Donovan's work was done. Donovan's assistant, Tom Debevoise, who had been with the case since the
summer of 1957, from the very first motions of Abel's defense, resigned. Debevoise had been elected attorney general in Vermont and time, as well as conflict of interests,
would not allow him to keep one foot up north and another down south with Abel. Like Donovan, this young
lawyer had come to know Abel quite well; his mind had
not been closed to the "spy" as a "bad guy" all those
years and he had, when he left, regrets, considerable
warm feeling for his client, and some strong opinions
about the whole business.

No, Debevoise would say, you could not call him nondescript, not with those eyes and that nose. No, he was
really very striking. But Debevoise thought more of his
mind when he described Abel to himself; he had come to
know that mind well. Highly trained, enormously intelligent, wryly humorous, interesting; Debevoise liked him.

Parts of the case bothered him. By the time Debevoise
withdrew, he had not found the answers, particularly to
the riddle of Abel's return to New York City in the spring
of 1957 after a trip to Florida, after Hayhanen had defected. Why, Debevoise wondered, had he allowed himself to be caught with so much evidence? Why, in light of
his careful conduct in the past, was he so vulnerable? If he
thought about leaving the country and seemed to have
made preparations for it, why did he change his mind?
Abel seemed to have acted in defiance of the idea that
Hayhanen might have defected. Why, went the riddle, did
he want to be caught?

Debevoise spent hours talking with Abel; they were
friendly hours; Abel gave him an oil painting; Abel spoke
freely, although not exhaustively, and still there was no

inkling of an explanation. No, Debevoise had decided, this was definitely not the spy who wanted to come in from the cold. He was very much a "Mother-Russia guy." Abel had schoolmastered discussions in his cell about the Americans and Soviets, the benefits and detractions of each system. He was not a hard-line dogmatic Communist. Debevoise felt that rigidity from Russian officials he had met, never from Abel. The colonel was too much a pragmatist and student of history to be that way. When someone would confront him with "less savory" aspects of Russian totalitarianism, he would say, "Well, all that's changed now." He spoke often of the details of Beria and Stalin, and his feeling about the future of his country was enormously optimistic.

What Debevoise saw and responded to in his client were many of the same qualities of character that the artists in Brooklyn Heights had been drawn to. Like those artists, Debevoise had to struggle within himself with the question of what Colonel Abel, a military man on a military mission, had done. He struggled; it was impossible, he said, to envision Abel involved in "strong-arm stuff." He recoiled from such a vision. It felt wrong. "He never told us of any of his activities," Tom Debevoise said, "but his role was surely evaluation and collation of some kind of information." Surely it was; for that was the only role the mind would allow to a man who, having come from the enemy, was likable.

The press reported first that a Powers-Abel exchange was under discussion, then it seemed unlikely. The word from Washington was that the Russians were not expected to agree to a trade because it would mean acknowledging that Rudolph Ivanovich Abel was indeed what he had been convicted of being; since there had been no "official" Soviet move toward Abel ever, the prospects were reported as dim. On the other side, American officials had not been allowed to see Gary Powers, and his captors were planning a public trial. There it seemed to sit, fossilized.

In June, Gary Powers's father wrote to Colonel Abel, in Atlanta, urging him to help engineer an exchange. He asked that Abel approach the "proper authorities" in the Soviet Union while Mr. Powers went to the State Department and President Eisenhower. Abel answered that Mr. Powers ought to communicate with the Abel family in

East Germany. Donovan announced this in a news conference, said he had turned the request over to "Washington," and that he was optimistic about an exchange
although officialdom was not.

Powers went on trial in Moscow, was represented by
an appointed attorney and judged by a military tribunal,
and was sentenced to ten years' imprisonment. Powers's
father, who attended the trial, described the procedures as
"shocking." The papers made much of the contrast between the two spy trials and mentioned that an exchange
was being discussed and then the story vanished. Not a
word in the press throughout 1960; one incident in 1961.
It seemed that the notion of a spy swap was scrapped by
the Russians or the Kennedy Administration that moved
into Washington, and that the principals, Gary Powers
and Rudolph Abel, were to retire into oblivion.

Oblivion was all there was for Reino Hayhanen. Still
protected by the government, which meant looked after
by CIA agents, Hayhanen had been moved around a little
from one New England town to another, his life, what
there was of it, the same. He had Hannah and a large dog
and an isolated house in Keene, New Hampshire. The
closest neighbor was a hundred yards away and Hayhanen lived as he always had, drinking, watching television. He was a little better by 1960, managing to remain
drunk most of the time but never to slip into a coma. It
had been more than two years since William Tompkins,
former government prosecutor, had seen the man he
called Gene and when he traveled to New England for
his second visit, he found Hayhanen in "better shape."
This time, the trip was a mercy mission like the first;
"they," Tompkins said, were trying to rehabilitate the defector. Tompkins—the "best friend you have in this
world, Gene, and you know it"—was asked to help. So up
he went and out into the lonely countryside to the isolated
house. Hayhanen's bodyguards faded away and the two
men were left to talk. Amenities, conversation, Hannah
drinking a lot of peach brandy, and Hayhanen always
with vodka in his hand; not getting anywhere. Tompkins
asked straightforwardly, at last, what Hayhanen would
like to *do*.

"Own a liquor shop," he said.

At that time, in another place, another full-scale espionage operation was about to be unmasked. This one, set down in history now as the "Naval Secrets Case," involved as interesting a set of characters as any film writer could have dreamed up: Henry Frederick Houghton, who worked at the Underwater Weapons Establishment in Southampton, England, a fellow much like Reino Hayhanen; Elizabeth "Bunty" Gee, who also worked at the Portland base, Houghton's "mistress," a spindly lady who resembled all the repressed spinsters in D. H. Lawrence's novels; Gordon Lonsdale, a man of many faces who had set himself up as a small businessman in London, involved with bubble gum machines and jukeboxes, and a student of Chinese at London University's School of Oriental and African Studies. Lonsdale's papers said that he was a Canadian. The other members of the cast were a suburban husband and wife team, Peter John Kroger, fifty years old, a dealer in rare and peculiar books (his antiquarian collection specialized in books on handcuffs, leg irons, and tortures; he did have a stock of more conventional volumes, Victorian and nineteenth-century Americana); and his wife, Helen Joyce Kroger, forty-seven, suburban matron, the perfect professor's wife, a bit strident, but well done up, the apparent strong partner. Her husband, white-haired, studious, clearly intelligent, had moved his rare-book collection to their suburban cottage, Cranley Drive, Ruislip, Middlesex, and the only unusual thing about their life style was the elaborate locks on the doors put there, so it seemed, to protect that book collection.

Enter the inspector, Detective Superintendent George Gordon Smith of Scotland Yard, just the type: quite British, quite effective, and he did get his man. Got more than one, in fact, on January 7, 1961. Lonsdale, Houghton, and Miss Gee were arrested as they came out of Victoria Station carrying, as Superintendent Smith and his staff of Doctor Watsons knew they would be, a shopping bag filled with secrets of the Royal Navy, among them details of the British atomic submarine plans. That same afternoon, Detective Superintendent Smith went out to Middlesex, talked his way into the Krogers' cottage, where for months he had been watching Lonsdale go, and arrested the Krogers. Helen Joyce Kroger tried pulling a fast one, going downstairs to stoke the furnace before she left the house, and one of Smith's men caught her in the act of

stuffing a handbag into the fire. Its contents were pulled
out in time and later introduced into evidence.

The five were taken to the Bow Street police station in
London and detained in custody; the official charge
against them read that "between April 14, 1960, and January 7, 1961, they conspired to commit breaches of the
Official Secrets Act." By Monday morning, March 13, as
their trial opened in Court Number One at Old Bailey before Lord Chief Justice of England, Lord Parker, a great
many facts were known to the public. The press in England and New York had devoted considerable space to
it; in England it was treated as an outrageous scandal re-
flecting the gross inadequacy of British security; in this
country, to an audience already accustomed to continuous
spy exposés, both real and fictional, there was no cause
for outrage, just interest.

Lonsdale was the central figure, the mastermind. His
background story, the Canadian documents, and the "legend" built around them were false. Lonsdale was in fact a
Russian and the destination of all the information he had
been collecting from Houghton and Miss Gee, passing
through the Krogers, was the Soviet Union. There were
odds and ends of espionage apparatus at the Krogers'
home, all of which were introduced into evidence. And
then some personal letters were read out to the court, all
of them having been seized on the day of her arrest when
Mrs. Kroger went down to stoke the boiler. The handbag
she had tried to destroy contained several microfilmed letters in Russian clearly addressed to Lonsdale and one, in
longhand, from him to his wife which, it was assumed,
Mrs. Kroger had not had time to reduce to microdot. Reporters of the trial said that when the letters were read,
Lonsdale sat with his head bowed, the only time during
the eight-day trial that he showed any sign of emotion.

A letter dated December 9, 1960, read:

Hello my darling. I congratulate you on the past forty-
third anniversary of the October Revolution. We were
expecting letters from you but it turned out that they
may come at the end of the month. . . . On November
3 we had an evening party at the place where I work
and sang. It reminded me of our life in Prague, and I
felt very sad. . . . We were all deeply sorry you were
not with us and so was I, especially. If my memory

does not deceive me, it is already seven Octobers and six May Day celebrations . . .

The rest of the letters were similar in tone. The wife complained that Lonsdale's son and daughter missed their father and that the son had said "what a stupid job Daddy has got." They were chatty letters, filled with the longing of the entire family for their absent daddy, reports on the children's progress at school, complaints about money, and requests for presents from the West. By themselves, they might have aroused some sympathy for the father on trial, but the letters do not exist by themselves and, hearing them, the echo is unmistakable. The "wife" of Colonel Rudolph Abel could have written them. Point for point, tone for tone, the similarity. At Lonsdale's trial nothing, of course, was to be made of it. Three years after the trial, in *The New Meaning of Treason*, Rebecca West noted the similarity and doubted that either set of letters was genuine.

It may seem far-fetched to suggest that both sets of letters were prepared in advance, to be discovered if and when the agent and his arsenal were discovered, to have just the effect that the Abel family letters had on the jury that was trying him: to make them regard the spy as a good patriot and a man like themselves, who is making the same sacrifices for his country as the soldier on a jungle post or the Navy man on an Arctic station . . .

In spite of her admission that it may seem farfetched, Miss West offers no other explanation. If it were only the letters that reminded you of Abel as you watched the Lonsdale case unfold, there would be no need of explanation. But there are many more connections. In the Krogers' home the tools of the trade that were hidden in every corner of it could have been issued by the same hand that gave Colonel Abel his paraphernalia: soft film, hollow flashlights, a schedule for radio broadcasting, several one-time cipher pads exactly like Abel's, a hole in the cellar with more equipment buried in it, just like Reino Hayhanen's in Peekskill, large sums of money in twenty-dollar bills, microdot reading equipment, and an impressive array of false passports and false identities. There are more connections. As soon as the Krogers

were arrested, the search for their real identities began
and the FBI came up with the answer: the couple were
Americans, their real names were Morris Cohen and
Lona Petka Cohen. At their trial, the Cohens' background was unraveled for public consumption and one
thread of that background connected them to Colonel
Abel. In 1950, the Cohens had given a dinner party at
which the most important guest was an English businessman called Milton. The other guests were not named in
the Old Bailey courtroom, but Milton was identified as
Colonel Abel. Toward the end of the year, the Cohens
disappeared from their East 71st Street apartment in New
York City. Milton remained. In 1957, when Milton was
unmasked as Colonel Rudolph Abel, KGB, and his possessions sifted, the FBI found what they listed as "brown
paper wrapper in zippered brief case, contains $4,000 in
$20 bills," and "two photographs—one of man, one of
woman, with names Shirley and Morris on the back."
Shirley and Morris were also Helen and Peter Kro-
ger/Lona and Morris Cohen. No one could explain why
Abel had the man's name right and the woman's name
wrong. A third link between the Cohens and Abel was a
silver locket hidden in their flat containing a picture of
their three children and a microdot film of newspaper
clippings about Abel's thirty-year sentence.

All these links. They hold. The Krogers and Lonsdale,
Elizabeth Gee and Harry Houghton were found guilty of
the conspiracy charges. Lonsdale was sentenced to
twenty-five years in prison, the Krogers to twenty, Houghton and Miss Gee to fifteen. Their connection with Colonel Abel, who languished in Atlanta, still was not
evidence of the particular charges of which they were
convicted, charges for which ample evidence was provided at Old Bailey. Still, it did make things coherent;
some pieces of the puzzle did fit; there was a Soviet espionage network. Like any large organization, it had a personality, and the trial of Lonsdale, the things he did and
said after the trial, the career and methods of the Krogers,
helped to define that personality.

It was in March 1961 that those sentences in the Naval
Secrets Case were handed down. That summer, another
member of the organization appeared again: Reino Hayhanen came briefly out of retirement to appear on television. The show had been arranged by the National

Broadcasting Company and the Department of Justice. Attorney General Robert Kennedy arranged through the CIA to have Hayhanen released from his "safekeeping" in New England, and to Washington then the defector came, drinking heavily, his hair returned to its natural light brown color; with his wife he came, Hannah, who had grown stout and now wore glasses, and with his keepers, two Ivy League types who worked for the CIA, one of whom guarded Hayhanen in the New England countryside. Various motives have been set down for the creation of this interview with Hayhanen for "David Brinkley's Journal"; among them, a likely one, that a show about Hayhanen also would be a show about Rudolph Abel and it was in our own interests to give Abel a great deal of publicity those months, to show him alive and well in Atlanta. The Soviets still had Gary Powers and we still wanted him back; the exchange was still under discussion. Brinkley's show was good news and good entertainment for television audiences; it was also politically strategic.

Hayhanen arrived in Washington. He was interviewed by Peter Maas, who wrote the show, first in a motel near the Key Bridge that links Georgetown and Arlington, then in the popular Marriott Motor Inn. This time no armed guards on the balconies. Inside each of those motel rooms, Hayhanen told his story again. He talked a lot about life in the country, about a big dog he had, and about the television set he watched a lot. He talked about Hannah and his fear, those long years before, of the Russians finding out or punishing him about her. He went over the story of his defection; said he had no idea at the time why he was being sent back; said he had made his KGB contact, as arranged, at a café in Paris, and then gone to the embassy; said that the embassy people did not seem to know what to do with him. He said all that in bits and pieces, and Maas had as much trouble making sense of the story as the Abel jury had. Eventually, the interviews were done; the show was taped with Brinkley.

Throughout one August morning the taping went on. When it was done, Maas and Hayhanen, accompanied by an entourage of CIA overseers and an FBI agent thrown in, went out to lunch in southeast Washington. Hayhanen was given his ration of vodka with the meal and the group returned, afterward, to the Brinkley studio. The first taping turned out to be partially unintelligible and a second was made. The two tapes were spliced to make the reasonably coherent sequence shown on the air. Hayhanen was paid two thousand dollars and left Washington.

That was half the job. The other half, more difficult, was Abel. The show was to include some commentary and film about Abel in Atlanta and, for that, permission of prison officials was needed. Peter Maas and Ed Guthman, Robert Kennedy's press secretary, saw Fred Wilkinson, who had become deputy director of the Bureau of Prisons. The request was unusual; if granted, it would be the first time a federal prisoner had been filmed in his habitat for television. Wilkinson was hesitant. Maas and Guthman persisted, pointing out the great interest Attorney General Kennedy had in the project.

"It's better to go along with this."

"The attorney general thinks it's important."

"All right," Wilkinson said, finally.

As they talked about how to arrange the filming, Wilkinson mentioned that Abel had been painting a portrait of President Kennedy. Would they perhaps want to film that? Maas was delighted. It would be a perfect way to end the show.

At Atlanta, a few days later, Maas arrived with a local NBC cameraman. They hid in the cellar of one of the cell blocks; out the window, the view was of the path Abel would have to walk on his way from the prison printshop where he worked, to the office of the warden where he was to be summoned. Wilkinson, who had acted as warden of that prison before moving to Washington, and who enjoyed a friendly relationship with Abel, came down to Atlanta. From the warden's office, he sent word to Abel that he wanted to see him and to show the portrait of President Kennedy to some people. Abel came out; the camera rolled. Under his arm he carried the portrait. The camera caught him and the canvas and then he disappeared into the office. He left the painting there. Maas and the cameraman went in and took some close-ups. Abel never knew what went on. Not then.

That afternoon, the camera was set up in a guard tower overlooking the big prison yard. In the late afternoon, after the prison workday was over, a guard spotted Abel. The camera went on. Abel came out of the printshop, down some steps into the yard, walked past the *boccie* courts and the Italians playing there, marched around by himself, then with another man, whom the guard could not identify, and finally sat down to play chess. With a great deal of footage, NBC packed up. At the studio the show was put together and scheduled to go on the air in November.

In the fall, David Brinkley received a telephone call from Colonel Stanley Grogan, director of Public Information for the CIA. Grogan had some private information for David Brinkley: Reino Hayhanen was dead. No specifics. Whether Brinkley still wanted to put the show on the air was up to him, but the CIA thought he ought to know about the death. He could, if he wanted to, say that Hayhanen was dead, but Brinkley of course could not, for the entire show had a "pitch" and that was to others with information of value to the CIA to come forward with the assurance that they, like Reino Hayhanen, would be well protected. The show went on without the footnote on November 8, 1961.

Brinkley introduced the story. He said that Colonel Abel was the "top Russian spy in the United States" and that he "collected defense and atomic energy information." Then he talked about Abel's assistant and his cover story—Eugene Maki, Enanville, Idaho. Maki appeared, his face kept dark, only his hands visible, his accent very thick.

"Would they like to kill you?" Brinkley asked. He meant the Russians. "Yes," the darkened face said. "Hard job to find me. They're trying hard."

They talked about Hayhanen's defection and to the straight question "Why did you defect?" he answered, "I wanted liberty."

They went over the spy's background and the tricks of his trade. Hayhanen described hollowed-out coins and microdots. He said that in the United States his "organization" had used nickels, quarters, or half-dollars. Then he talked about his training in Moscow. "Korotov told me when I first met him that the United States was our worst enemy and we are in war with them," he said. When he arrived in the country, Hayhanen avoided any Communist Party member. "If you are involved with them, you may be caught," he said, and added that the opinion of the Communist Party of the United States held by the Russians was, "It is a weak party."

Hayhanen told some of the best parts of the spy story to the television audience—the thumbtack in a sign in Central Park to signal his safe arrival; his payment of five hundred dollars a month in American money through a drop under a lamppost in Fort Tryon Park; and some of the recognition signals he was assigned. He was told to smoke a pipe, he said. He protested, "But I don't smoke," and was told by his superiors, "Do it anyway."

"What did they tell you it would be like here?" Brinkley asked.

"Don't be afraid of American counterintelligence. They are walking in children's shoes." Hayhanen had a little trouble getting that folk saying into understandable English, but he made it. Then he added, "Russian intelligence is also clumsy, careless, and stupid. Not some times, many times."

Then he talked about Abel. The anger and hate, unabated since the trial, came through strongly. Hayhanen described their first meeting at the Keith's Theater in Flushing and his feelings about Abel. "I didn't like him. He was sneaky."

"But," Brinkley said, "spies are supposed to be sneaky."

"Yes, but I'm not."

Hayhanen said that Abel had been sick when he knew him. He thought it was ulcers. Then he tried another old Russian saying and got it out—"You're a bad spy if you have not ulcers."

Brinkley asked how he felt when he took the witness stand at the trial and was asked to identify Abel in the courtroom. "He was the chief Russian spy in the United States." Hayhanen said with astonishing aplomb. "I was very glad to point him."

They talked a bit about communications. Hayhanen said that Abel had a radio in his Brooklyn Heights studio and that he transmitted by radio to the Russian Embassy in Washington. "I believe he got his answers through embassy, too," he said.

There the interview ended. The rest of the program was films of Abel in Atlanta, showing the warden his portrait of President Kennedy and walking the prison yard and playing chess. A tag line at the end of the program said that after his defection Hayhanen was "in the northeastern United States under the care and protection of the

Central Intelligence Agency. . . . We are authorized to say, indeed asked to say, that if any others like Eugene Maki care to step forward any time they will be guaranteed security, physical and financial."

Not a word about Hayhanen's death and certainly not about the ironies that death cast on the words spoken by both Brinkley and Hayhanen on the program. Indeed nothing appeared in print until two Washington newspapermen, David Wise and Thomas B. Ross, published their book about the CIA, *The Invisible Government,* in 1964. In it, Wise and Ross said that between the filming of Brinkley's show in July 1961 and its telecast in November, "word spread around the intelligence community that Reino Hayhanen was dead; the CIA's prize defector had been killed in a mysterious 'accident' on the New Jersey or the Pennsylvania Turnpike."

A difficult death to track down. The CIA, whom everyone who watched David Brinkley's television show knows, was in charge of Hayhanen. The obvious place to start asking. But Larry Houston, chief counsel of the agency, a man much involved in the Abel case all along, the man who received carbon copies of all correspondence James Donovan had with Russian officials, throughout the case, Larry Houston, who ought to know what happened to Hayhanen, says that the accident story is bogus and that Hayhanen did die, but of natural causes. He thinks it was cirrhosis of the liver. Plausible, considering the drinking and the state he was in when Tompkins went to see him. Still, a death like that leaves a record somewhere and there is none. Not in Keene, New Hampshire, where Hayhanen had been living; not in any of the surrounding towns. Houston can provide no data.

Donovan believes the accident story but cannot point the way to evidence of it. James Donovan's sole comment on reports of Hayhanen's "accident" was, "Well almost all of them go that way." The Pennsylvania and New Jersey turnpikes have no record of an automobile accident resulting in death to a white male of Hayhanen's description in the summer of 1961.

Tompkins remembers that he was called about the accident story soon after it appeared in print. That was the first he heard of it. The caller wanted details. So did Tompkins. So he called Larry Houston at CIA and was convinced, Tompkins says, that "Hayhanen died of natural causes; that is, nonviolently." The basis of that conviction seems to be trust in the source from which it came. Neither Tompkins nor Houston will produce a fact to substantiate the story. No one will. Neither the visible government nor the invisible one, nor private persons, as they are called. The people who watched over Hayhanen in New England claim they never heard of him. No one knows anything.

Faced with no-facts, the mind invents. Reino Hayhanen alias Eugene Maki is dead. Or probably dead. Perhaps he died in an accident. Perhaps the accident was just an accident—but one whose traces had to be removed from the record. Try not to invent, but the sinister note creeps in. Hayhanen said the Russians were still looking for him; they probably were. But then people in the Department of Justice start telling you chilling stories of what is done with informers and defectors who have outlived their usefulness. "They all go that way," Donovan says. You juggle the possibilities: the Russians got him, our guys got him, the bodyguards were careless and Hayhanen got himself, the bodyguards were deliberately careless. All this *if* there was an accident. Theme and variations. Everyone knows nothing.

At the beginning of February 1962 there were mysterious goings-on at the Atlanta penitentiary, in Washington, D.C., and in New York City. People spoke to one another in code—calling themselves Fred W. or Noah A. and making peculiar arrangements about what they referred to as "the package." At the prison, two inmates, Kurt Ponger and Morton Sobell, were suddenly denied visiting rights for a few days; the warden was directed not to let Ponger or Sobell have any contact with prisoners about to be released. Earl Peck, an officer at the prison, was given an assignment that he could not understand; he was told to be ready to make a trip to New York City. The clothing officer at Atlanta was asked to prepare prisoner 80016-A's civilian clothes. In Washington, Fred T. Wilkinson, deputy director of prisons, and Noah Alldredge, supervisor of Custodial Service for the Bureau of Prisons, went mysteriously in and out of their offices and had those coded conversations and went over to the passport bureau where they were issued passports that listed the countries for which they were destined as France, Spain, and Italy.

On the night of February 6, Wilkinson and Alldredge took a train from Washington to New York City. They arrived at Pennsylvania Station at half past one in the morning and went directly to a hotel where they waited for the telephone to ring. For several hours there was no ring on the hotel telephone. After the midnight count in the Atlanta prison, number 80016-A was taken from his cell, told to dress, given his commitment papers and, in in the company of Earl Peck, driven to the airport. The Delta jet left Atlanta at two in the morning; by half past five, Peck and his charge arrived at the federal detention house on West Street, New York. The prisoner was hidden away and orders were given that no one who had seen him or known him in the past was to be allowed out of the prison.

Wilkinson waited in his hotel room. Peck arrived just before sunrise and reported that everything had gone according to schedule. Throughout Wednesday, everyone waited. Phone calls came in. The men who called identified themselves by first names and last initials; Wilkinson double-checked by calling back before he got into a conversation. A time was set for departure; a call came through with an order to hold. On Thursday morning, Wilkinson and Alldredge went to the Public Health Service for inoculations against smallpox and typhoid. By Thursday afternoon, they were given the order to go.

They drove up 11th Street on the West Side. Wilkinson got out of his car and went up to the man waiting on the street.

"Are you ready to make a little trip?" he asked.

"Yes."

Noah Alldredge went to the detention center and picked up a package of firearms and handcuffs. The first car pulled away with Wilkinson, the big "package," and two people described as "government agency men." A car full of agency men went in front; another, with Alldredge and the smaller "package," behind. They crossed into New Jersey. Inside the middle car, Abel talked with Wilkinson and ignored the government agency men, one of whom spoke Russian and had been around before; Abel never liked him. For an hour and a half they drove. Abel told Wilkinson, "You're doing a good job in Atlanta, but you still have people suffering whom the authorities don't pay any attention to." Wilkinson, as always, thought that Abel's largest intellectual drawback, as it emerged in the many conversations like they had had, was that he could not measure progress. On the drive through New Jersey the conversation went easily and Abel began pointing out towns he knew along the way. At Bordentown, the cavalcade turned and Abel said that he had been there. But he had not been at the McGuire Air Force Base, which was their destination. The cars stopped; Abel and Wilkinson and the agency men and Alldredge were transferred to a station wagon and driven about a mile and a half down a runway, right up to the steps of a waiting plane.

The party boarded the plane, Abel's two brown suitcases, the luggage and equipment for the rest of the party, the plane's crew and pilot who had not been told where they were going. The plane belonged, Wilkinson said, to a general; it was a big Super-Constellation transport with eight seats, a kitchen, and lots of room to move around. Inside, settled, they waited, the curtains drawn, until six o'clock in the evening. Once the plane was airborne, someone went up to tell the pilot that he was flying a confidential mission; he was not told whom he was carrying. The "package," Abel, ate a good dinner and talked to Wilkinson for about two hours. More talk about the prison system. It was understood where Abel was going and when Wilkinson finally asked, outright, what he'd find waiting for him, Abel said, "I think I'll be all right."

Part of the procedure was a list of precautions against suicide—Abel was allowed to carry no sharp objects, he was never left alone, he was closely watched. Wilkinson said he "didn't feel in my heart that suicide was possible for him," but he followed the precautions. "Could be he was not in good standing in Russia," he said. They had to be careful.

The plane traveled across the ocean at a steady speed of 350-375 miles an hour and Abel spent the night sleeping restlessly. No one got much sleep. The plane landed at Wiesbaden, Germany, just after six in the morning. There was trouble with the radio. A conference was held to solve the problem of getting a repairman on board to fix the radio without letting him see Abel. Miraculously, there had not been a single news leak about any of these activities and the agency in charge was not about to risk one for the sake of a radio. Finally, simply, the curtains were pulled around the passengers' seats, Abel safely hidden inside, and the repairman allowed on board. The radio was replaced and, two hours after putting down, the plane was in the air again, negotiating the Berlin Corridor. Two additional passengers had come aboard at Wiesbaden: a doctor who was to examine Francis Gary Powers and a pilot who, Wilkinson later found out, was a friend of Powers, brought along to make the identification. It took two and a half hours to fly through the corridor and the plane was surrounded by MIGs which, Wilkinson said, "came out to look us over."

Just before three in the afternoon, Berlin time, the plane landed at Templehof Air Base, Berlin. The provost marshal was there and one of his staff cars backed up to the plane; Wilkinson, Abel, and companions got straight off the plane and into the car. They were driven to the United States Army Base; Abel's cell was examined and found satisfactory, his clothes were removed and Abel was left in a pair of pajamas without a string (suicide precautions) and with two men who took turns standing four-hour watches over him. Wilkinson and Alldredge were driven to an empty house where, as Wilkinson put it, "we slept as much as we could."

At seven the next morning, a bitter cold, sleeting morning, Saturday, February 10, Wilkinson and Alldredge returned to the army base. Only then had the point of exchange been fixed: the Gleinicker Bridge, formerly a route to the resorts around Potsdam, by 1962 closed to all but Allied traffic. It had been renamed the Bridge of Unity by the Communists. At the base, last-minute conferences and arrangements—Wilkinson was to participate in the actual exchange, along with Allan Lightner, chief of the United States Mission to Berlin, and James Donovan, who had acted all along as the unofficial representative of the United States government. They met in the morning, had their conference over coffee, and Donovan left for his last talk with Colonel Abel.

The party moved out at half past seven, Abel riding in a car with Wilkinson, nervous. The convoy again consisted of three cars, this time three small German-made ones. As they drove the twenty miles from the compound to the bridge, Abel began talking to the CIA man who had been along through the entire trip. Wilkinson was too tense to listen closely, but the other two were talking about "philosophies of government," he said, and Colonel Abel got so angry and heated that the two men had to be separated. Out the car windows you could see, as you rode along the border between West and East, barbed wire and police with binoculars. Both Donovan and Wilkinson were struck by the youth of most of the border guards they saw. The cars drove by more wire, more guards.

"Rudy," said Wilkinson. He hesitated. "Do you *want* to go back to that sort of thing?"

Abel looked out the window. "I won't have that sort of thing." Silence. Then, again, "I don't think it will disturb me." And the conversation went no further.

It was eight o'clock when the party arrived at the bridge. The supporting players were dropped off and the men who were to take part in the exchange drove up to the end of the bridge and got out: Abel, Wilkinson, Donovan, Lightner. An agency man was to have accompanied them, but as the car drew up its driver, a "goon," as Wilkinson called him, muscled the other man out of the way. The agency man was "too fine a person to make a scene," so the goon marched behind the exchange party and someone was excluded from his moment in history.

Were it not for the excruciating tension in the air, the movements made in the next few minutes would have looked very much like some formal dance—a minuet perhaps. Slowly, from each end of the five-hundred-foot steel span, a trio stepped forward. They detached themselves from the huddle of officials and United States Military Police and parked cars and walked toward the middle of the bridge—Lightner, Donovan, and someone who would identify Gary Powers. Slowly. Like the climax of *High Noon*, except there were no ballads playing in the background to propel the action along. Eyes on each end of the bridge focused on the trios marching forward; in the cold air you could see your breath smoking as you exhaled and you were surprised because you thought you were holding it. In the center of the bridge, each side stopped. Hands were shaken, solemnly, and again from each end of the span, a second trio stepped out. This one included the "package," Colonel Abel, Wilkinson, and the goon who had muscled his way in.

"At first," Wilkinson said, "we were a little formal. It was one of the most tense times in the whole project." Wilkinson was armed. When he reached the halfway point, he shook hands with the man in charge for the other side, a man called Schischkin—a big Russian, six feet four, who, Wilkinson said had "a great sense of humor" and Donovan said was "chief of the KGB in Western Europe," hiding behind the title of "Second Secretary of the Soviet Embassy in East Germany." Whoever Schischkin was, he was the man in charge on the bridge.

Schischkin announced that all prearranged conditions had been met. Frederic Pryor, an American student who had been held by the East Germans since August 25, 1961, accused of "economic espionage," had been released by the East Germans at Checkpoint Charlie. The exchange of Powers for Abel could take place. Confirmation of Pryor's release was called for. No, said the voices from the Allied side of the bridge, it had not yet come. Everyone waited.

Identifications were made on each side. The Russian who had come to identify Abel asked the colonel to remove his glasses. He did. A wave signaled that it was indeed Rudoph Ivanovich Abel. Powers's friend signaled the same. Still, they waited for word of Pryor. Powers and Abel changed sides on the bridge; there was a little "byplay," Wilkinson said, and joking as they waited. One of the Russians pointed to Wilkinson's hat, an American version of a Tyrolean hat with feathers. Wilkinson asked Abel to translate for him, to tell the Russian that he was willing to trade his feathered hat for the Russian's fur turban. Abel translated. The Russian nodded and reached for the hat.

"Nix, nox," said one of the Russian officials standing there. He scowled.

Someone shouted that Pryor had been released. The hat trade was never made. Wilkinson turned to business, drawing from his pocket the official pardon for Colonel Abel, signed by Attorney General Robert Kennedy and President of the United States John F. Kennedy. The document commuted Colonel Abel's sentence provided that he never reenter the United States. Wilkinson wrote the date and time of the release on the paper and handed it to Abel who took it, saying, "I'll keep this as a sort of diploma."

Abel shook hands all around and picked up his suit-cases. Powers lifted his and began to walk. Donovan, Wilkinson, Lightner, and the mysterious guard came back to their own side of the bridge and climbed into the wait-ing cars. It was nearly nine o'clock. As they pulled away, preparations were made to open the Bridge of Unity to morning traffic. No one looked back.

In the United States of America it was six hours earlier. There had been a party at the White House in Washing-ton, D.C., the night before, and it was still going on. Ste-phen and Jean Smith, President Kennedy's brother-in-law and sister, were the guests of honor; the Smiths were leav-ing Washington for New York and this presidential gala was one of the many farewells they had that week. Out-side, the lawns of the White House were drifted with snow. Inside, Lester Lanin and his orchestra were making music in the Blue Room and drinks were flowing in the Red Room. Around two in the morning, one of the guests noticed the party thinning out. Pierre Salinger had gone. Then McGeorge Bundy, Arthur Schlesinger, Jr., and Theodore Sorenson disappeared. The guest watched them go. He went to ask Kennedy if the evening were over.

"It's nothing," the President answered. "They're just letting Powers go."

The music continued and the guest had another drink.

In the Press Room, at three o'clock in the morning, Pierre Salinger announced that the U-2 pilot Francis Gary Powers had been released and turned over to Amer-ican authorities in Berlin and that President Kennedy had commuted the sentence of Russian spy Rudolph Ivan-ovich Abel, who had been returned to the Soviet Union.

THIRTEEN

THE spy came in and got a cold shoulder. Officially, the Soviet government had no spies and had never heard of the man called Rudolph Abel. That line persisted from the time of his trial in the United States until well after his exchange for Powers. But a few days after Abel's return to the Soviet Union, a peculiar letter appeared in the newspaper *Izvestia*:*

Esteemed Comrade Editor:

We, Helen and Lydia Abel, Rudolph Abel's wife and daughter, ask that our letter be published in your newspaper so that the whole public of the Soviet Union may know about the humane act of the Soviet government.

Our husband and father Rudolph Abel, while in the United States of America in 1957, was arrested without grounds upon the denunciation of a swindler and *provocateur*, accused of antistate crimes for allegedly performing intelligence work for the Soviet Union and illegally sentenced to thirty years of hard labour.

All of our numerous appeals, including appeals to the President of the United States, for the pardon of our dear father and husband who was sentenced even though he was innocent, failed to yield any positive results.

We then addressed ourselves to the Soviet government and established contact with the relatives of F. Powers, who was sentenced in the U.S.S.R.; they in turn addressed themselves to the Soviet government with a request for his pardon and asked the U.S. government to help them in every possible way.

The Soviet authorities took a sympathetic view of our request. As is known, F. Powers was released. Feb-

* *Izvestia*, February 23, 1962, p. 4. Translated by George J. A. Murray, Jr.

ruary 10, 1962, was a holiday for us as well. On this day the American government returned our father and husband to our family.

. With all our hearts, we thank the Soviet government and its chief, N.S. Khrushchev, personally for their human magnanimity.

H. Abel and L. Abel.

The letter was deliberately personal. It carefully skirted saying that Abel had been released in exchange for Powers by an agreement between the two countries. It insisted on the innocence of "dear father and husband" and was the last to be heard of Rudolph Abel, colonel or private citizen, for three years.

In the interim, the spy game changed. Washington's fumble over Gary Powers and his U-2 and the subsequent admission that our country was engaged in active spying and would continue to be so, set the tone. At the very least, by the 1960s everyone knew that the United States recruited, trained, and sent into the field a great many secret agents. Some of the mystery and some of the taint disappeared from the spy profession. It came of age and went respectable. Spies in their old school ties were part of the national defense.

By 1964, spies were much in the news. *The Invisible Government*—"the most extensive and revealing study of our intelligence and espionage system that has ever appeared in print"*—pinned the CIA wriggling on the wall of public scrutiny. Spies, both real and imagined, sold books and kept audiences at their television sets or on movie theater lines. The Cult of the Spy had once been primitive; it had its few chiefs and hordes of underlings, its sacred mysteries, venerable relics, and obscure rituals. Bizarre and unfathomable. But that was before. With a barrage of information about spies, things were changed. The more we knew the less interesting it was. The cult, photographed at close range, translated and popularized, lost its distinction. Spies became Everyman and worried about losing their jobs, their wives, their hair. Just like you and me. No wonder the spy finally came in from the cold sneezing and shrugged his shoulders.

Colonel Abel remained interesting, even became more

* *New York Herald Tribune.*

interesting because he was gone. Set against the two currents of spy thinking in the 1960s—spy as James Bond, unbelievable, or spy as Alec Leamis, too believable—the dim colonel grew more puzzling. *There* was a real spy; who *was* he? Hindsight diminished his importance— "Abel, I believe did not direct the entire Soviet espionage network in North America, but he was an important cog in their 'illegal' network here," said Allen Dulles. "There seems little or no evidence against him of important espionage," said *Newsweek*. Both statements seven years after his hullabalooed trial and two years after his return to the Soviet Union.

At the beginning of May 1965, two things happened simultaneously: Gary Powers was awarded a medal by the CIA and Rudolph Abel reemerged. The Powers award was given minimal coverage in the American press and the pilot himself was kept out of the public eye. In Moscow, just the opposite was done with Abel. There began a thaw in the Soviets' talk about their own espionage agents and an inundation of information about Rudolph Abel. First, in May, an unidentified general appeared on a Moscow television program talking about intelligence operators. Rudolph Abel, he said, had worked for Soviet state security since 1927; contrary to previous disclaimers, he *had* been exchanged for Gary Powers. The Communist Party and the Soviet government, reported the unknown general, had decorated Colonel Abel for his feats. Abel was reported living in Moscow.

A new propaganda war was under way. Our Spy Is Better Than Your Spy. Our Spy Fooled Your Counter-Spies. Something the Soviets had always been good at. The Soviet decision to award their secret agents the Order of Lenin or the supreme Hero of the Soviet Union, and the subsequent effort to glorify and glamorize those agents brought Rudolph Abel on stage again. In February 1966, on the same day that Soviet writers Andrei Sinyavsky and Yuli Daniel received jail sentences for their antistate activities and touched off protests around the world, *Molodoi Kommunist* (*Young Communist*) printed an interview with Colonel Abel. The magazine article introduced Abel to Soviet readers as a man who had worked for the Soviet intelligence service for more than thirty years. His decorations included "the Order of Lenin, two Orders of the Red Banner, the Order of the Red Banner of Labour, and several medals." James Donovan was quoted lauding Abel's accomplishments—"a patriot who has served his country carrying out exceptionally risky military assignments"—including his knowledge of the American idiom, five other languages, chemistry, nuclear physics and electronics, music, painting, mathematics, and ciphers.

Abel, speaking in the interview, "warned that for obvious reasons he must omit certain details. But those facts he gave are correct. 'I prefer omission to distortion,' he said."

The facts are not correct, either. The article is filled with details that serve the interests of the Soviet state—criticism of the McAllen detention center: the bleakness of Abel's cell, the boredom, unrest, and meaningless work of the guards there; the continued harassment of poor Mexican workers who cross into the United States in desperate search of a living wage. He says that FBI agents burst into his room at the Hotel Latham before he had a chance to open the door. He says that the night before his arrest he had contacted Moscow and was worried, with the FBI in his hotel room, about getting rid of his code: "I got rid of the code quite easily. It was small, so I hid it in my hand and said I wanted to go to the bathroom. There, under the 'watchful' eye of one of the agents, I dropped it in the toilet and flushed it down the drain." He says, too, that he was "interrogated" at McAllen for six weeks and then, "on my insistent demand" the arrest was "made official in accordance with United States procedural rules" and he was transferred to New York and given a trial.

The McAllen details are in tone and substance the kind of propaganda you read daily in the Soviet press. The description of his arrest is overdone: Abel opened the door to his hotel room, was more distracted than he allows, and spent less time talking with the FBI. He did not get rid of his code, for FBI agents found the tiny one-time cipher pad hidden in a sanding block and produced it at his trial. Finally, his removal from McAllen to New York and the decision to put him on trial was by no means made at Colonel Abel's insistence. On the contrary, if he was insistent about anything at McAllen, it was that he be quickly deported to the Soviet Union.

That he fooled the FBI and destroyed evidence under

their very noses became one of the repeated notes in the continuing Soviet releases about Abel. There was the code that he flushed down the toilet. There was also a radiogram that, Abel said, he had received from headquarters the night before and:

In my paintbox (I liked to paint) there was some paint left on my palette and I took the sheet containing the text of the radiogram from under the stack of paper and began to scrape off the paint onto it. When the pallette was quite clean, I crumpled the paper and sent it down the toilet after the code. I was, of course, very sorry that I could not do the same thing with the other papers, but the success I had had with the radiogram and the code buoyed my spirits considerably.

Abel said, too, that he destroyed two microfilms hidden in his tie clasp: one on the way to INS headquarters—"a strip of thin film with the text of a report on a very important matter"—that he dropped to the floor of the car and another, as he was being questioned and guarded at the INS building. There, he said, he talked with one of his guards about ways of fighting juvenile delinquency and "meanwhile, I checked my tie pin once again and discovered that the overzealous official [who had examined the tie clasp] had lost another bit of evidence."

In March 1966, Abel appeared at the Moscow press club and repeated this story. To it he added, "I was not the great master spy they made me out to be. I was only the radio operator. I was no second Sorge. The man who really masterminded the Soviet espionage network in the United States is still going strong." In April, Abel spoke on Moscow radio, repeating his story about duping the FBI. The Soviet press gave a lot of space to those stories. So did the American press. Eventually, the FBI answered: "Abandoning its earlier 'no comment' stand, the agency said that Abel was 'apparently attempting to vindicate himself in the eyes of his Red bosses by false, boastful statements,' " reported *The New York Times*.

Slowly, there began to filter from behind the propaganda a man. Lurking behind all the identities he had used in his career, lurking behind the Soviet news stories about him, the puppeteer who had pulled all the strings, was the man known as Abel. But, exposed and revealed, masks torn away, Abel remained a mystery. Nearly a decade after his return home, Abel remains a mystery. The simplest facts are still missing, in spite of a great deal of information pouring forth. Abel's life before he arrived in Quebec one fall day in 1948 is still unknown. Not only to the public, but to the government that captured and tried him and, with all their files and manpower and agents and defectors, is still trying to find out who he is. And what he did.

Who was he? There are statements on record about his birth, family, education, and career. Many statements. Second-hand, made by people who are guessing or lying or repeating what they have read elsewhere. After his capture, on trial and in custody, Abel said only what he needed to say. He did not, understandably, testify at his trial; he never spoke with reporters. To the attorneys who defended him Abel was cordial, but when it came to questions of background he replied only to those he thought relevant. All that was relevant, at the time, was that he was a Russian national illegally in this country who had committed certain acts that were judged conspiratorial and violations of the internal security of the United States. The rest, sadly, was not relevant.

What we know about Rudolph Abel's life is pieces, and they do not fit together. He said, consistently, that he was born on July 2, 1902. A fact perhaps. He told his attorney James Donovan that he came from "a proud family, prominent in Russia before the Revolution." At his deportation hearing before INS officials in Texas, Abel said that he had been born in Moscow. In the Soviet press, almost a decade later, he put his place of birth as St. Petersburg. The rest of the official Soviet biography of Rudolph Abel conforms to that government's present attitudes about what kind of life makes a good citizen of the Soviet state. Abel or his ghostwriter told it this way in one version:

I was born in St. Petersburg. My father was a factory worker. He and his friends were connected with revolutionary minded students and belonged to a circle of the League of Struggle for the Emancipation of the Working Class. This group, it will be recalled, was led by V. I. Lenin.

When the Czarist government arrested the group's members, my father was exiled to Archangel Gubernia and subsequently transferred to Saratov Gubernia, where he lived under police surveillance and where he met my mother.

That part of the story, aside from the proper "revolutionary" background, is something else that Abel was consistent about. He had told the INS investigators that his father (to whom he gave the absurd pseudonym of "Ivan Ivanovich Abel") had married a woman (Lubov Karneeva, Abel called her), who came from Saratov. Then Saratov it most likely was. That province of the Soviet Union and its capital city, also called Saratov, on the Volga River south of Moscow, east of Kiev, cultural center of the lower Volga region, has a population consisting of Russians, Ukrainians, and, before the Second World War, Germans. Much has been said about Colonel Abel's work in Germany during the war and the possibility has been raised that he was of German parentage. It seems a good possibility.

The Soviet-authorized version of Rudolph Abel's early years continues:

... Unending police persecution forced my father to move constantly, and we went with him from place to place.

All this naturally told on the development of my world outlook. I sympathized fully with my father and his friends, and helped them to distribute Bolshevik literature whenever I could. I was too young to do anything more serious.

In the early years after the 1917 Revolution, I worked among young political emigrés who had returned home. This not only helped me learn foreign languages, but subsequently played an instrumental role in the choice of my career.

In the McAllen detention center, Abel had told his questioners that during those years after the Revolution he had attended primary and secondary schools in Moscow.

Abel's story in Soviet publications of what he did between 1922 and 1926 traces his enrollment in the Young Communist League, his work as an "agitator," his struggle against Trotskyites "for influence among the young people," his army service in the radio engineering corps, and his demobilization in 1926. In that story, there is a touch of the man some people knew as Emil Goldfus:

Many of us were radio hams in our spare time. Those were the years of the crystal set and spark transmitter, as radio telephony was only in its infancy then. Young people today will find it hard to imagine how inventive radio amateurs were at that time. We got wire for our coils from discarded doorbells. We hunted for crystals in rocks and geological collections. Our capacitors were of innumerable odd shapes and sizes. I remember how in 1923 I once managed to dig up an R-5 tube, which took an incredible amount of electricity to heat up. We had to improvise no end to make the wet cells feed this tube. It glowed like a good burner when it was working.

Rudolph Abel must have written that paragraph himself. It reminds you of Emil Goldfus's skill at electronic repair and invention. It sounds like the man who stood his radio on end to make it work right and who said, "Whatever one fool can do, another can."

His official biography continues with a description of a moment of crisis after his demobilization. Abel had to decide on a career:

I received two offers, one from a research institute and the other from the foreign department of UGPU. I was attracted both by radio engineering and the adventure of secret service work. My comrades insisted that I must use my knowledge of foreign languages in the service of my country. Finally, I made my choice, and on May 2, 1927, I joined the Soviet intelligence service.

Abel's own chronology ends there. Whatever happened after his enlistment as an intelligence agent in 1927, the Soviets have not chosen to have him reveal it. Others have, however. Gordon Lonsdale, convicted by the British in 1961 for espionage activities and exchanged in 1964 for Greville Wynne, an English businessman who had been the channel for bringing Soviet Colonel Oleg Penkovsky's information to the West, published his memoirs in 1965.* Lonsdale's book is regarded as unreliable but it does indicate what the Soviets wanted known about their spies, particularly Lonsdale and Abel, that year. Lonsdale tells a fantastic story about being captured by the Germans outside Minsk in 1943 and taken to a command post where an officer of the Abwehr, German Army Intelligence, questioned him and recruited him to work for the Germans behind the lines of the Red Army. The Abwehr officer turned out to be a Russian agent who had been planted in Germany and infiltrated the Abwehr. That was Rudolph Abel but, Lonsdale says, he knew him then only by his code name, Alec. Lonsdale worked as Alec's radio operator. Alec was "quiet, somewhat elderly"; he "easily lost himself in any crowd." Lonsdale admired his self-control and tenacity. Alec's interests, according to Lonsdale, were science and art. His knowledge was encyclopedic and he was clever with his hands.

An article in *Pravda* commemorating the "Great Patriotic War" repeats this assertion about Rudolph Abel's service in Germany:

> On the eve of the great victory holiday (V.E. Day), one cannot fail to express special appreciation and profound gratitude to the valiant Soviet intelligence agents who, like Hero of the Soviet Union Richard Sorge or the agent known by the name of Rudolph Abel, performed difficult but honorable tasks in the struggle against the enemy. This was truly labor demanding great mental effort, audacity, determination, boundless love and loyalty to the homeland. The time has not yet come when the names of all these intrepid people can be mentioned, but history will be as generous to them as they rightfully deserve. After all, it is to their selflessness, their extremely difficult service in complex conditions—far from homeland, family, and friends—that we are indebted for the disclosure of Hitlerite Germany's insidious plans not only against the Soviet Union, but also against those who entered the coalition against Hitler.†

* Gordon Lonsdale, *Spy: Twenty Years in the Soviet Secret Service* (London: Spearman, 1965).

† V. Semichastny, Chairman of the USSR Council of Ministers' State Security Committee, "Soviet Chekists in the Great Patriotic War," *Pravda,* May 7, 1965, p. 4.

Then comes the period of mystery in the life and times of Colonel Rudolph Abel. He arrived in the United States in 1949; he was arrested in 1957. For eight years he did his work here. But *what* work? As the Soviet government continued to unveil their Master Spy Abel these last years, the expectation was that they would reveal or invent something about Abel's mission in the United States. That revelation would certainly not lead to the truth, but it would go somewhere. It would tell us what the Soviets want the West to think about Abel's accomplishments. It never came.

In the memoirs, the television program, the radio talk, and a recent film in which Abel appears, seated behind a desk, to introduce the film story of Gordon Lonsdale's spy career, there is not a word about what Abel accomplished. Unlike the talk of heroic accomplishment that accompanied the public presentation of Sorge, Lonsdale, Burgess, Maclean, and Philby, not a word about Abel's spying. Nothing about what he was assigned to do, what he had access to, how successful he was. Abel talks in his own voice in those propaganda pieces about intelligence work in general:

> Everyone knows that an intelligence man has to operate in hostile surroundings, running constant risks. He must be erudite, have a broad outlook, and a knowledge of foreign languages.
>
> Intelligence work is not a series of riproaring adventures on an entertaining trip abroad. It is above all hard and painstaking work, demanding intense effort, perseverance, stamina, will power, knowledge, and great skill.

Skill at what? We know that Abel was skillful at remaining undetected for nine years; we know that he hid his identity. We know about his mechanical skill—all those hollow containers; all his lectures to Hayhanen about soft film and codes. He was skillful at playing his role: the right look, the right accent, the right personality. But, beyond that, what use were his skills to the KGB? What did he get those nine years?

The question—and it is the first one asked by those who know Abel's story—is based on the assumption that

spies get information and that the information is important. That the espionage networks spread out by both
sides in the Cold War give some return for the money that
goes to support them. That spies *do* something and that
what they do helps their side in the war and that the
whole business of spying—the financial cost, the training,
the dedication, and the personal price some men must pay
to themselves—is *for* something.

It may not be. Persuasive arguments have been put
forth that pick the spy game down to its wasteful, sterile,
and miserable bones:

> The spies, it seems, are like the nuclear deterrent,
> simply engaged in canceling each other out. In the last
> resort, the espionage establishment . . . has exactly the
> same aim as any other establishment: jobs for the
> Boys. Spying pays high salaries and gives an illusory
> self-esteem to its operators. For those outside the game,
> it does no good and some harm.
>
> In wartime there may be some use for spies, though
> even this is doubtful. Intelligence services studying
> public information probably arrive at better results than
> are produced by secret agents. . . .
>
> The whole set-up is a great waste of money and con-
> ceivably of ability.*

No crank argument that, no silly gadfly Mr. Taylor.
Nor John Le Carré:

> . . . there is no victory and no virtue in the Cold War,
> only a condition of human illness and a political mis-
> ery. †

Nor the hosts of journalists, or former members of the
American or British secret services whose plaint has been
loud this last decade in opposing the myth created by the
KGB, from whom we expect myths, and the CIA, from
whom we are learning to expect them—the myth that se-

* A. J. P. Taylor, "Bogey Man," *The New York Review of
Books,* December 7, 1967.

† John Le Carré, "To Russia, With Greetings," *Encounter,*
May 1966.

cret intelligence is *for* something, whoever is made to suffer, whatever the cost.*

Turn all this on the story of Rudolph Abel. Our press and our government called him the biggest spy ever caught. Master Spy. Yet it is more than possible that Abel never got a piece of secret information. Information, yes; but secret, or valuable, no. Intelligence work depends on getting all kinds of information; anything, everything counts. Hayhanen told that to the jury at Abel's trial. Although *The Spy Who Came in from the Cold* is fiction, what it reveals about intelligence in the Cold War is not. In that novel, British agent Alec Leamis, who appears to have defected, is being interrogated by an East German intelligence officer:

> There are, as you know, two stages in the interrogation of a defector. The first stage in your case is nearly complete: you have told us all that we can reasonably record. You have not told us whether your Service favors pins or paper clips because we haven't asked you, and because you did not consider that answer worth volunteering. There is a process on both sides of unconscious selection. Now it is always possible—and this is the worrying thing, Leamis—it is always entirely possible that in a month or two we shall unexpectedly and quite desperately need to know about the pins and paper clips.

Perhaps Rudolph Abel was assigned to the United States, given a code and a series of hiding places for secret messages, sent an assistant who bumbled so badly he eventually brought Abel down with him, lived in danger, endured behind his mask—all for the purpose of finding out about pins or paper clips.

* For example: In the history of nations the influence of spying had been generally exaggerated. It is true that the secret services of states have played exciting underhand roles throughout modern history. But their clandestine activities were seldom formative or decisive: what most of the dramatic achievements of secret agents amount to is the gathering of precious fragments that may or may not confirm, but that do not formulate, already existing diplomatic and strategic policies.
John Lukacs, *A History of the Cold War* (New York: Doubleday & Company, 1962), p. 178.

That is what white espionage is all about.* Agents are sent out to report on everything they can. If Rudolph Abel had special access to secret information himself or had recruited agents with such information, something of that would have leaked out by now. No, it is more likely that he read *The New York Times* and rode the subways and read *Scientific American* and used his skill—his ability to interpret and select, his thirty-year knowledge of what his superiors in Moscow would consider good intelligence—to pack all that stuff into microdotted messages and speed it to KGB headquarters in Moscow. In terms of what might change the course of history—as far as *anyone* knows—Abel was a minor figure. As most spies are.

And the man, Abel, the man who did all this, whatever it was—who was that man? Watch the newspapers as the Soviets continue to bring Abel out in the open. Look at his face as he appears in a film. Sympathetic. Someone you might want to know. Perhaps have dinner with. Talk about painting with. Listen to as he plays the guitar. The more you look, the more you learn about him, the less you know.

If you believe the Soviet reports, Abel is all over the globe. Sometimes he lives in retirement in Moscow playing his guitar and painting. Sometimes he is teaching espionage trainees at one of the mysterious KGB schools. Once he was said to have gone to Saigon and once to be

* "The collection of foreign intelligence is accomplished in a variety of ways," Allen Dulles wrote in *The Craft of Intelligence* (New York: Harper & Row, 1963), "not all of them either mysterious or secret. This is particularly true of overt intelligence, which is information derived from newspapers, books, learned and technical publications, official reports of government proceedings, radio and television. . . . In countries that are free, where the press is free and the publication of political and scientific information is not hampered by the government, the collection of overt intelligence is of particular value. . . . Since we are that kind of country ourselves, we are subject to that kind of collection. The Soviets pick up some of their most valuable information about us from our publications, particularly from our technical and scientific journals. . . ."

This collection of overt intelligence is also known as white espionage.

stationed in Leipzig as liaison officer between Soviet intelligence and the East German High Command.

He remains masked. The more exposure he gets in public the more the list of identities extends. Rudolph Abel is a pseudonym. The man behind that pseudonym is also: Mark; Martin Collins; Emil Goldfus; Milton; Master Spy Trapped by the FBI; The Accused; The Prisoner; The Man Traded for Gary Powers; The Invisible Man; The Invisible Man Made Visible; Star of Radio, Television, and the Silver Screen; Memoir Writer; Wearer of the Order of Lenin; Propagandist; Hero. Pieces of a puzzle.

EPILOGUE

On the first of September 1967, Burt and I arrived in Moscow looking for Rudolph Abel. By evening we were ensconced at the Hotel National—a place known in the "old days" as the center of spy activity in the capital because the building next to it was the American Embassy. The embassy has since moved, but the shadow—or glitter—of intrigue remains with the National. There we settled ourselves, had a grim meal in the dining room (face to face with the Kremlin), and in the morning, began.

We had two solid leads: the Novosti press bureau, whose job it is to deal with journalists from the West; and a man called Victor, whose job is ambiguous. Victor's name had been insistently put to us as we slogged about offices in the United States asking who might help arrange an interview with Colonel Abel. Victor was then being described in the American papers as an agent of the KGB. Most people whom we respected thought of him as an unofficial mouthpiece through whom the Soviet government releases information for which they wish no official responsibility; his own posture is that he is an independent operator, entrepreneur-businessman-journalist, with good connections in high places.

Novosti first that Saturday, because we knew where it was. Pushkinskaya Ploschad, past a statue of the poet himself we went, through throngs of people, going there on foot because we wanted to see part of the city and the distance, according to the map we had purchased from Intourist, was short. It turned out to be a great distance. We walked and walked, cursing the map. (Later an "old Moscow hand" joked that the maps were deliberately misleading, thereby discouraging potential espionage agents from finding anything in Moscow.) We arrived, exhausted, at Pushkin Square and found the Novosti building. Inside, the first bit of style we had seen: a receptionist behind her desk, bedecked with mascara, lipstick, a

1950s teased hairdo. To this lady we presented ourselves
and said with assurance that Novosti knew all about our
request, for we had written explaining our mission.

To whom, she asked, had we written?

Yevgeny Ruzhnikov, director of the American Section,
we promptly said.

Yevgeny Ruzhnikov? He was gone.

"Oh?"

The man we now wanted to see was called Valery K.
Yuryev, she said.

Okay. Yuryev, then.

Yuryev appeared, smiling.

We learned that the detailed letter we had written explaining our mission to Moscow had either arrived or not
arrived. If it had arrived, it had either been discarded or
misplaced. Probably by Yuryev's predecessor. Himself,
he had never heard of us.

We were standing in the reception hall still, people
were coming and going with briefcases tucked under their
arms. We were waiting to be invited into Yuryev's office.

Having had a great deal of experience with Yuryev's
comrades in the United States—every official representing the Soviet Union in Washington or New York had behaved this way—we held our ground and told our story
again: Burt's friendship with Abel, known to him as Emil;
the book we were writing; the groundwork we had set
down back home; the request for an interview; the limitations we would respect about such an interview. By then,
the speech was coming out rote.

Yuryev smiled.

"But. Yes, but I don't understand what we at Novosti
can do for you."

We held our ground some more and told him: he could
help arrange an interview. Simple.

"Yes, but after all, Abel is in semiretirement now. You
know, he is leading a quiet life."

Yes, we knew.

"He is, ah, perhaps fishing."

So was Yuryev.

"Why don't you just call him on the telephone?"

"Why don't you . . ."

"In any case," he said—the meeting was about to end,
there in the reception hall, quite abruptly—"we shall

have to check on your original letter and I shall let you know tomorrow or Monday."

Sure.

Frustrated, enraged, we tried to cool off at a café. Grunted our order, then pointed at what we wanted, fumbled with the money, and were stared at. Then on toward Gorky Street.

Our plan was to find Victor. Like Colonel Abel, this Victor either was or was not in Moscow. Unlike Colonel Abel, though, we were sure he existed. To him we had three routes of access: a British newspaper for whom he was an occasional correspondent where we had left a message; an American business associate of Victor's who had been due to arrive in Moscow at the time we did and with whom we had spoken before leaving New York. Our third route was the direct one. Victor had a home just outside Moscow; we could simply telephone.

Burt spoke. The voice on the other end belonged to Victor's wife. Although the connection was barely audible, she seemed to be saying that Victor was, indeed, in Moscow; that he was on his way to meet his friend the American businessman at the Hotel Rossyia; he could be reached there.

Burt thanked her and hung up. One connection, mercifully, finally, made. We *had* it. Burt dropped another coin into the box and dialed the businessman's room. No answer.

We continued down Gorky Street, now beginning to slope toward the Kremlin, finding the next several booths occupied. Then an empty one. Coin, dial, ask for the room. No answer. Try the wife again.

Oh, said Victor's wife, she had just heard from him. He was on his way to meet the businessman in the lobby of the Hotel National instead. She told us to proceed there straightaway.

None of the faces in the hotel lobby looked right, none resembled the photographs we had seen. We caught our breaths, watched the people come and go, then decided that Victor might try to telephone. Burt went upstairs to his room to wait; I remained in the lobby. As he opened the door to his room, Burt had a brief vision of Victor and the businessman lounging inside, encircled by heavy Russian smoke. Instead, only the whiff of hotel cleanser.

Downstairs, I watched the circular front door; I watched
the house KGB man, planted next to a pillar, his hands
behind his back, watching the same door and watching
me watch him.

Upstairs, Burt went at the telephone again. This time,
the conection was very clear.

"Yes, of course, Mr. Silverman. He's definitely on the
way over to the National."

"What does his friend, this businessman, look like?"

"Oh, he is close to fifty," she said, "gray, close-cropped
hair. An uplifted head that always seems a bit nervous. . . . Yes, all right. Then you'll both be waiting in
the lobby?"

"Yes," Burt said.

"No, no bother."

She rang off. Burt shuttled back downstairs and reported. That gray-haired fellow, we remembered, we had
seen, we thought we had seen, coming into the lobby. He
had looked around, disappeared into the Intourist Bureau
office, reappeared, and left. More anxiety. Had we missed
him? Where was Victor? We sat down to wait. I pointed
out the house agent watching the lobby. We waited some
more. The agent watched Burt and Burt watched his
watch.

"I'm going to call again."

Through the National's front door, just then, came a
youngish man, tall, wearing a distinctly Western costume,
fashionably Western, likely French—raw silk sports
jacket, dark slacks, well-fitting (unlike every other pair on
the streets of Moscow), steel-rimmed glasses, and crown-
ing touch, a silk ascot. He came forward, paused, surveyed the lobby, and strode directly toward us.

"Mr. Silverman, I'm Victor."

We three walked out of the hotel. The day had been,
until then, warm and sunny, but there was a sudden spat-
tering of rain. Victor led us to his car, a maroon Merce-
des, parked halfway across the boulevard, and the rain
stopped as we climbed in.

"I have a rather interesting problem," Burt was saying.

"Yes, but you know, interesting problems are not always so easy."

We had not yet explained our mission. Victor obviously
knew all about it, yet we had to play the game. He listened and drove around to Moscow's newest hotel, the

Rossyia. From the crowd in the lobby emerged a dapper man with an unmistakable New York accent.

"Hi, everybody."

He seemed to know us, too. Still, Victor introduced us and we four rode to a suite high in the hotel, overlooking St. Basil's cathedral. The New Yorker poured some scotch and Victor began to complain to us about his travels in our country, the restrictions imposed upon him (he wanted to visit Las Vegas and Miami Beach and was denied permission to do so until he appealed somehow to Vice-President Hubert Humphrey who made it possible). He said, too, that the American press had vilified him, that he had been called a secret agent, that he had been accused of sponsoring Western-oriented artists who somehow soon landed in jails and of stealing plays from the West for royalty-less productions in Moscow.

On and on he went, while we sipped our scotch and looked interested, perhaps sympathetic.

"Well," said Victor. "I mean, if I'm an agent, why don't they just arrest me? I tell them that; why don't they put me on trial? Why couldn't I go to Las Vegas and Miami?"

We suggested that Victor write his own story and vindicate himself in the Western press. He seemed to like that idea. Burt mentioned our connections with a magazine in New York that wanted the Abel interview if we could get it and Victor warmed to the possibility that *we* might help *him* to get his own story published. We were noncommittal; by then we had learned the game, too.

On to our project. Burt drew from his manila folder of "documents," without which we never went anywhere, several brochures from shows of paintings and drawings he had had in New York (we had been conditioned, from the first days of our enterprise, to carry proof of our authenticity, whatever that was; no one in Moscow ever fully believed what we said we were; so we carried documents); Burt turned over to Victor a copy of an article he had written for *Esquire* magazine several years before, and the illustration, a painting of Abel, that went with it. He gave Victor, too, our written statement of intentions. Victor took them.

"Yes, but why do you come to me? After all, *I'm* still trying to see Kim Philby."

Another deal? Was Victor simply sharing the frustrations of being a working journalist with us, or was he asking our help again? We did not know. Again, we looked sympathetic.

"Why should I do anything if *The New York Times* says those things about me?"

And all the while he was putting our brochures and reprints and written statements away. He continued disclaiming and stuffing those things in his pocket, saying something about photostating them and getting them back to us, while we drained our drinks and took a last look at the view of St. Basil's. The American businessman was doing his own business by then, going over papers and making phone calls. He was cordial, but he left us to Victor. We rose and smiled and walked with Victor to the elevator, where he turned and, as though he had just thought of it, said, "Why don't you go to the Caucasus? Why don't you take a trip and have a good time?"

Hastily, both Burt and I tried to translate that remark. Victor had asked us, somewhere along the way, how we knew that Abel was in Moscow and we had said that we did not know for certain, but all indications were that he was. Victor had not contradicted that. Was this, then, this suggestion that we take a trip, his answer? By then we were taking everything said to us as coded information. Did Victor mean that our quest was fruitless and we might as well spend our money having a good time— which is what he said? Or was he privy to some information that our friend the colonel had himself gone south for a holiday? When we got back to the hotel, Burt and I explored that remark with all the Talmudic sensitivity we could muster. In the end, we dismissed it, and waited in Moscow.

We spent thirteen days in the capital of the Soviet Union. Victor remained our major hope—we called him our "contact man"—but we tried everything else we could think of, too. We began visiting some resident journalists in that city, people to whom we had been sent by people back home. A peculiar thing happened. We discovered, very quickly, that we were lepers. Except for one wire service correspondent and a textile-business Englishman whom we often met at dinner, no one trusted us. Americans seemed unable to decide whether we had been sent by the KGB or CIA. In either case, they wanted nothing to do with us. The correspondent for a major New York

City newspaper would not let his Russian wife be seen with me. The representative of an international airline, for whom I was writing a traveler's guide to Moscow, asked me to please disappear.

Russians, too, recoiled. On one of those days, someone told us that there had been a book about Colonel Abel published that year in Moscow. Oh yes, we said, could we see one? Well, the person who told us did not have one, but was willing to write out, in Russian, the question; we could then take the written message to Moscow's bookstores. We did. Each time, we would enter the bookstore, thrust forward what we hoped was a written request for Abel's book, and be stared at with incomprehension. We left. Eyes followed us.

Or did they? Everyone was behaving oddly; but so were we. We had noticed peculiar behavior on our own part long before we came to Moscow. At first we were two normal civilians making inquiry into a spy story. We thought facts were facts; that there were aspects of intelligence and Colonel Abel's case that we would never know, but that we would acknowledge that right from the beginning. We thought we had a footing. But, as we went along, we ran into a topsy-turvy world. We would ask simple questions, like— What is the name of the motel that Reino Hayhanen was taken to for his pretrial interview with counsel for the defense? Routine question, just a detail, just for the record. And we got answers that seemed to indicate we had uncovered a state secret. Got them about simple questions and more so about complicated ones: How did Reino Hayhanen die? The secrecy and evasiveness that clung to the people we had been meeting as we worked on our book were contagious. By the time we arrived in Moscow, we had caught the disease.

Our trip was a "mission." We shied away from introducing each other as "my collaborator." We carried that envelope of top-secret documents—brochures from Burt's painting shows and vague letters of introduction from people whose vagueness we interpreted as not wanting to be implicated in anything if we were caught. We had a code system with a magazine that wanted to buy the story of our interview with Colonel Abel: a telegram signed by Burt saying "send more yellow oil paint" meant our prospects did not look good; "more red paint" meant that they did. Minor symptoms; they grew worse.

The world we found in Moscow was scripted by Kafka (when it frightened us), Lewis Carroll (when it amused us), and Pirandello (when it did both). Our immersion in that world made us mad. Let it be said: confused about our own identities. We were not agents for CIA, KGB, or SMERSH. Or were we?

There was no way of knowing what was true and what was not. No yardstick for reality. Our decision to go looking for Abel was either stupid or whimsical or the only responsible thing a journalist could do. There was or was not a chance of seeing him. Victor could or could not help us. Someone was putting us on; we were putting ourselves on; we put them on. Or none of the above. Halfway through those thirteen days we realized that we did not know anything about what was happening to our quest and decided to stop trying to know.

In the interim, Victor told us that he was "working on it" and agreed to be postman for us if Burt wanted him to see if he could deliver a letter to Abel. Yes. Burt wrote the letter out and put it in the mail, although neither of us believed that anything moved through the Moscow mails. Victor had given an address in Moscow, although he lived in a *dacha* on the outskirts, explaining that the address he gave us was his "office" and correspondence was picked up there and brought out to him. It was no more ambiguous and peculiar than other arrangements we had made along the way, so we dropped the letter in a box and waited.

On Friday, Burt called to ask if the letter had been received.

"No," said Victor, "but maybe I get it this afternoon."

On Sunday we called Victor's *dacha* and got his English wife, who spoke as though we were old friends by now and asked why had we not come out to visit. Then she put Victor on the phone.

He was sullen.

"How are you?"

Pause.

"I still haven't gotten your letter."

Pause. We were not surprised.

"Now, Mister Silverman," he said, and I saw Burt stiffen, "why do you go around with stories about our meeting? I have had here a British reporter to ask me what is my motive to come seeking you out. This is not true, as you well know. I have wanted to help you if I could, but I don't see how under these circumstances."

Burt asked what Victor was talking about. What British reporter? The only reporter he had spoken to, Burt said, was an American from the Associated Press. And he hadn't mentioned Victor.

"I'm astonished. I tried to be discreet." Burt was sweating. I watched, trying to piece together the conversation from what I could hear, and it sounded ominous. "I don't know how this could have gotten out."

"Well," Victor said, "I'm telling you this just happened. I think this doesn't help you any. I'm sorry. I can't understand it. Besides, why did this man come to me for a story? I don't see why he was told I initiated our conversation. It is absolutely false. These things go on all the time."

"All I can say, Victor, is that I understand your feelings and I regret terribly this happened. But look," Burt said, and I watched him make a gesture of reaching out toward the space beyond the telephone.

"But, look—I'd like to see you—this phone has a terrible connection—can't we come out to talk?"

We couldn't come out to talk because Victor lived in an area tourists were not allowed to visit and to which there was no transportation. We agreed, instead, to be at our hotel the next morning. We searched our memories of those few days between our first cordial visit with Victor and this new rage of his. What the hell was he talking about? What British journalist? And then we found out that the young Englishman we had dined with and made evening tours with had decided, as he said when we confronted him, to "help us out" by asking a friend of his, a correspondent for a British newspaper, to put in a good word with Victor. Recriminations. Accusations. Suspicion that our good English friend was not a businessman at all. Much heaving of shoulders all around over the damage— and we were not quite sure of that either; perhaps Victor was having a temper tantrum and the unclear success we thought we enjoyed with him would not be destroyed.

Monday morning we were in our hotel room. Victor's wife called to say he could not see us. Undaunted, Burt composed his last letter to Colonel Abel and we made a long journey out to Victor's office address to deliver it ourselves. The letter said:

Dear Emil:

I am writing to you once again, this time from Moscow, and this time with almost no expectation that we can get together. (I hope you are aware that I have been trying to arrange a meeting for over a year, with no success.) This trip was a gamble. I hoped that some minor miracle would take place. Perhaps this is a measure of my naïveté. I now realize the enormous difficulty of such a reunion. As I said before, however, I'm sometimes pretty stubborn. There's some ego involved as well. I couldn't believe that friendship and human curiosity were not stronger than practicalities. But I see now that this was not even involved.

I have been in Moscow for ten days, and will probably leave this coming Thursday. Before going, and in the hope that this letter does get to you, I should like to tell you a few things more. First, about things long past. I'm sorry I didn't write to you in Atlanta. In defense of that, I can only say that they were different times, and I was not above fear. I was also counseled by what I thought were wiser heads. Hindsight, and a changed political climate, have made those decisions and that counsel seem excessively cautious or worse. Maybe the reason I'm here now is to make up for that.

The book about you will, I think, be a truthful and honest one. It will try to explain why you are remembered so clearly by many of the people you met. Certainly all my friends have that memory and think of you affectionately.

I hope that all of this will not cause you any difficulty. I must say that at some points along the way in the last year and a half, I've thought of giving up the project, but always came back to it because it seemed more pertinent than ever.

It is almost ten years to the day since your trial started back in Brooklyn. Many things have happened to all of us since then—to me, my friends Harvey and Dave, and to you as well. I had hoped to talk to you about all of it. I had also fantasized a trip we could have made to the Hermitage to talk about art and painting once again. I also thought we could talk about your feelings about America and the people you met there. Apparently, this is not to be. Some other time perhaps—when the two of us can meet simply as old friends.

I will not say good-bye, just *au revoir.*

Sincerely,
Burt Silverman

Our last conversation with Victor was on Wednesday, the day before our departure. We had not given up; we were willing, stubbornly willing, to stick it out beyond our scheduled return, if Victor would hold out a possibility. He did not. "I'm very sorry," he said. "Nothing can be done at this time."

At this time.

If not now, when? Victor had not slammed the door; what did that mean? We did not know any of the following: whether Victor was capable of arranging an interview; whether Victor had tried and been rebuffed or tried and been put off; whether Victor was honest with us; whether our friend the colonel was alive; or in Moscow; or ever existed.

Or ever existed. We left Moscow without having seen Colonel Abel, but having glimpsed our story. In that peculiar uncertainty about what was real that hounded us—from our arrival in Moscow to Victor's "nothing at this time"—we had our landscape. In our own escapade—the back-street meetings and the coded communications and the double-talk, double-think, double-faced operation of ourselves and the people we met—Victor; the United States Embassy staff; Soviet officials; the most experienced journalists in the Western world—we had our plot. In the parts of the puzzle, pieces that never coalesced, prisms of ourselves, other people's selves, we found Colonel Rudolph Abel. If he ever existed.

APPENDIX A

The following letter was written in Russian and translated by the government. It is dated "6th April":

My Dear:

I am writing a second letter. Up till now I only heard [from you] from the trip. I want very much to find out how are you? How is your health?

I am gradually beginning to come to myself. I am able to do some things around the house and am thinking about the summer home.

I could go for a rest but I am afraid to move alone, so that I have not yet decided, although I passed the medical board. How necessary you would be to me now. And how good it is that you do not yet feel the need of being with me?

Everything is the same with us. The children meanwhile live in friendship, and move around one after the other, when they are together.

Evelyn does not work steady yet, it takes a long time to process, but is doing translations at home and has a pupil.

Free time from her husband and work, she takes me to the doctor and at the same time she herself had a checkup. Spring here will again be late. Up till now, it has been cold, damp and snow. The winter was simply horrible, and I am worried about my flowers.

Evunya [diminutive for Evelyn?] says the plum trees froze, and it's hard to get to the pears.

Our acquaintance spent the winter at the summer home alone. It was very hard for her, and of course cold with such frosts, but she is feeling cheerful. She is sending you regards and wishes for an early return. Your father-in-law arrived long ago, he is well-established, and they are very pleased. He is now awaiting your earliest return, and I, although I know it is silly, I am counting off the days of the known period. Your gift—the dog feels very well and is fully accustomed to us. I have not received your package yet and for that reason am not going to thank you, since I do not know what will be there. A childhood friend visited us; he was here on business for a week, and every day when he was free he visited us. We talked a lot, reminisced, and most of all day dreamed. Don't let us down! It is not clear yet about the apartment. We are waiting . . . And in general, our whole life, constant waiting . . . That's the way it is my dear. My servant is leaving. I am seeking a new one, and I'm not especially sorry. Write often as possible. The children, there are two now, send greetings and all the best for you. 'Son' is very disturbed, what kind of an impression he will make on you; he might not appeal to you at once. I am ending now. I kiss you firmly. I wish you luck, health, and most of all a speedy return.

Elya.

Attached to that was another letter, this one in English:

Dear Papa,

I am very lonesome and await a letter from you. I married. My husband is an engineer in communications, the same as you he likes to fool around with the radio. He likes photography.

Now we are getting ready to make an electronic exposure meter for the automatic determination of exposure while printing. Write what you think of this. We want also to make a densitometer for color printing, but as yet we have not determined if two will be needed to determine the sharpness of color and for the determination of general sharpness—or whether one will do. Write!

My husband sends a big greeting and the best wishes. He wants very much to meet you as soon as he can. I also very much want that you will come soon.

I am getting set for a job in technical translation and review. Up till now I have not been approved and am sitting at home.

I await your letter and your arrival.

Our maid sends her greetings.

I kiss you firmly.

Your, Evelyn.

The next letter, also a translation from Russian, is dated 21 June.

My dear,

At last we received your small package. Everything pleased us very much and as usual whatever you do, successfully with care and attention. Thank you, my good one. We were also very glad to have received a letter from you and to learn that everything is fine with you. It is a pity that you have not had letters from us in such a long time. I sent you several. I think that you will receive them all. We congratulate you on your birthday. Remember, on this day we will drink a toast for your well-being and your early promised return. We are at the summer place. In this raw, in many respects, year, our garden has suffered. On the best apple trees, from which last year you called a plentiful harvest, only now have the leaves started to appear. The pears, plums, also barely coming to life and they certainly are not yet blooming. In this year I do very little in the garden and house, I feel very bad, I have no strength. I am still fighting with the house servant and do not have a new one. How sad that the hyacinths traveled so long and dried out very much. Nevertheless, I planted them and am waiting for next to find out if they died or not. Also, the daughter of our childhood friend is visiting with us. She entered the academy and passed to the second course with good marks. With her I will send a knife. Everyone very much wants to see you soon and to even kiss you a lot.

Herman—the husband of Ev, sits beside me and is drying my ink blotches. The television works. Our whole family sits around and watches, but I seldom look at it, I become very tired and my head starts to hurt. We put off for a while the plan for bigger gates, because the street is all upturned and it is difficult to approach in a car. I am now without a house servant, she left for a vacation. Still the same one. Although she does not satisfy me—she is very rude, but you can't find another. Our female winterer herself remodeled the room—some room—and it looks very good. She lives there during the summer time with her—our cat and two children of Syunul (ph). The dog—Carrie, who was given to you by the husband of my sister is with us. She is a wonderful creature with thoughtful eyes. She behaves very well and resembles our Spotty

in character. She too awaits her master, and I also wait.
It is desirable to have a husband at home, at the present
time I feel your absence much more, especially since I
have been with you, remember what you had promised
me before your departure. I am finishing writing. I kiss
you firmly and all of our relatives and friends also do so.
I wish you success and health. Our new chef is wonderful,
attentive and tactful so that you can be calm.

I kiss you.
Elya.

The next letter is undated and it is also a translation
from Russian:

My dear.
See again has begun our endless correspondence. I do
not like it so much, it would be better to sit down and to
talk. From the letter of Ev you know about our luck during your short absence. We arrived safely with the exception that the train bounced up and down and from side to
side so that our bodies for a long time couldn't come to
their balance. Now, I am no longer a traveler on this type
of transportation. You already for sure imagine my ab-
sentmindness and grief when I discovered the forgotten
lunch, and certainly this was my fault. It was necessary at
once to place it in my pocket. After your departure, I certainly was ill. There was a hardening of the arteries of the
heart or hypertension crisis. I was in bed relatively a
month and a half. Now I go and do a little but my nerves
are not fully recovered. I sleep poorly and do not go out
on the street. I walk on the balcony. It seems in this year
that I will not be able to do anything with the summer
home, although my children Evunya and Herman say that
they will help, but you know that they will be working
and of course tired. And yourself know what this is. My
pupil will play two new pieces. Sometimes I approach
your instrument and look at it and want to again hear
you play and I become sad. For the remaining money I
asked basically to have them send it all to you, just as we
talked. Daughter and I have everything except you. And
she after getting married always says there are no such
men as her papa and therefore she is not too much in
love with her husband. You are the best of all for us.
And don't frown, everyone says this who knows you. See

the enlightenment in life came out funny, isn't it true? Yes, with us it was also funny. I didn't move to the apartment quickly, and an error occurred. They showed one apartment, but gave another. One was more or less evenly priced ours then the last one lacked a lot. It is good that our chef was with me and I was ashamed to cry and hardly to suffer. So that the things remained packed. If you look at everything with a philosophical viewpoint, then, taking hair from your head doesn't pay, or in the future you have better luck, and in general in the apartment there will be a general clean-up. This is the worst and it is not so bad. To ask for and to talk about a new apartment, I am not going to do. Nevertheless, according to the new rules they can give you an equally priced one. This does not suit me and to go to a lesser one it is unnecessary. Especially effort for us to make an exception is not pleasant, and bothers our friends. Even so made an exception for us with the first apartment and gave us an apartment one and a half meters greater than ours. That is the funny stuff that occurred with us. Much ado about nothing. I am getting ready to go with my pupil to the North Sea and to rest and cure my heart, but I don't know how this will be. I am afraid to go alone and the little daughter is working. She got the job through her niece and her husband. She is very pleased with her work which pays well. Already she grieves that you are not here. Maybe tomorrow I will receive a letter from you. When I think about this my heart dies. I kiss you firmly and congratulate you. Try to arrange everything so that you do not delay the period of our meeting. Years and age will not wait for us.

Your Elya kisses you. Son and daughter and all your friends congratulate you and send you the best of everything.

Now the move to the new apartment will bring trouble and care. I asked for three rooms but didn't get them. My friend drove me over to look. The rooms by our estimation were smaller than ours but according to official data they must be larger by one meter. As soon as we receive permission to move we will once more go there to look and to measure everything. It would be necessary to discuss this matter with you. After, in the first place, where you were promised and it will not be suitable to go to the summer home. Such is the news with us. How are you there? How is your stomach? I think much about everything, that even Evunya's happiness does not make me happy. Take care of yourself. I want to live together with you for ourselves. The servant just as you figured is not old and although she left us she returned. It is very difficult for me without anyone now. Everything is very good at the summer place. Our old dweller is simply a hero and I am so grateful to her for everything. Well, I finished my dear. See what kind of letter I wrote, and most important, what I wanted to. I kiss you and ask you to take care of yourself.

Elya.

The next letter also is a translation from Russian, dated 20 August, no year.

My Dear:

How glad I was to learn that you finally received one of my letters. Which one in particular I am not sure, but it is good that you received it and I hope that you will receive the rest.

In the congratulations I wrote little, certainly because it was inconvenient and not because I would not write in general, you are making this up. Once more I thank you for the package. We received it in May. Everything is all right and we liked everything very much. It is a shame that the hyacinths traveled long and two of them perished altogether. The rest are planted and already have rooted, further, leaves are in pairs, firm, and I go to them to talk with you, you know this is a live greeting from you. Next year they will bloom.

Our garden suffered a great deal this year. But the trees nevertheless remained whole. The pear, which you pruned, did not suffer at all, because the branches were close to the ground. The apples which I bought with you also survived all right. I just now arrived from a northern resort where I was once before. I went with my people. Evunya couldn't because she is working and I was afraid to go alone. Now I feel all right, so don't worry about me.

Take care of yourself and come soon. We count every month that passes and you remember this. Now we have guest from the city from where you left. All remember you, especially the niece with the wife of your brother;

they grieve that there is no one to play with and to set our solitaire with.

The next letter is in English:

Dear Dad:
I was very glad to receive your letter and know that you have at least received our letter, though only the first one. I hope that by the time you receive this one all letters will have reached you already.

We got our parcel in May, and thank you very much for it. We liked your presents very much. We planted the hyacinths that have survived and by now three of them have sprouted. You say that you want to have more particulars about my husband.

I shall try now to give you a better picture of him. He is short, green-eyed, dark-haired, and rather handsome. He is rather gay and talkative when the conversation considers cars or football. He works as an engineer in communications, mostly telephone. He seems to be a good specialist though he has no higher education. He is capable though rather lazy. My first task is to make him study. I am afraid that it would be a difficult one. Well, I must say that he is a nice chap, that he loves me, and loves mother, though he is not very warm toward his own parents. He has an old Opel Olympia and spends most of his spare time repairing it. He likes photography.

You asked whether I am happy with him. As one of our greatest poets once said, there is no happiness in life, but there is peace and free will. As regards my freedom and will, they are not hampered in any respect. But as regards peace, I seem to possess an immense ability to find or invent troubles.

My husband is liable to all sorts of fantastic ideas, such as to build a bar of brick in the pond that is in our forest. Thank the Lord, he has forgotten about it. I am very glad that he likes Mother and the whole of our family. The only thing that troubles me is that I find him boring sometimes.

Now about my in-laws. They are awful. The mother is anxious to persuade me that she loves me dearly, but somehow I don't believe her. The father likes to make the great man of himself and to poke his nose in other people's business. I have had a couple of warm conversations

with him. He started making plans about our bungalow
and garden and I told him that it was not his own, and
nothing of his business, and that we could very well do
without his advice, opinion or permission.

I do wish you were with us. Everything would be much
easier for me then. I am missing you very much. I thought
at first that my husband could substitute you more or less
in some respects, but I now see that I was mistaken.

Now about my work. I like it fine. It is very difficult,
but anyhow it is very interesting. I translate articles on
aeronautics, aerodynamics, air frames, and so forth. Recently I have translated an article on boundary layers,
and it was a hell of a job. I have a splendid boss. He is a
very interesting man, clever, talented, tolerant, and handsome. We like each other and spend much time talking
about various things. He knows literature and arts, and
many other things. He is 44, single, and rather unhappy.
I wish you could see him and talk with him.

My health is okay. Sometimes when I am overtired I
have headaches but it is not very often. I work much and
with pleasure. My boss knows the language, though he
cannot speak very well. I help him to learn the language
better and often talk with him in the language.

Our hibernator sends you her best regards, and wishes
to see you as soon as possible. All our friends send you
their regards. My husband hopes you will like him when
you come home.

With all my love, Evelyn.

P. S. I have started writing poetry in this language.
Next time I shall send you a sample.

The last letter is handwritten in English.

Dear Dad:

I wish you many happy returns. Many thanks for the
parcel, and all you sent us. It all came in very handy.
Daddy, dear, I am missing you so much. You just cannot
imagine how much I need you.

It is about four months since I have married, and to me
it seems it is eternity. So dull it sometimes is. In general
he is a good chap, but he isn't you, or even like you. I
have already got used to the fact that all people must remind you somehow, but in this case it isn't so.

I have got a job, and a very interesting one. I work as

an engineer referent in aviation. My boss is a very good man, and we like each other. We often talk about all sorts of things. He is a bit like you, though not so broadminded and not a very great erudite, though very clever. Goodbye. Forgive me please for the awful letter. I am in a great hurry as I have to go to work. With all my love, Evelyn.

APPENDIX B

Excerpts from U.S. Supreme Court Opinions in the case of Rudolph Ivanovich Abel, Also Known as "Mark," and Also Known as Martin Collins and Emil R. Goldfus, versus United States of America. Decided March 28, 1960.

Mr. Justice Frankfurter delivered the opinion of the Court:

The question in this case is whether seven items were properly admitted into evidence at the petitioner's trial for conspiracy to commit espionage. All seven items were seized by officers of the Government without a search warrant. The seizures did not occur in connection with the exertion of the criminal process against petitioner. They arose out of his administrative arrest by the United States Immigration and Naturalization Service as a preliminary to his deportation.

We have considered the case on the assumption that the conviction must be reversed should we find challenged items of evidence to have been seized in violation of the Constitution and therefore improperly admitted into evidence. We find, however, that the admission of these items was free from any infirmity and we affirm the judgment. (Of course the nature of the case, the fact that it was a prosecution for espionage, has no bearing whatever upon the legal considerations relevant to the admissibility of evidence.)

I

The underlying basis of petitioner's attack upon admissibility of the challenged items of evidence concerns the motive of the Government in its use of the administrative arrest. We are asked to find that the Government resorted to a subterfuge, that the Immigration and Naturalization Service warrant here was a pretense and sham, was not what it purported to be. According to petitioner, it was

not the Government's true purpose in arresting him under
this warrant to take him into custody pending a determination of his deportability. The Government's real aims,
the argument runs, were (1) to place petitioner in custody so that pressure might be brought to bear upon him
to confess his espionage and cooperate with the F.B.I.,
and (2) to permit the Government to search through his
belongings for evidence of his espionage to be used in a
designed criminal prosecution against him. The claim is,
in short, that the Government used this administrative
warrant for entirely illegitimate purposes and that articles
seized as a consequence of its use ought to have been suppressed.

Were this claim justified by the record, it would indeed
reveal a serious misconduct by law-enforcing officers. The
deliberate use by the Government of an administrative
warrant for the purpose of gathering evidence in a criminal case must meet stern resistance by the courts. The
preliminary stages of a criminal prosecution must be pursued in strict obedience to the safeguards and restrictions
of the Constitution and laws of the United States. A finding of bad faith is, however, not open to us on this record.
What the motive was of the I.N.S. officials who determined to arrest petitioner and whether the I.N.S. in doing
so was not exercising its powers in the lawful discharge of
its own responsibilities, but was serving as a tool for the
F.B.I. in building a criminal prosecution against petitioner,
were issues fully canvassed in both courts below. The
crucial facts were found against the petitioner.

. . . To be sure, the record is not barren of evidence
supporting an inference opposed to the conclusion to
which the two lower courts were led by the record as a
whole: for example, the facts that the I.N.S. held off its
arrest of petitioner while the F.B.I. solicited his cooperation, and that the F.B.I. held itself ready to search petitioner's room as soon as it was vacated. These elements,
however, did not, and were not required to, persuade the
two courts below in the face of ample evidence of good
faith to the contrary, especially the human evidence of
those involved in the episode. We are not free to overturn
the conclusion of the courts below when justified by such
solid proof.

Petitioner's basic contention comes down to this: even
without a showing of bad faith, the F.B.I. and I.N.S.

must be held to have cooperated to an impermissible extent in this case, the case being one where the alien arrested by the I.N.S. for deportation was also suspected by the F.B.I. of crime. At the worst, . . . circumstances reveal an opportunity for abuse of the administrative arrest. But to hold illegitimate, in the absence of bad faith, the cooperation between I.N.S. and F.B.I. would be to ignore the scope of rightful cooperation between two branches of a single Department of Justice concerned with enforcement of different areas of law under the common authority of the Attorney General.

The facts are that the F.B.I. suspected petitioner both of espionage and illegal residence in the United States as an alien. That agency surely acted not only with propriety but in discharge of its duty in bringing petitioner's illegal status to the attention of the I.N.S., particularly after it found itself unable to proceed with petitioner's prosecution for espionage. Only the I.N.S. is authorized to initiate deportation proceedings, and certainly the F.B.I. is not to be required to remain mute regarding one they have reason to believe to be a deportable alien, merely because he is also suspected of one of the gravest crimes and the F.B.I. entertains the hope that criminal proceedings may eventually be brought against him.

The I.N.S., just as certainly, would not have performed its responsibilities had it been deterred from instituting deportation proceedings solely because it became aware of petitioner through the F.B.I., and had knowledge that the F.B.I. suspected petitioner of espionage. The Government has available two ways of dealing with a criminally suspect deportable alien. It would make no sense to say that branches of the Department of Justice may not cooperate in pursuing one course of action or the other, once it is honestly decided what course is to be preferred. For the same reasons this cooperation may properly extend to the extent and in the manner in which the F.B.I. and I.N.S. cooperated in effecting petitioner's administrative arrest. Nor does it taint the administrative arrest that the F.B.I. was not barred from continuing its investigation in the hope that it might result in a prosecution for espionage because the I.N.S., in the discharge of its duties, had embarked upon an independent decision to initiate proceedings for deportation.

The Constitution does not require that honest law en-

forcement should be put to such an irrevocable choice between two recourses of the Government.

We emphasize again that our view of the matter would
be totally different had the evidence established, or were
the courts below not justified in not finding, that the administrative warrant was here employed as an instrument
of criminal law enforcement to circumvent the latter's legal restrictions, rather than as a bona fide preliminary step
in a deportation proceeding. The test is whether the decision to proceed administratively toward deportation was
influenced by, or was carried out for, a purpose of amass-
ing evidence in the prosecution for crime. The record pre-
cludes such a finding by this Court.

II

The constitutional validity of the long-standing administrative arrest procedure in deportation cases has never
been directly challenged in reported litigation. . . . The
Court seems never expressly to have directed its attention
to the particular question of the constitutional validity of
administrative deportation warrants. It has frequently,
however, upheld administrative deportation proceedings
shown by the Court's opinion to have been begun by arrests pursuant to such warrants. . . . In the presence of
impressive historical evidence of acceptance of the validity
of statutes providing for administrative deportation arrest
from almost the beginning of the Nation, petitioner's dis-
avowal of the issue below calls for no further consideration.

III

Since petitioner's arrest was valid, we reach the question whether the seven challenged items, all seized during
searches which were a direct consequence of that arrest,
were properly admitted into evidence. This issue raises
three questions: (1) Were the searches which produced
these items proper searches for the Government to have
made? . . . (2) Were the articles seized properly subject
to seizure, even during a lawful search? . . . Was the Government free to use the articles, even if properly seized,
as evidence in a criminal case, the seizures having been
made in the course of a separate administrative proceeding?

We take as a starting point the cases in this Court deal-

ing with the extent of the search which may properly be
made without a warrant following a lawful arrest for
crime. The several cases on this subject in this court cannot be satisfactorily reconciled. This problem has, as is
well known, provoked strong and fluctuating differences
of view on the Court. This is not the occasion to attempt
to reconcile all the decisions, or to re-examine them. . . .
It would be unjustifiable retrospective lawmaking for the
Court in this case to reject the authority of [earlier] decisions.

. . . Were the officers of the I.N.S. acting lawfully in
this case when, after his arrest, they searched through petitioner's belongings in his hotel room looking for weapons
and documents to evidence his 'alienage'? There can be
no doubt that a search for weapons has as much justification here as it has in the case of an arrest for crime, where
it has been recognized as proper. . . . Nor is there any
constitutional reason to limit the search for materials
proving the deportability of an alien, when validly arrested, more severely than we limit the search for materials probative of a crime when a valid criminal arrest is
made. . . . According to the uniform decisions of the
Court deportation proceedings are not subject to the constitutional safeguards for criminal prosecutions. Searches
for evidence of crime present situations demanding the
greatest, not the least, restraint upon the Government's
intrusion into privacy; although its protection is not limited to them, it was at these searches which the Fourth
Amendment was primarily directed. We conclude, therefore, that government officers who effect a deportation arrest have a right of incidental search analogues to the
search permitted criminal law-enforcement officers.

Judged by prevailing doctrine, the search of petitioner's
hotel room was justified. . . . The only things sought here,
in addition to weapons, were documents connected with
petitioner's status as an alien. These may well be considered as instruments or means for accomplishing his illegal
status, and thus proper subjects of search. . . .

Two of the challenged items were seized during this
search of petitioner's property at his hotel room. The first
was item (2), a forged New York birth certificate for
"Martin Collins," one of the false identities which petitioner assumed in this country in order to keep his presence here undetected. This item was seizable when found

during a proper search, not only as a forged official document by which petitioner sought to evade his obligation to register as an alien, but also as a document which petitioner was using as an aid in the commission of espionage, for his undetected presence in this country was vital to his work as a spy. Documents used as a means to commit crime are the proper subjects of search warrants and are seizable when discovered in the course of a lawsuit search.

The other item seized in the course of the search of petitioner's hotel room was item (1), a piece of graph paper containing a coded message. This was seized by Schoenenberger as petitioner, while packing his suitcase, was seeking to hide it in his sleeve. An arresting officer is free to take hold of articles which he sees the accused deliberately trying to hide. . . . When an article subject to lawful seizure properly comes into an officer's possession in the course of a lawful search it would be entirely without reason to say that he must return it because it was not one of the things it was his business to look for.

Items (3), (4), and (5), a birth certificate for "Emil Goldfus" who died in 1903, a certificate of vaccination for "Martin Collins," and a bank book for "Emil Goldfus" were seized, not in petitioner's hotel room, but in a more careful search at I.N.S. headquarters of the belongings petitioner chose to take with him when arrested. This search was a proper one. . . . And items (3), (4), and (5) were articles subject to seizure when found during a lawful search. They were all capable of being used to establish and maintain a false identity for petitioner, just as the forged "Martin Collins" birth certificate, and were seizable for the same reasons.

Items (1)–(5) having come into the Government's possession through lawful searches and seizures connected with an arrest pending deportation, was the Government free to use them as evidence in a criminal prosecution to which they related? We hold that it was. Good reason must be shown for prohibiting the Government from using relevant, otherwise admissible, evidence. There is excellent reason for disallowing its use in the case of evidence, though relevant, which is seized by the Government in violation of the Fourth Amendment to the Constitution. . . .

These considerations are here absent, since items (1)–(5) were seized as a consequence of wholly lawful conduct. That being so, we can see no rational basis for excluding these relevant items from trial: no wrong-doing police officer would thereby be indirectly condemned, for there were no such wrongdoers; the Fourth Amendment would not thereby be enforced, for no illegal search or seizure was made; the Court would be lending its aid to no lawless government action, for none occurred. Of course cooperation between the branch of the Department of Justice dealing with criminal law enforcement and the branch dealing with the immigration laws would be less effective if evidence lawfully seized by the one could not be used by the other. Only to the extent that it would be to the public interest to deter and prevent such cooperation, would an exclusionary rule in a case like the present be desirable. Surely no consideration of civil liberties commends discouragement of such cooperation between these two branches when undertaken in good faith. When undertaken in bad faith to avoid constitutional restraints upon criminal law enforcement the evidence must be suppressed. That is not, as we have seen, this case. Individual cases of bad faith cooperation should be dealt with by findings to that effect in the cases as they arise, not by an exclusionary rule preventing effective cooperation when undertaken in entirely good faith.

We have left to the last the admissibility of items (6) and (7), the hollowed-out pencil and the block of wood containing a "cipher pad," because their admissibility is founded upon an entirely different set of considerations. These two items were found by an agent of the F.B.I. in the course of a search he undertook of petitioner's hotel room, immediately after petitioner had paid his bill and vacated the room. They were found in the room's wastepaper basket, where petitioner had put them while packing his belongings and preparing to leave. No pretense is made that this search by the F.B.I. was for any purpose other than to gather evidence of crime, that is, evidence of petitioner's espionage. As such, however, it was entirely lawful, although undertaken without a warrant. This is so for the reason that at the time of the search petitioner had vacated the room. The hotel then had the exclusive right to its possession, and the hotel management freely gave its consent that the search be made. Nor was it unlawful to seize the entire contents of the wastepaper basket, even though some of its contents had no connection with crime. So far as the record shows, petitioner had abandoned these articles. He had thrown them away. So far as he was concerned, they were bona vacantia. There can be nothing unlawful in the Government's appropriation of such abandoned property. These two items having been lawfully seized by the Government in connection with an investigation of crime, we encounter no basis for discussing further their admissibility as evidence.

Affirmed.

Mr. Justice Douglas, with whom Mr. Justice Black concurs, dissenting.

Cases of notorious criminals—like cases of small, miserable ones—are apt to make bad law. When guilt permeates a record, even judges sometimes relax and let the police take shortcuts not sanctioned by constitutional procedures. That practice, in certain periods of our history and in certain courts, has lowered our standards of law administration. The harm in the given case may seem excusable. But the practices generated by the precedent have far-reaching consequences that are harmful and injurious beyond measurement. The present decision is an excellent example.

The opening wedge that broadened the power of administrative officers—as distinguished from police—to enter and search people's homes was Frank v Maryland. That case allowed a health inspector to enter a home without a warrant, even though he had ample time to get one. The officials of the Immigration and Naturalization Service (I.N.S.) are now added to the preferred list. They are preferred because their duties, being strictly administrative, put them in a separate category from those who enforce the criminal law. They need not go to magistrates, the Court says, for warrants of arrest. Their warrants are issued within the hierarchy of the agency itself. Yet, as I attempted to show in my dissent in the Frank Case, the Fourth Amendment in origin had to do as much with ferreting out heretics and collecting taxes as with enforcement of the criminal laws.

Moreover, the administrative officer who invades the privacy of the home may be only a front for the police who are thus saved the nuisance of getting a warrant. . . . The administrative official with an administrative warrant, over which no judicial official exercises any supervision and which by statute may be used only for deportation, performs a new role. The police wear his mask to do police work. That, in my view, may not be done, even though we assume that the administrative warrant issued by an administrative rather than a judicial officer is valid for an arrest for the purpose of deportation. We take liberties with an Act of Congress, as well as the Constitution, when we permit this to be done. The statute permits the arrest of an alien on an administrative warrant "[p]ending a determination of deportability." The Court now reads the Act as if it read "Pending an investigation of criminal conduct." Such was the nature of the arrest.

With due deference to the two lower courts, I think the record plainly shows that F.B.I. agents were the moving force behind this arrest and search. For at least a month they investigated the espionage activities of petitioner. They were tipped off concerning this man and his role in May; the arrest and search were made on June 21. The F.B.I. had plenty of time to get a search warrant. . . . But the F.B.I. did not go to a magistrate for a search warrant. They went instead to the I.N.S. and briefed the officials of that agency on what they had discovered. On the basis of this data a report was made to John Murff, Acting District Director of the I.N.S., who issued the warrant of arrest.

No effort was made by the F.B.I. to obtain a search warrant from any judicial officer, though, as I said, there was plenty of time for such an application. The administrative warrant of arrest was chosen with care and calculation as the vehicle through which the arrest and search were to be made. The F.B.I. had an agreement with the officials of I.N.S. that this warrant of arrest would not be served at least until petitioner refused to "cooperate." The F.B.I. agents went with agents of the I.N.S. to apprehend petitioner in his hotel room. Again, it was the F.B.I. agents who were first. They were the ones who entered petitioner's room and who interrogated him to see if he would "cooperate"; and when they were unable to get him to "cooperate" by threatening him with arrest, they signaled agents of the I.N.S. who had waited outside to come in and make the arrest. The search was made both by the F.B.I. agents and by officers of the I.N.S. And when petitioner was flown 1,000 miles to a special deten-

tion camp and held for three weeks, the agents of the
F.B.I. as well as I.N.S. interrogated him.

Thus the F.B.I. used an administrative warrant to
make an arrest for criminal investigation both in violation
of §242(a) of the Immigration and Nationality Act and
in violation of the Bill of Rights.

The issue is not whether these F.B.I. agents acted in
bad faith. Of course they did not. The question is how far
zeal may be permitted to carry officials bent on law enforcement. As Mr. Justice Brandeis once said, "Experience should teach us to be most on our guard to protect
liberty when the Government's purposes are beneficent."
The facts seem to me clearly to establish that the F.B.I.
agents wore the mask of I.N.S. to do what otherwise they
could not have done. They did what they could do only if
they had gone to a judicial officer pursuant to the requirements of the Fourth Amendment, disclosed their evidence,
and obtained the necessary warrant for the searches which
they made.

If the F.B.I. agents had gone to a magistrate, any
search warrant issued would by terms of the Fourth
Amendment have to "particularly" describe "the place to
be searched" and the "things to be seized." How much
more convenient it is for the police to find a way around
those specific requirements of the Fourth Amendment!
What a hindrance it is to work laboriously through constitutional procedures! How much easier to go to another
official in the same department! The administrative officer
can give a warrant good for unlimited search. No more
showing of probable cause to a magistrate! No more limitations on what may be searched and when!

The tragedy in our approval of these short cuts is that
the protection afforded by the Fourth Amendment is removed from an important segment of our life. . . .

This is a protection given not only to citizens but to
aliens as well, as the opinion of the Court by implication
holds. The right "of the people" covered by the Fourth
Amendment certainly gives security to aliens in the same
degree that "person" in the Fifth and "the accused" in the
Sixth Amendments also protects them. Here the F.B.I.
works exclusively through an administrative agency—the
I.N.S.—to accomplish what the Fourth Amendment says
can be done only by a judicial officer. A procedure designed to serve administrative ends—deportation—is clev-

erly adapted to serve other ends—criminal prosecution. We have had like examples of this same trend in recent times. Lifting the requirements of the Fourth Amendment for the benefit of health inspectors was accomplished by Frank v Maryland, as I have said. Allowing the Department of Justice rather than judicial officers to determine whether aliens will be entitled to release on bail pending deportation hearings is another.

Some things in our protective scheme of civil rights are entrusted to the judiciary. Those controls are not always congenial to the police. Yet if we are to preserve our system of checks and balances and keep the police from being all-powerful, these judicial controls should be meticulously respected. When we read them out of the Bill of Rights by allowing short cuts as we do today and as the Court did in the Frank and Carlson Cases, police and administrative officials in the Executive Branch acquire powers incompatible with the Bill of Rights.

The F.B.I. agents stalked petitioner for weeks and had plenty of time to obtain judicial warrants for searching the premises he occupied. I would require them to adhere to the command of the Fourth Amendment and not evade it by the simple device of wearing the masks of immigration officials while in fact they are preparing a case for criminal prosecution.

Mr. Justice Brennan, with whom the Chief Justice, Mr. Justice Black, and Mr. Justice Douglas join, dissenting.

This is a notorious case, with a notorious defendant. Yet we must take care to enforce the Constitution without regard to the nature of the crime or the nature of the criminal. The Fourth Amendment protects "The right of the people to be secure in their persons, houses, papers, and effects, against unreasonable searches and seizures." This right is a basic one of all the people, without exception; and this Court ruled that the fruits of governmental violation of this guarantee could not be used in a criminal prosecution. The Amendment's protection is thus made effective for everyone only by upholding it when invoked by the worst of men.

The opinion of the Court makes it plain that the seizure of certain of the items of petitioner taken from his room at the Hotel Latham and used in evidence against him must depend upon the existence of a broad power, without a warrant, to search the premises of one arrested, in connection with and "incidental" to his arrest.

. . . I think it plain that before it can be concluded here that the search was not an unreasonable one, there must be some inquiry into the over-all protection given the individual by the totality of the processes necessary to the arrest and the seizure. Here the arrest, while had on what is called a warrant, was made totally without the intervention of an independent magistrate; it was made on the authorization of one administrative official to another. And after the petitioner was taken into custody, there was no obligation upon the administrative officials who arrested him to take him before any independent officer, sitting under the conditions of publicity that characterize our judicial institutions, and justify what had been done. Concretely, what happened instead was this: petitioner, upon his arrest, was taken to a local administrative headquarters and then flown in a special aircraft to a special detention camp over 1,000 miles away. He was incarcerated in solitary confinement there. As far as the world knew, he had vanished. He was questioned daily at the place of incarceration for over three weeks. An executive procedure as to his deportability was had, at the camp, after a few days, but there was never any independent inquiry or judicial control over the circumstances of the arrest and the seizure till over five weeks after his arrest, when, at the detention camp, he was served with a bench warrant for his arrest on criminal charges, upon an indictment.

The Fourth Amendment imposes substantive standards for searches and seizures; but with them one of the important safeguards it establishes is a procedure; and central to the procedure is an independent control over the actions of officers effecting searches of private premises. It is one thing to say that an adequate substitute for this sort of intervention by a magistrate can be found in the strict protections with which federal criminal procedure surrounds the making of a criminal arrest—where the action of the officers must receive an antecedent or immediately subsequent independent scrutiny. It goes much further to say that such a substitute can be found in the executive processes employed here. The question is not whether they are constitutionally adequate in their own terms—whether they are a proper means of taking into custody one not charged with crime. The question is rather whether they furnish a context in which a search generally through premises can be said to be a reasonable one under the Fourth Amendment. These arrest procedures, as exemplified here, differ as night from day from the processes of an arrest for crime. When the power to make a broad, warrantless search is added to them, we create a complete concentration of power in executive officers over the person and effects of the individual. We completely remove any independent control over the powers of executive officers to make searches. They may take any man they think to be a deportable alien into their own custody, hold him without arraignment or bond, and, having been careful to apprehend him at home, make a search generally through his premises. I cannot see how this can be said to be consistent with the Fourth Amendment's command; it was rather, against such a concentration of executive power over the privacy of the individual that the Fourth Amendment was raised.

. . . The Court's attitude here must be based on a recognition of the great possibilities of abuse its decision leaves in the present situation. These possibilities have been recognized before, in a case posing less danger: "Arrest under a warrant for a minor or a trumped-up charge has been familiar practice in the past, is a commonplace in the police state of today, and too well-known in this country. . . . The progress is too easy from police action unscrutinized by judicial authorization to the police state." Where a species of arrest is available that is subject to no judicial control, the possibilities become more and more serious. The remedy is not to invite fruitless litigation into the purity of official motives, or the specific direction of official purposes. One may always assume that the officers are zealous to perform their duty. The remedy is rather to recognize that the power to perform a search generally throughout premises upon a purely executive arrest is so unconfined by any safeguards that it cannot be countenanced as consistent with the Fourth Amendment.

One more word. We are told that the governmental power to make a warrantless search might be greater where the object of the search is not related to crime but to some other "civil" proceeding—such as matter bearing on the issue whether a man should forcibly be sent from the country. The distinction is rather hollow here, where the proofs that turn up are in fact given in evidence in a criminal prosecution. And the distinction, again, invites a trial of the officers' purposes. But in any event, I think it perverts the Amendment to make this distinction. The Amendment states its own purpose, the protection of the privacy of the individual and of his property against the incursions of officials: the "right of the people to be secure in their persons, houses, papers, and effects." Like most of the Bill of Rights it was not designed to be a shelter for criminals, but a basic protection for everyone; to be sure, it must be upheld when asserted by criminals, in order that it may be at all effective, but it "reaches all alike, whether accused of crime or not." It is the individual's interest in privacy which the Amendment protects, and that would not appear to fluctuate with the "intent" of the invading officers.

. . . Since evidence was introduced against petitioner which had been obtained in violation of his constitutional guarantees as embodied in the Fourth Amendment, I would reverse his conviction for a new trial on the evidence not subject to this objection.

INDEX

ABOUT THE AUTHOR

Louise Bernikow was educated at Barnard College, the University of California at Berkeley, Oxford, and Columbia. She has been a Fulbright Scholar to Spain, photographer's model, and college English instructor. She is also the author of THE WORLD SPLIT OPEN, AMONG WOMEN, and LET'S HAVE LUNCH.